YIDDISH IN AMERICA

Essays on Yiddish Culture in the Golden Land

YIDDISH IN AMERICA

*Essays on Yiddish Culture
in the Golden Land*

Edited by:
Edward S. Shapiro

Weinberg Judaic Studies Institute
University of Scranton

University of Scranton Press
Scranton and London

Library of Congress Cataloging-in-Publication Data

Yiddish in America : essays on Yiddish culture in the Golden Land /
edited by Edward S. Shapiro.

   p. cm.
  ISBN 978-1-58966-137-0 (pbk.)
   1. Jews, East European—United States—Intellectual life.
2. Jews—United States—Intellectual life.   3. Immigrants—United
States—Intellectual life. 4. Yiddish language—United States—
History.   5. Yiddish literature—United States—History.   6. United
States—Ethnic relations.   I. Shapiro, Edward S.
  E184.36.I58Y53 2007
  305.892′4073—dc22

                                  2007047798

Distribution:

University of Scranton Press
Chicago Distribution Center
11030 S. Langley
Chicago, IL 60628

DEDICATION

"To the Memory of Murray Friedman"

CONTENTS

INTRODUCTION

Edward S. Shapiro

In the fall of 2003, Leon Gildin, a retired lawyer living in Phoenix, contacted Murray Friedman, director of the Feinstein Center for American Jewish History at Temple University, with a proposal for a book on secular Yiddish culture in America. Gildin had grown up within this culture in the East Bronx during its Jewish heyday of the 1930s and 1940s, and he had fond memories of the borough's Yiddish-speaking schools, Yiddish summer camps, Yiddish newspapers, Yiddish theater, and housing projects where Yiddish was the language of the courtyard and the playground. He believed such a book would fill an important gap in the historiography of American Jews and be a fitting tribute to a once vibrant and treasured culture, now only a faint memory to most American Jews.

Friedman thought Gildin's suggestion worthwhile, and his center attempted to find a person both qualified and free to undertake the project. He was unsuccessful. Of the scholars capable of writing such a book, none were able to assume a task which, if done properly, would occupy them for many years. So agreement was reached about an alternative proposal to produce a book of essays by specialists on various aspects of Yiddish secular culture in America. This still left the problem, however, of finding funding and a publisher for the volume. Marc B. Shapiro, the Harry Weinberg Professor of Jewish Studies at the University of Scranton, stepped into the breach. He provided funds from the Weinberg endowment to underwrite the project and approached the director of the University of Scranton Press, Jeff Gainey, who was enthusiastic about publishing it—provided the essays received positive response from outside reviewers.

Dozens of potential contributors were contacted. Of the twenty who agreed to contribute essays, about half ultimately submitted content for the book. The missing essays were to cover such important subjects as Yiddish politics, Yiddish labor unions, Yiddish schools, Yiddish summer camps, Yiddish publishing houses and book stores, the Yiddish popular press, and Yiddish-speaking agricultural colonies, topics vital to the understanding of secular Yiddish culture in America. This volume, therefore, makes no claim to be exhaustive. It is rather a step toward a more complete view of the cultural world of first- and second-generation American Jews. Hopefully, it will provide information and encouragement to others wishing to delve more deeply into this culture. There are many books on secular Yiddish culture in America, but only Irving Howe's justly acclaimed 1976 volume, *World of Our Fathers,* examines it in a comprehensive manner.[1] But no single volume, even one such as Howe's, at nearly 650 pages, can do justice to the topic. *World of Our Fathers* emphasizes literature, politics, and journalism, but neglects Yiddish movies, radio shows, poetry, and political cartoons. The essayists in this volume cover these and other topics.

The contributors were told that their essays should discuss "secular Yiddish culture in America." In other words, they should address not only the Yiddish culture that Jews brought with them from Europe, but also what happened to it when it was transplanted across the Atlantic. How did Yiddish culture in America differ from its counterparts in Eastern Europe, Palestine, London, Paris, and Buenos Aires? How did it evolve in the United States? How did Yiddish writers, artists, publishers, and movie producers and directors respond to the unique social, economic, and political conditions of their new land? What effects did capitalism, individualism, rapid social and economic mobility, the absence of officially sanctioned anti-Semitism and a strong socialist movement, and other salient American factors have on Yiddish secular culture? What was lost and what was gained as Yiddish secular culture gradually adapted to this new habitat?

---

[1] For the response of both Jews and Gentiles to *World of Our Fathers,* see Hasia Diner, "Embracing *World of Our Fathers:* The Context of Reception," in Jack Kugelmass, ed., *Key Texts in American Jewish Culture* (New Brunswick, NJ: Rutgers University Press, 2003), 210–212.

Howe noted that Yiddish-speaking immigrant Jews were often be-fuddled by America. "The world interests them intensely, though they are frank, with one another, to admit they often find it beyond com-prehension." In Abraham Cahan's 1917 novel, *The Rise of David Levin-sky*, one of the great novels of immigrant acculturation in America, the central figure says, "The United States lured me not merely as a land of milk and honey, but also, and chiefly, as one of mystery, of fantastic experiences of marvelous transformations." Take politics, for exam-ple. In 1936, the socialist true-believing readers of the hitherto social-ist newspaper the *Forward* were surprised when the paper, edited by Cahan, came out in support of the re-election of Franklin D. Roo-sevelt. They would rather have had their right arms wither than vote for the presidential candidate of a capitalist party. But they should not have been surprised by the paper's stance. By 1936, as Howe wrote, the *Forward*'s socialism had "faded into Sunday ceremonials, as the social-ism of the garment-union leaders faded into pragmatic American poli-tics. With the advent of Franklin Roosevelt's New Deal, the *Forward* became, in effect, an organ of Jewish liberal-labor opinion. Its opposi-tion to Zionism also waned and, like almost every other Jewish paper, it became a warm, though not uncritical, partisan of the new Jewish state." The realities of American politics had convinced Cahan that the socialist pieties of Europe were an anachronism. Were the experiences of other Yiddish writers, artists, and filmmakers similar to Cahan's? How, the contributors were asked, did these individuals come to terms with American realities, and how was this reflected in their work?[2]

Between 1881 and 1924, when Congress drastically reduced im-migration from Eastern and Central Europe, somewhere between

---

[2] Irving Howe, *World of Our Fathers: The Journey of the East European Jews to Amer-ica and the Life They Found and Made* (New York: Simon and Schuster, 1976), 542, 638. This American, socialist, Yiddish world of schools, newspapers, fra-ternal and mutual-aid societies, workers' education societies, parades, politi-cal clubs, lecture series, and labor movements is the subject of Tony Michels, *Fire in Their Hearts: Yiddish Socialists in New York* (Cambridge, MA: Harvard University Press, 2005). By 1920, Michaels said, the Yiddish socialists of New York City had "not only built a popular movement; they also molded the posture and character of the world's largest Jewish community in an era punc-tuated by upheavals and crises on both sides of the Atlantic." (p. 253).

two and a quarter and two and a half million Jews immigrated to the United States, primarily from the Eastern-European Jewish heartland. This was part of a massive demographic revolution during which two-thirds of Eastern-European Jews moved to somewhere else in Europe or crossed the Atlantic. "America was in everybody's mouth," wrote Mary Antin in her autobiography *From Plotz to Boston* (1899). "Businessmen talked of it over their accounts; the market women made up their quarrels that they might discuss it from stall to stall; people who had relatives in the famous land went around reading their letters for the enlightenment of less fortunate folk." Immigration, however, was discouraged by Jewish religious authorities in Eastern Europe, who believed America, Canada, and the countries of Western Europe were unfit for religious Jews, and who feared for the future of their institutions and communities should a significant number of Jews depart.

In 1894, Rabbi Israel Meir Ha-Kohen, the most revered Orthodox figure in Eastern Europe at the time, published his *Niddehei Israel* (*Dispersed of Israel*), warning Jews of the dangers to their souls should they permanently relocate to such *trefa* (religiously impure) lands: "The true and correct way for anyone desiring to acquire genuine merit with God is to have the fortitude not to settle in one of these countries. . . . Truly, the heart of any righteous man will shake within him once it arrives in those countries, at the sight of the breakdown of religion among many people there." The rabbi recognized that economic necessity might force Jews to migrate to the West, but in such cases their stay should only be temporary. "If he is compelled to go there on account of need, then once God helps him he may return home, and trust in God, who provides bread for all flesh, to sustain him also at home. Let him not listen to the seduction of his instinct, that he should stay there until he amasses a fortune, for then he is exchanging the Everlasting World for the transient world."[3] Ha-Kohen, however, was preaching to the unconverted. By the late nineteenth

---

[3] Lloyd P. Gartner, "Jewish Migrants en Route from Europe to North America," in Moses Rischin, ed., *The Jews of North America* (Detroit: Wayne State University Press, 1987), 33–34.

century, secularism, acculturation, and a variety of political ideologies had undermined the authority of spokesmen for religious orthodoxy, and this process would be accelerated once Yiddish-speaking Jews from Central and Eastern Europe arrived in the United States.

The migration of 1881–1924 was the most significant factor in American Jewish history. During these years, the number of Jews in the United States increased thirteen-fold and, by 1924, they comprised over three percent of the American population. American Jewry was transformed from an exotic religious sect, fated to disappear, to a permanent component of American religious life alongside Protestantism and Catholicism. Because of this immigration, New York City would have, by the twentieth century, the largest number of Yiddish speakers ever gathered in one city, and the United States would have more Yiddish-speaking persons than any other country in history.

This immigration was unique not only in its size, but in its composition. In contrast to that of other ethnic groups at this time, which consisted mostly of young men, Jewish immigration was a family affair. One-quarter of the Jewish immigrants were children under the age of fourteen, and over forty percent were females. No other immigrant group from Central or Eastern Europe came close to the Jews in this regard. Coming over as families, the Jewish immigrants had consciously severed ties to the old country. They saw America as their permanent home, and learned English and became citizens more quickly than other immigrants. In America, they established supplementary Yiddish schools for their children, but they did not create Yiddish day schools. Their children would go to public schools where they would learn English and U.S. history and become good Americans. Not surprisingly, their rate of repatriation, despite the entreaties of Ha-Kohen, was far lower than that of other immigrant groups. Europe offered little to entice Jews back. It is not coincidental that the classic portrait of the Americanization school—Leo C. Rosten's *The Education of Hyman Kaplan* (1937)—focuses on the tribulations of a Yiddish-speaking immigrant in learning English. (Hyman Kaplan is convinced that the sixteenth president is a Jew named Abraham Lincohen.)

In 1918, a Yiddish variety show featured a song "*Lebn Zol Kolombus*" ("Long Live Columbus"). Israel Baline, who had emigrated from Russia to New York City's Lower East Side with his family when he was five years old, would provide the most popular version of this sentiment. He would change his name to Irving Berlin and become best known for writing "God Bless America." This sense of having come to America to stay encouraged Yiddish-speaking immigrants to establish a variety of cultural and philanthropic institutions familiar to them in Europe. By the 1920s, America had a flourishing Yiddish stage, Yiddish radio programs, Yiddish movies, and Yiddish publishing houses, and Yiddish movies and books were being sent from America back to Europe. These things would not have happened if the Jewish immigrants were merely planning to visit—not settle and stay—in the United States.[4]

The American Yiddish-speaking generation saw portrayed on stage and in movies—and heard broadcast over the radio—their deepest desires and anxieties, including their nostalgia for the old country and their yearning to become part of their new land. Here they experienced what the literary historian Donald Weber has described as "the emotional costs of Americanization." These shows, films, and programs, Weber noted, continue to speak to us today "not merely as sentimental artifacts indulging our own needy nostalgia, but rather as texts that open up a world where the claims of memory, the rawness of generational struggle, the ravening impact of shame remain palpable, alive."[5]

The most important of these cultural artifacts was the newspaper. In 1922, the eminent sociologist Robert E. Park, referring to the Yiddish popular press, said, "No other foreign-language press has succeeded in reflecting so much of the intimate life of the people which it represents, or reacted so powerfully upon the opinion, thought, and aspiration of the public for which it exists."[6] A host of Yiddish newspapers, each with a distinctive political and religious outlook, sprang up in major American cities. They included papers for socialists, communists, anarchists, Zionists, the religiously Orthodox, and middle-

[4] Paul Kriwaczek, *Yiddish Civilization: The Rise and Fall of a Forgotten Nation* (New York: Alfred A. Knopf, 2005), 310–316.
[5] Donald Weber, *Haunted in the New World: Jewish American Culture from Cahan to the Goldbergs* (Bloomington: Indiana University Press, 2005), 51–53.
[6] Robert E. Park, *The Immigrant Press and Its Control* (New York: Harper and Brothers, 1922), 89.

class strivers. The most successful was the Jewish daily *Forward* of New York, the most important ethnic newspaper in American history. At its peak, the paper had eleven separate editions, including one in Chicago, and its circulation surpassed that of all other Yiddish papers combined.

The *Forward* reflected the values and outlook of Abraham Cahan. Cahan had no illusions that a Yiddish newspaper could last much beyond the first generation of immigrant Jews. "He also found no virtue in Yiddish," his biographer Moses Rischin noted. "The Jewish folk tongue was . . . no more than a workaday language for propagating socialism among Yiddish-speaking immigrants that inevitably would be superseded by English." Like many of his generation, Cahan believed traditional Jewish life, including the Yiddish language, was obsolete and destined to disappear in America with the passing of the immigrant generation.[7]

Cahan was an Americanist and the first teacher of English to Yiddish-speaking immigrants in the New York City public school system. He saw the paramount task of the *Forward* to be facilitating the adaptation of Jews to their new home. Its advice on how to behave in America and the information it provided about the American social and political system, with suitable guidance on whom to vote for, softened the shock of Americanization and facilitated the entry of immigrant Jews into the American mainstream. The *Forward*'s role was thus paradoxical, as was that of Yiddish secular culture in America in general. As Irving Howe noted, the paper simultaneously attempted to educate its readers in Yiddish culture while tearing them away from it "in behalf of American fulfillment." "The sooner it began to realize its visions, the sooner it would destroy them."[8]

The most important section of the *Forward* in facilitating this acculturation was its letters-to-the-editor column, the "Bintel Brief." At a time when many Jews viewed traditional Judaism as an anachronism, fresh authority figures were needed to assist the immigrants in navigating

---

[7] Moses Rischin, "Abraham Cahan: Guide Across the American Chasm," in David Berger, ed., *The Legacy of Jewish Migration: 1881 and Its Impact* (New York: Brooklyn College Press, 1983), 76.
[8] Howe, *World of Our Fathers*, 524.

their way in this strange land. The *Forward*'s letters-to-the-editor column helped fill this need. Introduced in 1906, the column became the
most popular section of the *Forward,* and other Yiddish newspapers
soon introduced their own letters-to-the-editor columns. The *Forward*'s readers trusted the paper, and they asked advice on the most intimate of matters, including sex, marriage, family relationships, and
the raising of children.

One reader, for example, wanted to know whether intermarriage, which in Eastern Europe resulted in ostracism from the Jewish
community and alienation from one's family, was acceptable in America. Another letter-writer feared that her daughter, who had fallen in
love with a man from a Republican and church-going family, was about
to enter into a disastrous marriage. What should the mother do? The
editor responded that while he agreed with the mother, her daughter
was obviously infatuated with her beau, "and when one is in love, then
all the sensible arguments are worthless." A third reader wondered
whether it was acceptable in America, in contrast to Europe, for her
husband to prevent her from going to evening high school twice a
week. The editor sided with the woman. "Since this man is intelligent
and an adherent of the women's emancipation movement, he is
scolded severely . . . for wanting to keep his wife so enslaved." Another
woman was worried that her husband planned to divorce her because
she was childless after six years of marriage, grounds for divorce under
Jewish law. She was told by the *Forward* that not only did American civil
law not recognize Jewish law, but that "a civilized man doesn't cast out
his faithful wife just because she has no children." A young man asked
whether he should marry his girlfriend, who had a dimple in her chin.
"It is said that people who have this lose their first husband or wife."
"It's truly shameful," the paper responded, "that a young man who was
brought up in America should ask such questions."

The most mundane aspects of life prompted questions to "Dear
Editor," this new wisdom figure. One reader asked how he should respond to the admonitions of his brother-in-law and a friend not to read
a Yiddish newspaper on the subway because other riders would view
him as a "greenhorn." The paper advised him to continue reading the
paper in public since there was nothing evil or improper about doing
so. A reader wished to share the embarrassment suffered by him and

his siblings when his parents insisted on speaking Yiddish, even while shopping on Fifth Avenue in New York City. The paper answered that there was nothing wrong with speaking Yiddish in public, although the parents should also become more proficient in English. Another reader wondered whether he should allow his son to play baseball, this "wild and silly game" in which children "can get crippled." In America, he complained, educated men "run after a leather ball like children." He did not want his son to become "a wild American runner. But he cries his head off." Chess and dominoes are fine for Jewish children, but baseball? The *Forward* replied that there was nothing wrong with playing the American national pastime. Jewish parents should allow their sons to play baseball "as long as it does not interfere with their education or get them into bad company." Their children must not grow up as "foreigners in their own birthplace."[9]

The Yiddish writer Isaac Bashevis Singer shared Cahan's doubts regarding the future of Yiddish in America. Singer, who had moved from Warsaw to New York City in 1935, published an essay in 1943 titled "Problems of Yiddish Prose in America." Here he argued that the Yiddish familiar to him in Poland was obsolete in the United States. "Life here is so rich and varied," Singer wrote, "that English words and phrases inevitably have crept into Yiddish while, at the same time, hallowed Yiddish terms and expressions have disappeared." Jewish immigrants have "vulgarized the language . . . and created a gibberish which no self-respecting Yiddish writer could use in good conscience." "The stubborn few who insist on speaking 'pure Yiddish,'" Singer said (perhaps writing from personal experience), have become "objects of ridicule and the butt of jokes." The American lover of Yiddish was thus forced to dine on leftovers: "Only food prepared in the old world can

---

[9] Isaac Metzger, ed., *A Bintel Brief: Sixty Years of Letters From the Lower East Side to the* Jewish Daily Forward (Garden City, NY: Doubleday, 1971), 109–111, 121, 149–150, 158–159, 165–166, and 182–183; Peter Levine, *Ellis Island to Ebbets Field: Sport and the American Jewish Experience* (New York: Oxford University Press, 1992), 87. "Bintel Brief" means "a bundle of letters." The letters were often revised and edited by the *Forward,* and some were even written by the *Forward*'s staff. Howe, *World of Our Fathers,* 533–537.

nourish him in the new." If, as Singer claimed, Yiddish literature was "a product of the ghetto . . . and it can never leave the ghetto," then its future was bleak indeed. While Singer was writing these words, the Eastern-European Yiddish heartland was being cruelly obliterated.[10]

Singer noted that in America "the dream of a secular Jewish culture . . . has played itself out."[11] The leftism so central to the Yiddish political and cultural scene of the late nineteenth and early twentieth centuries was alien to the individualistic and capitalistic ethos of America. The secular definition of Jewish identity, espoused by the militant Yiddishists, was also inappropriate for the United States. In 1955, Will Herberg, a historian of the American Yiddish labor movement, published *Protestant-Catholic-Jew,* the most influential book of that decade on the sociology of American religion. His title reflected the mid-century consensus that Jewishness in the United States was no longer a matter of culture and politics. What made American Jews distinctive, Jews and Gentiles agreed, was Judaism, not the Yiddish language or Yiddish culture.

It is the great paradox of Yiddish in America that its last remaining major redoubts are a couple of Brooklyn neighborhoods inhabited by Orthodox sectarians. There, one can purchase tickets for the city's subways from vending machines offering Yiddish as a language option. For the sectarian Orthodox, Yiddish is not, as it was for the pioneers of Yiddish literature and culture a century earlier, a means to liberate Jews from the tyranny of religious obscurantism and a way for Jews to join the world of literary modernism and high culture. As Aaron Lansky, the founder of the National Yiddish Book Center, remarked, the founders of Yiddish literature sought "to reinterpret and reconstruct Jewish tradition in a modern context—an endeavor that, while not without precedent in Jewish history, was nonetheless anathema to the blackcoated defenders of tradition." Today, however, the sectarians value the Yiddish language because it embodies the heritage of Eastern European Orthodoxy, and because it helps them live in an isolated and encapsulated world governed by ancient religious texts and

---

[10] Isaac Bashevis Singer, "Problems of Yiddish Prose in America (1943)," translated by Robert H. Wolf, *Prooftexts,* 9 (1989), 5–10.

[11] Singer, "Problems of Yiddish Prose in America," 11.

marked by distrust of Gentiles and non-Orthodox Jews. To preserve the sanctity of their surroundings, the Orthodox have developed their own Yiddish songs, children's literature, and popular songs.[12]

There is a contemporary revival of interest by Americans, Israelis, and Europeans in Yiddish language and culture, but this is largely a hothouse affair restricted to academic and quasi-academic institutions such as the National Yiddish Book Center in Massachusetts, the YIVO Institute for Jewish Research in New York, and academic programs in Yiddish at Harvard, Columbia, Oxford, and other universities. Except for the Orthodox, the users of Yiddish as a vernacular language have not increased. Few members of the audience for *Fiddler on the Roof* understand the language in which the stories of Sholem Aleichem were written and on which the musical was based. Those involved in this Yiddish revival often have a political agenda for which Yiddish has great symbolic importance. They identify with a literature and culture which, they believe, embodied opposition to racism, imperialism, and capitalism. By returning to Yiddish, these new devotees are paying tribute to the type of Jewish politics that once reigned in the East Bronx and the Lower East Side. At a time when Jews are more likely to be found in the fleshpots of Scarsdale and the Hamptons, interest in Yiddish culture has become a subversive activity.

Ironically, this Yiddish revival is taking place during a period of diminishing American anti-Semitism and racism, and it is funded by the beneficiaries of American capitalism, many of whom vote Republican. More ironic is the fact that Isaac Bashevis Singer, who won the Nobel Prize for Literature in 1978 and was the most prominent Yiddish writer of the second half of the twentieth century, was a political conservative who distrusted the utopian enthusiasms of the Left.[13]

----

[12] Aaron Lansky, *Outwitting History: The Amazing Adventures of a Man Who Rescued a Million Yiddish Books* (Chapel Hill, NC: Algonquin Books, 2004), 24–25.
[13] For the current state of Yiddish in America, see Jeffrey Shandler, *Adventures in Yiddishland: Postvernacular Language and Culture* (Berkeley: University of California Press, 2006). Shandler emphasizes the contemporary symbolic role of Yiddish. "The very fact that something is said (or written or sung) in Yiddish is at least as meaningful as the meaning of the words being uttered— if not more so." (p. 22)

UPS AND DOWNS OF YIDDISH IN AMERICA

Ruth R. Wisse

The fate of Yiddish in America is usually described as a crisis of language. Since the vast majority of Yiddish-speaking Jewish immigrants did not pass the language on to their children and grandchildren, there developed an unfortunate breach in the transmission of culture between one generation and the next. This left a heritage without its heirs and heirs without access to their heritage. A valuable Yiddish formal and folk culture risked being lost to posterity. To mitigate the effects of this loss, those of us who work professionally in the field of Yiddish translate and transpose as many of its treasures as possible into English, hoping to compensate in some small measure for the erosion of Yiddish as a vernacular.

To the extent that the problem of Yiddish *is* confined to language, it is being remedied in various ways. American university presses have been publishing English editions of the works of major Yiddish writers, including Mendele Mocher Sforim, Sholem Aleichem, I. L. Peretz, Sh. Ansky, Itsik Manger, David Bergelson, Eliezer Shteynbarg, Kadya Molodovsky, and many others.[1] The impetus of Holocaust

---

[1] Books by the first five authors form part of the New Yiddish Library being published by Yale University Press that is also readying additional volumes by David Bergelson, Jacob Glatstein, I. I. Trunk, and others. Syracuse University Press has issued *Classic Yiddish Stories of S.Y. Abramovitsh, Sholem Aleichem, and I.L. Peretz,* ed. and trans. Ken Frieden, (2004); Eliezer Shteynbarg, *The Book of Fables,* ed. and trans. Curt Leviant (2003); Chava Rosenfarb, *Bociany* and *Of Lodz and Love* (2000); Yehuda Elberg, *The Empire of Kalman the Cripple* and *The Rose Rabbi* (1997). Wayne State University Press issued *Paper Bridges: Selected Poetry of Kadya Molodovsky,* ed. and trans. Katherine Hellerstein (1999). This is by no means an exhaustive list.

commemoration and historiography inspires the translation, from Yiddish into English, of many important memoirs, diaries, and historical documents.[2] Klezmer groups mine collections of Yiddish music looking for new additions to their ever-expanding repertoires. Libraries and research institutions, such as the YIVO Institute for Jewish Research, continue to build and organize their archival collections. Courses and programs in Yiddish at major universities are turning out a new generation of teachers who are integrating Yiddish studies into the disciplines of history, anthropology, music, and folklore, as well as literature programs in American, European, and comparative studies. The National Yiddish Book Center, as its founder Aaron Lansky describes it in his memoir, *Outwitting History,* collects Yiddish books for redistribution and generates creative programming to stimulate interest and disseminate information. The following are only some of the works by Yiddish scholars to appear in English during the past five years: *Words on Fire: an Unfinished History of Yiddish; Early Yiddish Texts 1100–1750; Storm in the Community: Yiddish Polemical Pamphlets of Amsterdam Jewry 1797–1798; Yiddish Theater: New Approaches; Yiddish Fiction and the Crisis of Modernity; Yiddish and the Creation of Soviet Jewish Culture 1918–1930; Yiddish After the Holocaust; Journeys Beyond the Pale: Yiddish Travel Writing in the Modern World; What Must Be Forgotten: The Survival of Yiddish in Zionist Palestine; Yiddish South of the Border: An Anthology of Latin American Jewish Writing;* and *Defining the Yiddish Nation: The Jewish Folklorists of Poland.* This wide range of books greatly expands our understanding of Yiddish literary history and culture.

But, while celebrating these developments, I would also like to consider an unsettling aspect of this transposition. When Charlotte Simmons, the eponymous, small-town heroine of Tom Wolfe's 2004 novel, goes off to study at a top-tier college, she expects to be challenged by her peers. Her mantra, "I am Charlotte Simmons," expresses her confidence that she will realize her fullest potential among

---

[2] Of particular interest is *Awakening Lives: Autobiographies of Jewish Youth in Poland Before the Holocaust,* ed. Jeffery Shandler (New Rork: YIVO Institute for Jewish Research, 2002) that incorporates fifteen biographies from a much larger YIVO collection.

people who share her intellectual aspirations. Instead, in order to fit in among her classmates, she compromises herself in so many ways that the phrase, "I am Charlotte Simmons," takes on a hard-edged irony. Likewise, when Yiddish—the vernacular of Ashkenazic Jews and their descendants—moved into the American mainstream, it underwent profound changes in accommodating itself to its new surroundings. Those changes affected not only the reputation of Yiddish, but its very nature.

Earlier this year, an earnest graduate student—a young woman wearing a small silver cross—stopped me to ask about Isaac Bashevis Singer's novel *The Family Moskat* that she had just finished reading at the suggestion of a Jewish friend. Fascinated by Singer's panoramic study of three generations of Warsaw Jews, she was puzzled by the book's enigmatic conclusion—a conversation between two leading characters during the German bombardment of the city in September 1939 that signaled the start of the Second World War:

> Hertz Yanovar burst into tears. He took out a yellow handkerchief and blew his nose. . . . "I've got no more strength," he said apologetically. He hesitated for a moment and then said, in Polish: "The Messiah will come soon."
> Asa Heshel looked at him in astonishment. "What do you mean?"
> "Death is the Messiah. That's the real truth."[3]

The sobriety of this ending is no surprise. Writing this book after the war, Singer must have felt that he was memorializing his destroyed community of Polish Jews. In the end, the novel's main character, Asa Heschel, has not managed to escape the city, although he had thought about it often and could have managed it earlier. Nonetheless, the student was justified in wondering about the identification of death as the Messiah. Was Hertz Yanovar voicing the author's view that the Messiah had come to European Jews in the form of the Shoah? Was this a comment on the Jews' misguided hopes for redemption? Were we meant to accept this as a verdict on modern Jewry as a whole?

---

[3] Isaac Bashevis Singer, *The Family Moskat,* trans. A. H. Gross (New York: Farrar, Straus and Giroux, 1978), 611.

My questioner could not have known that the Yiddish version of *Di mishpokhe mushkat,* serialized in the Jewish daily *Forverts* (*Forward*) between January 1946 and May 1948, had concluded on a redemptive note.[4] As the Yiddish version of the novel draws to a close, the narrator salutes a group of young Jewish pioneers who were on their way to Eretz Israel.

> The Jewish land was far away. The desert was closed to them. No pillar of cloud showed the way by day, no pillar of fire by night. God had hidden his face. Jacob had been defeated. His enemies mocked him: Where is your God, O Israel? Why is your Protector silent? Where is His justice? Where is His covenant? Your Prophets have betrayed you. God Himself is a Nazi. . . .
>
> Jacob has been cremated, Dinah—ravaged, Shimon and Levi—gird your loins. Don't expect any pity. Amalek stalks you. Pharaoh is readying his chariots. Everything remains as of yore: Israel and the Canaanite, God and the Idols, Egypt and the fleshpots. Moses is dead, but he calls out to you: arise, remnants of Israel, and ready yourselves for the final battle. The house of Jacob is aflame and the House of Esau is made of straw. Go forth and fear not. The final victory will be yours. Messiah is on his way to you.

The Yiddish version repudiates despair. Jews must now conquer the Land because they can no longer wait for divine guidance. Appearing in the very month that the State of Israel came into being, this Yiddish novel invoked the victory of Jews who fight on their own behalf. The Yiddish Messiah points the way, not to death, but to Zion.

When I translated the original ending for the student, she could not understand why Singer had introduced such a radical change, giving the English audience a wholesale Jewish catastrophe in place of a national resolution? While we cannot know all the considerations that went into Singer's decision, we may be certain that the translator was conveying the author's intention. In effect, Singer wanted to reinforce the confidence of the Yiddish public by pointing them to the single

---

[4] For Bashevis Singer's publications during this period, see David Neal Miller, *A Bibliography of Isaac Bashevis Singer 1924–1949* (New York, P. Lang, 1983).

bright spot on the horizon, but to downplay the national project for those who might be indifferent or hostile to the Jewish struggle for sovereignty. David Roskies speculates that Bashevis Singer "expunged the parochial message of hope and continuity" and pointed the American English readership toward a despondency that would find its apotheosis in the increasingly popular image of the Holocaust.[5]

Half a century earlier, the first Yiddish writer to break through to an American reading public was the poet Morris Rosenfeld, whose book, *Songs of the Ghetto,* was translated into English in 1898 by Harvard Professor of Slavic Studies Leo Wiener. Rosenfeld was by then very popular in the immigrant community. Drawing upon his own travails as a tailor—first in London, then in America—and hardships that included the loss of several children in infancy, Rosenfeld wrote a new kind of personal lyric that voiced the social and national sorrows of his fellow Jews. In poems that were often set to music, a modern cantor seemed to be standing at the head of an immigrant congregation not to recite the traditional liturgy, but as "the teardrop millionaire," to express its sentiments and apprehensions. At a time when ideological conflicts fractured Jewish society, Rosenfeld blended socialist and nationalist themes, mourning alike the Jew in exile and the worker tied to his machine.

In the Jewish day school that I attended in Montreal, where Jewish subjects were taught in Yiddish, Rosenfeld's song, "*O, ir kleyne likhtelekh,*" was part of the Chanukah repertoire:

> *O, ir kleyne likhtelekh! Ir dertseylt geshikhtelekh, mayselekh on tsol, ir dertseylt fun blutikayt, beryeshaft un mutikayt, vunder fun amol.*

> O, little candles, what stories you tell, of blood and courage and bygone miracles. Whenever I see you flickering, I recall how Jews once fought, how Jews once triumphed. It's hard to believe that we were once a people who ruled sovereign in our land! O little candles, your stories stir me to pain. Our people once did more than complain. We showed the enemy how to do battle. Bravely we struggled for our

---

[5] David G. Roskies, *Against the Apocalypse: Responses to Catastrophe in Modern Jewish Culture* (Cambridge, MA: Harvard University Press, 1984), 301–302.

faith, and raised the flag of victory. Generations passed and we have since grown weak. In exile we lost our former might. Yet the fire of the Hasmoneans is in our blood. We may be weak as flies, but our ideal still burns in us. The nations of the world will never defeat us![6]

Like the flickering candles that it invoked, this song was meant to rekindle the ideal of Jews as a sovereign people. When I later read more of Rosenfeld, I discovered many poems on the sufferings of exile, longing for Eretz Israel, and the stirrings of modern Zionism.

Rosenfeld divided his poetic self into three equal parts—the Jew, the satirist, and the poet of social protest—but those encountering the poet in English were to discover only the last of the three. The English Rosenfeld figured almost exclusively as the "singer of Labor," who sings in weary accents "to the maimed spirit of the Jewish slums." He lets us hear "the pathetic cry of the bright spirit crushed in the poisonous air of the ghetto."[7] Leftist anthologists presented him as a poet of the "American Jewish working people."[8] Irving Howe, who championed the translation of Yiddish literature into English, characteristically interpreted Rosenfeld as one of several "poets of the sweatshop."[9] As a number of critics have by now pointed out, Howe's affectionate study of the immigrant generation, *World of Our Fathers*, emphasized the socialism of the Lower East Side at the expense of its Jewish religion and Zionism. "[He] was writing an elegy not only for a vanished culture, but for American Jewry."[10] Howe emphasized the aspect of Jewish life that bound him to the socialist movement, while airbrushing out of

---

[6] Morris Rosenfeld, "Di khanike likht," in *Shriftn* (Works), vol. 1 (New York: Forverts edition, 1909): 132–134.
[7] Hutchins Hapgood, *The Spirit of the Ghetto: Studies of the Jewish Quarter of New York* (New York: Funk & Wagnalls, 1902), ch. 4, "A Singer of Labor."
[8] Aaron Kramer, *Moses: Poems and Translations* (New York: O'Hare Books, 1962), table of contents.
[9] Irving Howe, *World of Our Fathers* (New York: Simon and Schuster, 1976), 421.
[10] Edward Alexander, *Irving Howe—Socialist, Critic, Jew* (Bloomington: Indiana University Press, 1998), 186.

the picture the religious and national faith that continued to sustain American Judaism.

We find yet another example of this trend in the career of Abraham Cahan, founder and long-time editor of the *Forverts,* who more than anyone else brokered the marriage between the immigrant Jews and America. No one in American life before or since so effectively worked both sides of the street, introducing Americans to the Lower East Side while interpreting America to his fellow Jews. Cahan's most noteworthy English fiction about the Jewish immigrant community was the 1917 classic *The Rise of David Levinsky,*[11] a rags-to-riches story about a penniless newcomer who works his way up in the clothing industry to become a large-scale manufacturer of women's coats. In the course of his climb, he betrays some of his benefactors, tries to crush the unions, and seduces another man's wife. He finds no satisfaction in his achievement, however, and looking back over his life, concludes, "[My] present station, power, the amount of worldly happiness at my command, and the rest of it, seem to be devoid of significance."[12] Late in the tale he says, "Sometimes when I am alone in my beautiful apartments, brooding over these things and nursing my loneliness, I say to myself: 'There are cases when success is a tragedy.'"[13] In much of Western fiction, the rush to economic success similarly results in moral failure, a formula exploited by one of Cahan's American mentors William Dean Howells in his novel *The Rise of Silas Lapham.* Cahan adapted the Jewish immigrant experience to the requirements of this genre, punishing his hero with remorse for the crime of "making it."

Yet Cahan's own trajectory demonstrated another side of the American Jewish experience. Starting out as a socialist with a vengeance, Cahan once called socialism the *neshomeh yesireh* of Judaism—the additional soul that some Jews believed inhabited them on the Sabbath.[14] The ears of his newspaper (the boxes on either side of

---

[11] The most recent edition in the series of Modern Library Classics (New York: Random House, 2001) has an introduction by a former editor of the English *Forward,* Seth Lipsky.

[12] Ibid., 3.

[13] Ibid., 517.

[14] Abraham Cahan, *Di neshome yesire* (New York, s.n. 1913?).

the paper's name) bore the motto: "Workers of the world, unite! You have nothing to lose but your chains." Cahan spread this message through what he grew into the largest-circulation Yiddish paper in history, with an estimated readership in the 1920s of almost one million. But as he liked to say of himself, he never placed ideology above the interests of the Jews. By the end of World War I, the paper specialized in bringing news of Jewish crises and the spread of anti-Semitism in Europe. After initial enthusiasm for the Bolshevik takeover in Russia, the *Forverts* exposed the repressiveness of the Soviet dictatorship. For all its enthusiasm about acculturation to America, the *Forverts* also tracked nativist sentiments in post-war America that dramatically slowed Jewish immigration to this country. Unlike the Jewish-owned *New York Times* that underplayed the dangers to the Jews as a subject unworthy of general interest, the Yiddish *Forverts* exposed threats to the Jews of Europe and Palestine.

By the mid-1920s, Cahan conceded that the single bright spot on the Jewish horizon was the new pioneering community of Palestine. His first visit to Palestine in 1925 coincided with the wave of immigration triggered by worsening conditions in Poland that brought 33, 801 people into the *Yishuv* that year.[15] Realizing the potential importance of favorable coverage from the *Forverts,* the leaders of the Jewish community in Palestine arranged for Cahan to see the best of what had been created, including the *kibbutzim* and the agricultural settlements, and to meet with the most influential Jewish personalities. Cahan's dispatches to the *Forverts* seemed exceptionally reliable because he had arrived there as an unbeliever. He determined to cover the country thoroughly from top to bottom, describing all the shades of life and each and every corner, so as "to get deep down into the problems and understand the situation correctly."[16] Although Cahan could not bring himself to espouse Zionism outright, his reportage conveyed "his great sense of moral elevation, the enthusiasm that gripped him

---

[15] Much of this information is contained in Yaacov Goldstein's valuable introduction to his edited book, *Jewish Socialists in the United States: The Cahan Debate 1925–1926* (Brighton, England and Portland, Oregon: Sussex Academic Press, 1998).
[16] Ibid., 72.

and the deep appreciation he evinced for everything he saw in the country."[17] From this point onward, the *Forverts* covered Eretz Israel as the emerging homeland of the Jewish people.

Following a second trip to Eretz Israel in 1929, Cahan issued a small book in English based on his *Forverts* reportage, but this English polemic never enjoyed anything like the success of *Levinsky* and remains unknown to English readers. A recent biography of Cahan typically mentions the book in a perfunctory discussion of Cahan's Yiddish journalism, devoting the bulk of its 170 pages to Cahan's English writing, culminating, of course, in *David Levinsky*.[18]

In sum, Abraham Cahan, as we know him in English, pronounces the same harsh verdict on the Jewish future as Bashevis Singer's revised English novel and Morris Rosenfeld's revised English reputation. We read in English a woeful verdict on Jewish destiny and Jewish survival, but in Yiddish, an often passionate struggle for Jewish rescue and for the Land of Israel. I do not mean to suggest that all Yiddish writers were necessarily patriots or defenders of Judaism. Not at all. American Yiddish writers were sometimes tendentious in their opposition, let alone their indifference, to Jewish nationalism. Yet writers in the Yiddish orbit were drawn back to Jewish concerns while working in English drew writers away from those concerns. Confinement to a Jewish immigrant audience and to a European Jewish language exerted a centripetal pressure on Yiddish writers that contrasted with the opposing centrifugal forces governing the move outward into American society. Language was not merely a vehicle of expression, but a determinant of identity. Whether out of aesthetic, commercial, or ideological considerations, whether initiated by the author, the translator, or the editor, the shift from Yiddish into English routinely suppressed the national/religious component of Judaism.

Turning now from aspects of Judaism and Jewishness that routinely *didn't* make it into English translation, we may look at the aspect

---

[17] Ibid., 24.

[18] Cahan's last book is a mild but firm attack on the writer Sholem Asch for espousing the Christian version of history in his trilogy on the life and times of Jesus. See *Sholem ash's nayer veg* (New York, s.n., 1941).

of Yiddish that most assuredly *did*—its comic image, the idea that Jews are funny. In the late 1960s, sociologist Sig Altman was watching a television talk show when one of the panelists, in the course of a totally serious discussion, remarked that he had found his information in the *Jewish Encyclopedia*. He described it this way:

> There immediately followed a burst of laughter from the studio audience, which obviously sensed a joke about to materialize, or perhaps saw one already born. The laughter rather suddenly subsided, however, as the collective realization apparently dawned that no joke was in fact intended at all. Nevertheless, the comic quality of the word, "Jewish" in the public consciousness had been perfectly demonstrated.[19]

Alerted by this incident, Altman began to monitor the mass media for several years to substantiate his insight that the very word "Jewish" had become laden with humorous overtones. A subsection of his inquiry concluded that Yiddish played a dominant role in identifying Jews with comedy. In their *Big Book of Jewish Humor,* Bill Novak and Moshe Waldoks wrote that "Yiddish has frequently been celebrated for being so rich in comic possibilities that even those who don't understand it are apt to chuckle at many of its terms." They note that F. Scott Fitzgerald used to wander into a Jewish delicatessen just to hear the word *knish*.[20]

No one did more to promote this association of Yiddish with comedy than Leo Rosten, whose *Joys of Yiddish,* first published in 1968, has almost never since been out of print. Arranged as a selective dictionary of Yiddish terms, the *Joys of Yiddish* intersperses terms that relate to Judaism—such as *daven* (to pray) and *minyan* (a prayer quorum)—with juicier items that supply the promised "joys" of the title. There are separate entries for Yiddish exclamations, such as *aha!*, *Ai-yi-yi, oy-yoy-yoy,* and *hoo-ha,* not to mention *feh* and *gevalt!* Words are chosen for their comic sound and then spun for their comic potential, as in this typical entry:

---

[19] Sig Altman, *The Comic Image of the Jew* (Rutherford: Farleigh Dickinson University Press, 1971), 11.
[20] Ibid., xviii.

farblondjet:

> Lost (but *really* lost), mixed-up, wandering about without any idea where you are. I include *farblondjet* not because English lacks adequate words for what *farblondjet* describes, but because *farblondjet*'s euphony exudes an aroma all its own. It refers not simply to being lost, but to having-gotten-way-the-*hell*-and-gone-off-the-track. . . . "He drove toward New Rochelle but got so *farblondjet* that he ended up in White Plains." "His appeal to the jury? Man, was he *farblondjet!*"[21]

Farblondjet is followed by *farchadat, farpotshket, farshtinkener* (sic, sic, sic) and *fartootst* ("a synonym for *tsedreyt*"), each illustrated by a little story.

> Professor Prescott asked a colleague in the philosophy department, Professor Minkus, what does *farblondjet* mean?"
>
> "Wandered way off course, lost, gone far astray," said Professor Minkus. "When I started my career, for instance, I was really *farblondjet:* I was a Reform rabbi for six years."
>
> "Really?" said Professor Prescott. "Were you then unfrocked?"
>
> "No," sighed Minkus, "just unsuited."

Rosten reinforces the connection between speaking Yiddish and being funny, just as Jewish comedians from the borscht belt to the comedy clubs did when they reached for a laugh by saying *shtik* or *shmuk*. On the whole, American Jews seemed to enjoy this comic association. Only an occasional Yiddish scholar objected that this comic Yiddish was mainly an American phenomenon, and not a savory one at that: "Sadly, ludic users of Yiddish think they are continuing traditional Yiddish humor, but the humor is often pseudo-humor just as the language is often pseudo-Yiddish."[22] The scholar objected that such treatment reduced Yiddish language and culture to the status of buffoonery.

One casualty of this association of Yiddish with comedy was the high culture that Yiddish poets and writers in the generation after

---

[21] Leo Rosten, *The Joys of Yiddish,* originally published by McGraw Hill 1968 (New York, Pocket Book, 1970), 112.
[22] Leonard Prager, "Ludic Yiddish" on *Mendele.* Yiddish literature and language website, Jan 26, 1992.

Morris Rosenfeld had begun to create in America at the end of World
War I. (In thinking about high culture I follow Mathew Arnold's definition: knowing "the best that has been said and thought in the
world.") The accents of these Yiddish writers may have sounded funny
when they spoke English, but in their native tongue they competed
with T. S. Eliot, Ezra Pound, and W. H. Auden, irrespective of whether
they were ever acknowledged in turn. Yiddish literature had a late
start, thanks in part to Russian censorship that stifled publishing and
the press, but once it took off, toward the end of the nineteenth century, it compressed into a few decades developments that had spun out
in Western Europe over several centuries. Confirmation of this contention came with the award in 1978 of the Nobel Prize for Literature
to the Yiddish writer Isaac Bashevis Singer, one of several Yiddish writers who had been nominated. Thus, Yiddish poets were creating timeless works of literature in the same culture that Jewish comics were
mining for comedy. But how could one expect Americans, including
American Jews, to imagine a high culture in a language that was being
played strictly for laughs?

The American Yiddish poet Jacob Glatstein (b. 1896), two years
younger than Jack Benny (b.1894), hit his stride in the 1930s while
the comedian was experiencing his first radio success. Glatstein was
then experimenting with Yiddish rhyme and diction, compressing his
ideas and emotions with modernist complexity. A brilliant example of
his wordplay, the lyric "*Zing Ladino*" ("Sing Ladino"), purports to be
about the language of the Sephardic Jews—Ladino (or Djudezmo)
being the vernacular of Jews of Spanish descent, just as Yiddish is the
vernacular of Jews of Central and Eastern Europe. In the opening
stanza of the poem, the "Western" poet invites his imaginary "Eastern" counterpart to show off the challenges and opportunities of *his*
Jewish vernacular:

> Zing ladino, blonder *zenger*
> Unzer *tsoyberzhargonino*
> *Alkolirte rederay*
> *Altsetsungte shprakheray*
> *Zunfargino, gino-gino,*
> Gingoldiker oyfshtral, oyfpral—

Algefarbgedankeray.
Ale broytn, ale toytn,
Ale teygn, ale *tundren,*
Ale *vundren alkolirn,*
Alkharuzin,
Alushpizin,
Ale knoytn, ale hoytn,
Gelroyt un *falashino,*
Palestino daberino,
Unzer, unzer *universladino,*
Blonder *aladino* zing.

I have put into italics all the words that Glatstein "invents" through changes in vowel amalgamation, grammatical alteration, or other devices. The preponderance of such terms makes it clear that, at first reading, Yiddish speakers are no more likely to fully understand this poem than people unfamiliar with the language. The verse mimics the sounds of Ladino, called our *tsoyberzhargonino* (our magical jargon)—the word *zhargon* rendered to sound Sephardic. Ostensibly praising his sister language (the "blond" language of the East as opposed to the "darker" language of the West), the singer shows off his own Yiddish, demonstrating through a run of composite words, soundplays, and neologisms, the marvels of our *universladino* (universal vernacular), our aladino—a tongue as miraculous as Aladdin's lamp. People say of jargon that it is not really a language, that the Jewish vernaculars do not have a grammar and are simply mishmashes of other languages. But the composite term *algefarbgedankeray* argues the opposite side of this proposition: the Jewish vernacular is so inclusive that it accommodates *gedankeray*—the creation of ideas—in every conceivable hue (*ale farbn*).

The poem's playfulness also registers serious undercurrents. The phrase *Palestino daberino* alters the Hebrew root *dbr* (to speak) to form a witty protest against the motto, "Speak Hebrew in Palestine." People say that Jews are a mongrel people, but their *falashino* mixture, evoking the term for Ethiopian Jews, *falasha* (*stranger*), enriches the Jews, just as their languages are enriched by the fusion of their sources. The Yiddish language has traveled with the Jews through many centuries of their life in exile, experiencing the bread (*broytn*) of good days and the death (*toytn*) of bad days and all the history in between. How extraordinary, then, that this language should be abandoned by its native speakers at the very moment that it is proving its genius. The encompassing joke of the poem is that the exoticism of Ladino to Yiddish readers is just how exotic Yiddish is becoming to its own children. The poet knew that his modernist poetry was already beyond most of his contemporaries' abilities to appreciate it.

Whereas Benjamin Kubelsky shed every trace of his Jewishness in the process of winning radio fame as Jack Benny, Jacob Glatstein denied himself even the prospect of translatability in exploiting the full potential of his Yiddish idiom. And the success of the one determined the fate of the other. The more the Jewish comedian was able to associate Jews (in the public mind) with his culturally undemanding comedy, the less the Yiddish modernist could expect readers to expend any effort on his culturally specific verse. This competition between comedian and poet was never acknowledged, since the Jewish comedian was unaware of his Yiddish literary rival. But Yiddish speakers could not simultaneously follow their comedians into the common culture and develop the Yiddish proficiency that was required for reading Glatstein. Not surprisingly, the majority opted for the easier alternative.

As the threat to European Jewry mounted in the 1930s, Yiddish writers shared the growing anxiety of the European Jews who shared their language. In 1934, Glatstein's contemporary, the American Yiddish poet H. Leivick, expressed his fearful sense of isolation in a poetic drama on the theme of Abelard and Heloise. In the play, the noted twelfth-century philosopher has been punished by castration and imprisonment for carrying on a love affair with his gifted student, Heloise. The play's setting is a cell to which Abelard has been confined. In Leivick's version of the story, Abelard was castrated at the instigation of the Church, and incarcerated in the monastery under the sadistic supervision of its head, Father Gregory. One day, a young priest, who turns out to be Heloise in disguise, visits Abelard. After an emotional exchange between the lovers, at the point of wishing to embrace her, Abelard discovers that Heloise has wrapped her torso in chains. "Why have you done this?" he asks. She replies:

To be your equal partner in pain.
The world submitted your body to brutal torture—
Mine should be tortured no less than yours. And if
The executioner's hand has left me untouched,
Forgive me—though I
Shall never forgive myself.
I sought a chain of necessary length,
And wound the rings stiff around my body
An excommunication of self,
A hallowed excommunication.[23]

In a note to the play, Leivick explained that the yearning of Abelard and Heloise for one another became "a symbol of a martyred love that was never betrayed. They who were not destined to be united during their lifetime were finally joined when they were buried in a common grave."[24]

To be sure, a number of personal factors may have drawn Leivick's attention to this subject. He suffered from tuberculosis and, around the time of writing this play, was himself condemned to a monkish existence in a sanatorium. Before escaping to America in 1911, he had served a life sentence in Siberia for revolutionary activity; the conflict with authority had absorbed him from the time he began to write. But composing this play in 1934, as Hitler's Germany isolated the Jews from the rest of humankind, Leivick surely recognized the plight of Jews as greater than his own. In the play, Heloise cannot rescue the solitary prisoner who is denied the possibility of procreation. What she *can* do is to join herself to his fate, to show her conviction in their justice and in their love. When at the end of the play Father Gregory places himself between the lovers and says, "I command you to separate this very minute," Heloise responds: "Separate, separate. You will never keep us apart. You are not the one who can divide us.

---

[23] H. Leivick, "Abelar un heluiz," in *Alev verk* II (Complete Works) (New York: Posy-Shoulson Press, 1934), 488. My translation.
[24] Ibid., 421.

Neither the cross, nor your cane, nor this prison cell."[25]

Though Heloise cannot undo the torture inflicted on her lover, she tries through her act of self-disfigurement to forge a common resistance against the world's cruelty by joining herself in flesh to the man she is already joined to in spirit. Rather than call on the spirit to compensate for the body as in the original legends surrounding Abelard and Heloise, Leivick called on the those still living in freedom to unite themselves physically and defiantly with those being tortured abroad.

Yoked to the language, culture, and fate of European Jewry, Yiddish writers in America like Glatstein and Leivick were increasingly aware of the differences between themselves and most other American Jews. In 1940, the Yiddish poet Kadya Molodovsky addressed a wry "Proposition" to God.

> One of your worlds doesn't please me at all,
> I'm afraid of its rulers . . . don't let the word get out.
>
> You play such odd jokes
> On your lovely flower garden,
> And on your people Israel, even in New York,
> Who weep over our destruction, and keep on playing cards.
>
> Just be sure to send your loveliest angel
> To make it easy for me to soar to your Temple,
> Do send your very loveliest angel,
> So that my vision may shut down with a smile.[26]

Kadya (as everyone referred to her) addresses the folksy God of her childhood, looking forward to all that was promised in the legends about the afterlife. She is dismayed at the "odd jokes" (*modne shpasn*) of mass destruction in one part of God's flower garden, while in another, Jews indifferently fritter away their time. Written as if from the

---

[25] Ibid., 496.

[26] Kadya Molodovsky, "Onbot," translated "Proposition," by Kathryn Hellerstein, *Paper Bridges: Selected Poems* (Detroit, MI: Wayne State University Press, 1999), 370–371.

edge of the grave, the poem identifies with the tragedy of the Jews, much as Leivick's Heloise does with her tortured lover. Despite her unhappiness with the way God is running His world, the poet's complaint is addressed strictly to Him; the Jewish card players are merely the object of her contempt, no longer even a party to her protest. Addressing God was one way that American Yiddish poets and writers turned their backs on their disappointing, Anglicizing fellow Jews.

In describing the effects of the switch from Yiddish to English, I am not bemoaning the decline of Yiddish in America, but merely pointing out that the trade-off involved a change of life and not merely language. Jews had spoken their own vernaculars in Europe and the Middle East because their way of life was so essentially different from that of their neighbors that it had generated a separate tongue. Had there been no need for that degree of separation, Jews would not have maintained a separate language; the proof is that they no longer maintained a separate language once they felt no need for it. That separate language exemplified a discrete consciousness, still shared by the immigrant generation in America that wrote in Yiddish, though no longer by those who were writing in the language of the land.

Jews changed their language to English in America much as people adapt their wardrobe to a new climate. America was so much warmer and so much more welcoming than Europe, Jews did not feel they needed insulation from their neighbors. Yiddish had learned to resist persecution, to defend its constituency with cunning and courage. But America proved relatively hospitable; why shouldn't Jews function in the common language of the land, amusing their fellow citizens in the process? However, the accommodation to English created its own realities. Just as a separate language emboldened the Jewish national consciousness, so writing in English for English readers seemed to require a distance from Jewish national concerns—even when writers were translating themselves, as in the cases of Abraham Cahan and Bashevis Singer.

What does all this imply for American Jews? Does it mean that because they now function in English they can no longer foster a Jewish national consciousness? Does America require Jews to forfeit their Jewishness, including their visceral connection with the Land of Israel?

And what especially does it mean for the Jewish writer who wants an American audience? When we know that even Yiddish writers diluted the national impulse of their work in order to satisfy an English readership, can we expect Jewish-American writers to risk alienating their potential readership by riveting their attention to the Jewish fate?

I think the answers are obvious, though hard to accept and harder yet to implement. Fostering Jewish consciousness of an intensity that once generated a separate language requires a tremendous—some would say unnatural—effort. Yiddish writers did not have to attend synagogue to speak to God; like Kadya Molodovsky, they had absorbed the Jewish *got* in their native tongue. Yiddish writers did not have to join AIPAC to express their attachment to Israel: their attachment inhered in the sources of their language. They could not, even if they tried, avoid responsibility for their fellow Jews. By contrast, those American Jews who function in English resemble members of all other ethnic and religious minorities in having either to safeguard their particularism or else see their children flow into the mainstream. If they want to know the God of the Jewish sources, they have to create and support the schools, synagogues, and organizations that will evoke His presence through word, deed, and atmosphere. If they want to experience the solidarity of the Jewish people, they will have to create and maintain the institutions that sustain that solidarity.

Since the English language does not promote Jewish religious civilization, and American culture does not actively foster Jewish solidarity, Jews who function in English have to supply the Jewishness that Yiddish contains and that speaking Yiddish used to reinforce. Translating from Yiddish may satisfy connections with the Jewish past, but the *direction* of translation indicates that these materials are being adapted to English culture. Sustaining the kind of life that Jews experienced in Yiddish means infusing English with the spirit and culture of Judaism and the Jews. Literature can be part of this project, but only if it is prepared to go—as Ludwig Lewisohn would have said—"upstream," making English respond to Jewish priorities.

Mark Helprin's short story "Perfection" is an eye-popping example of how Jewishness can, if it wishes, impose itself on American literature.[27] The protagonist of the story, Roger Reveshze, a fifteen-year-old student in the *yeshiva* of the fictional Hasidic Saromsker Rebbe, is locked in a theological trial with God. The setting is New York City in the year 1956. Sent on an errand to the butcher, Roger overhears on the radio a report of the impending decline of "the House that Ruth Built." What he understands by this term is the Davidic dynasty from which the Messiah is destined to emerge. The butcher—a pious Jew, like Roger—knows only that the once-greatest team in the world, the *Yenkiss,* is dying, and is not expected to win the "pennant" or the "series." Roger determines to become the champion of the *Yenkiss* in order to save the House of Ruth. The story relates how Roger not only takes the Yankees to victory, but turns them into a moral force. Hard-bitten manager Casey Stengel is won over to Roger's faith. Yogi Berra's cockeyed declarations ("You've got to be very careful if you don't know where you're going because you might not get there") acquire the power of mystical pronouncements. Inspired by Roger's ability to hit every ball that is pitched to him out of the stadium and into the stratosphere, the Yankees learn that they are playing to achieve a kind of perfection that reaffirms God's abiding presence in the universe.

Roger is a child survivor of the Majdanek extermination camp. At the age of three, just before the end of the war, he was taken with his parents to be shot. Although he escaped from the mass grave and was brought by the Saromsker Rabbi to the United States, he is not satisfied with his own survival. He demands demonstration of God's redemptive powers in the here and now. Roger's attempt to rescue the *Yenkiss* has less to do with the ball team than with the covenant between the Almighty and His people.

> What the Yankees did not know was that this boy who knew
> nothing about baseball had come into their midst to test an ancient
> compact that of late had been broken. The Yankees did not know that

[27] Mark Helprin, "Perfection," *Commentary* (October, 2004). Reprinted in *The Pacific and Other Stories* (New York: Penguin Press, 2004). References are to this edition.

their stadium had been turned into a court of justice in which the prosecutor was an odd little boy and the defendant was the creator of the universe. In Christian theology—and the Yankees were Christians—this is inconceivable. God does not appear in the dock. He does not dispute with those over whom He holds absolute sway. In Jewish theology, however, he does.[28]

The two thousand consecutive pitches that Roger hits out of Yankee stadium one afternoon, the literally miraculous season to which he treats the Yankees and their fans, is a latter-day version of Elijah providing proofs of God to the priests of Baal. It is also Helprin's proof of Judaism's power, not merely its presence. Just as Roger takes over Yankee Stadium to prove the enduring value of the Jewish contract, the author takes over American myth, literature, and language to demonstrate the power of the Jewish idea.

Yiddish—and the sounds of Yiddish in English—play in this story the kind of comic role that fueled so much of borscht-belt comedy. The confusion between Babe Ruth and Ruth the biblical babe, Roger's pronunciation of Mickey *Mental* and Casey *Stengele,* are standbys of the style of humor I was describing earlier. Ah, but when Mickey Mantle, who has a feature role in the story, describes the black-coated Roger as a *hasid,* it comes out *hayseed,* which is how his teammates refer to *him.*

> "*You* were a hayseed before you got into baseball," Yogi Berra said, expressing the almost universally held impression that Mantle was, somehow, the paradigm of American agriculture.
> Mantle looked sharply at the catcher. "I was *not.*"
> "Sure you were. Everyone knows it."
> "A hayseed?"
> "Yeah. Ask any baseball fan in America."
> "With the hat, and the sideburns and everything?" Mantle asked.
> "That's right," Berra said, thinking of straw hat and rural aspect.[29]

So now the joke goes in two directions. From the perspective of the story, all Americans may have an accent. The Oklahoman is as likely to

---

[28] Ibid., 156.
[29] Ibid., 154.

be tripped up on pronunciation as the Brooklyn Jew. And the more Roger works his way into the team, the more we see this kind of reciprocity at work. America saved the Jews, but the Jews also save America. Roger uses sport to make his point, but warns his teammates against thinking that sport *is* the point: "If [games] are taken as a universe in themselves, what a meager universe that is. This offends God, who worked for six days to make the universe we have. Can you imagine what would come of the work of an omnipotent being for six whole days? What is the infinity of detail, the infinity of extent, the infinity of connectedness, and the infinity of surprise, times six?"[30]

There is nothing more American than baseball, no team more American than those named the Yankees, and yet here we see that, had the believing Jew not come to their rescue and imbued them afresh with appreciation of God's living grandeur, they might have crumbled. Helprin's story joins the fate of both Houses of Ruth to one another, but shows in the process how much effort is required by a community and its writers to supply the missing national consciousness of Yiddish.

Yiddish writers had trouble *escaping* the atmosphere of Jewishness, whereas Jewish writers in English have to resist the allure of English to *remain* within the Jewish sphere. The very features of America that we most appreciate—its tolerance of pluralism, its welcoming embrace—work to dissolve the Jews' special connection to their people. On the other hand, with sufficient effort and faith, Jews may invigorate the country that gave them refuge. Translation from Yiddish will do nothing in itself to perpetuate the kind of Jewishness that Yiddish embodied. Jewishness can only be perpetuated by the religious and national fortitude that created Yiddish in the first place.

---

[30] Ibid., 185.

IMAGES WITH TEETH: THE POLITICAL INFLUENCE OF ARTWORK IN AMERICAN YIDDISH PERIODICALS, 1910s–1930s

Lauren B. Strauss

It has often been said that a picture is worth a thousand words. There was a time in the history of American Jewish activism during which a group of pictures were worth a thousand slogans in the fight to further a progressive agenda. During the early decades of the twentieth century, the Yiddish press in America boasted a number of long-running illustrated periodicals that enjoyed a fairly wide circulation. Many of these had a left-wing bent, though the extent of their devotion to specific political platforms differed depending on their sponsoring organizations and editorial boards. One common characteristic of these publications was that their artwork contributed greatly to the impact of their message, by succinctly expressing widely-held beliefs, conveying great emotion in times of tragedy or stress, and cleverly summarizing the central issues and conflicts of the "Yiddish street." These somewhat ephemeral works on paper used powerful images to translate American concerns and world events for the Yiddish-speaking public. In doing so, they served as a powerful agent of acculturation for those Yiddish-speaking Jews who preferred less establishmentarian routes to becoming American. Humor and social criticism (often combined in a single publication) provided a vehicle for secular Jews to comment on American values. The resulting commentary made creative use of Jewish religious and historical references, which resonated even for most of the secular arrivals from Europe's Jewish communities.

A survey of the range of illustrations in American Yiddish journals of the early twentieth century reveals the ideals and challenges of the Yiddish-speaking immigrant Jewish community. One can draw

important conclusions about the evolving relationship of Jewish immigrants to the left-wing agenda in the United States during those years
by comparing the subject matter of an earlier journal's illustrations
with the visual content of a later one. This is particularly true for the
satiric journal *Der groyser kundes* (*The Big Stick*) in the nineteen-teens,
the Communist-sponsored illustrated daily newspaper *Freiheit* (*Freedom*), and the monthly magazine *Der hamer* (*The Hammer*) in the mid-
nineteen-twenties and -thirties.[1]

In the annals of illustrated American Yiddish periodicals, a special place is reserved for the unique qualities of *Der groyser kundes*.
Founded in 1909 by humorist Joseph Tunkel, editor of the earlier
satiric periodical *Der kibitzer* (*The Kibbitzer*), *Der groyser kundes* met the
needs of a politically astute, secular, left-wing, Jewish immigrant audience whose heads were aligned with American progressives while
their feet were often (metaphorically) still planted in the soil of their
East European *shtetls*. Religious references, folklore, and news of coreligionists still living under the Tsarist fist were welcome material for
serious news consumption and sometimes for the communal funny
bone. Even confirmed anarchists and less well-educated Jews could
often relate to the trope of suffering and the Jew's special relationship
to God, books, and wandering that figured so prominently in the
history and religious traditions of their people. Such themes were
reflected in the paper's illustrations, particularly through their judi-
cious contemporary applications of familiar Bible stories and Jewish
customs.

With its wealth of sources and its willingness to skewer everything
from public figures to religious symbols, the paper was received enthusiastically almost from its inception. Though Tunkel was the leading
force behind the establishment of *Kundes*, he soon returned to Europe
to edit the Warsaw Yiddish paper *Moment*, leaving *Kundes* under the ed-

---

[1] Although current Yiddish transliteration favors the use of an "ay" rather
than an "ei," I refer here to the Communist-sponsored Yiddish daily newspaper as the *Freiheit*, not the *Frayhayt*. In doing so, I have chosen to retain the
original English spelling on the newspaper's masthead during the years that
are covered in this essay.

itorial hand of Jacob Marinoff. Marinoff cut a more cosmopolitan figure than the often bitterly satiric Tunkel, whose chosen pseudonym was *Der tunkler*—the dark one.[2] Under Marinoff's direction, *Kundes* (which had begun as a biweekly) began weekly publication in November 1910 and maintained this schedule until it folded in 1927. In its first three years, the journal boasted approximately 35,000 subscribers—a comparatively healthy number for the Yiddish press. By comparison, the daily *Freiheit* (renamed the *Morgn Freiheit* in June 1929) estimated that it had nearly 65,000 subscribers at its height in 1930, while the *Forverts* (*Forward*), the world leader in circulation among Yiddish publications, reportedly reached 200,000 subscribers.[3]

Despite Marinoff's determination to spoof what he regarded as self-important figures in society, the editor was sympathetic to the efforts of the Yiddish literary movement *Di yunge*—"the young ones."[4] This group of poets and writers included, among others, Zishe Landau, Reuben Iceland, the celebrated Mani Leyb, Moyshe Leyb Halpern, and literary impresario David Ignatoff. Their movement was bent on demonstrating the flexibility and artistic potential of the Yiddish language. They ambitiously applied its thousand-year mosaic of Hebrew letters and words, Slavic color, and Germanic structure and vocabulary

---

[2] Marinoff's sister, actress Fania Marinoff, was married to writer and cultural critic Carl Van Vechten. The pair hosted a salon in their home in which some of the most important figures in jazz and modern art could be found socializing.

[3] For figures on *Freiheit* subscribers, see Arthur Leibman, *Jews and the Left* (New York: John Wiley & Sons, 1979), 346. Leibman calls the *Freiheit's* estimate of 64,500 "highly suspect and probably inflated." On the other hand, the number of subscribers rarely equaled the number of readers, since copies of the most popular Yiddish newspapers were often passed around between families and friends, thus "stretching" a single subscription. For the estimated circulation of the *Forverts* and *Der groyser kundes,* see Aaron Rubinstein, "Devils & Pranksters: *Der groyser kundes* and the Lower East Side," *Pakn Treger,* 47 (Spring 2005/5765): 18.

[4] The most comprehensive study of *Di yunge* is in Ruth R. Wisse, *A Little Love in Big Manhattan: Two Yiddish Poets* (Cambridge, MA: Harvard University Press, 1988). Also see the discussion of *Di yunge's* relationship to Joseph Tunkel and *Der groyser kundes* in Rubinstein, 18.

to the task of describing life in the modern world—particularly in Manhattan, the apex of a new, raw culture. Several of the writers were involved with more highbrow journals, most notably *Shriftn* (*Writings*), whose *raison d'être* was to create a forum for modernist expression in the Yiddish language. In addition to works by its own cadre of poets and essayists, some of whom were primarily visual artists, *Shriftn* published translations of works by modern English-language writers such as Amy Lowell and Edgar Allan Poe. Its most exalted place was reserved, however, for American poet Walt Whitman, who represented to the young immigrants an iconic combination of brash individualism and entitlement, as simultaneously an elite individualist and a champion of democracy and the masses.[5] The illustrations in *Shriftn* were likewise fairly high-minded and cerebral. Max Weber's woodcuts of lone, African-influenced nudes and faces coexisted with Abraham Walkowitz's ecstatic sketches of dancers (inspired by the embodiment of modernist free expression, Isadora Duncan) and figures drawn with a heavier impasto in black ink, portraying street scenes, pensive faces, and what Walkowitz would later term "faces from the ghetto."[6]

It would seem that a periodical like *Der groyser kundes,* devoted to disemboweling the pretensions of intellectuals and other figures, would be anathema to this group of self-conscious young literary lions. In fact, however, there were many commonalities, not the least of which was their devotion to the marriage of written words and visual images as a tool to achieve maximum impact on their readers' psyches. *Di yunge* saw themselves in the pages of *Shriftn* (and elsewhere) challenging stagnant patterns of Yiddish poetic expression that had em-

---

[5] In the Yiddish literary community, *Shriftn* was certainly not alone in this adulation of Whitman. *Albatros,* an avant-garde Yiddish journal of art and poetry published in Warsaw and Berlin during the early 1920s, included in its credo this statement: "For us, modern poets, Walt Whitman is the first and last poet, because he spoke the first and last word." See reference in Leonard Prager, *Yiddish Literary and Linguistic Periodicals and Miscellanies: A Selective Annotated Bibliography* (Darby, PA: Norwood Editions, 1982), 35.

[6] Abraham Walkowitz, *Faces from the Ghetto* (New York: Machmadim Art Editions, Inc., 1946).

phasized the proletarian themes of the sweatshop poets and revolutionary balladeers. They imagined that in addressing life in the urban environment and the fate of the individual, they were diving into the ebb and flow of modern society. The satiric elves behind *Der groyser kundes* exposed and challenged current assumptions and community institutions in a more concrete fashion, criticizing specific events and figures as well as the general hypocrisy and corruption of their milieu. Because Yiddish could not help but evoke multiple historical associations with every word, both publications balanced precariously—and often opportunistically—between the crucible that had formed them in Eastern Europe and the blank slate that awaited in the New World.

Like several of its contemporaries in the American Yiddish press, *Kundes* favored the progressive side of the political spectrum. However, it was more nuanced and less beholden to a specific dogma than some other periodicals, particularly those established following the birth of the American Communist Party after World War I. In its blend of social and political commentary, the paper addressed its readers' European origins as well as their immigrant troubles. A fundamental characteristic of the cartoons that appeared throughout the journal's existence was the tendency to observe world events and developments through a Jewish lens, either referencing the Bible and Jewish history, or by implicitly asking an age-old question—"Is this good for the Jews or bad for the Jews?" If the situation required the artist to choose between Jewish constituencies—European versus American (even recent immigrants), or poor versus rich—the poor and European were invariably favored.

Like much of the press at the time, *Der groyser kundes* relied on its writers to offer pieces appropriate to different moods and situations and, if necessary, to assume a variety of personas, complete with pseudonyms and inside jokes. Its illustrators were no different. Several of them used a variety of names, signed in English or Yiddish, and discussed a wide range of topics, from the ridiculous to the merely humorous to the tragic. Working in the spirit of their most revered predecessor, nineteenth-century French artist and political cartoonist Honoré Daumier, a number of the artists elevated their medium to a level worthy of the best social commentary. Some of the illustrations, however, were taken from other sources (presumably without the permission or knowledge of their creators) and given appropriate Yiddish captions.

Out of a long roster of artists whose work was published in *Kundes,* three stand out as the most influential. The best known of these, Saul Raskin, had a long and varied career that moved rather notably from the Left to the establishment. In the second decade of the twentieth century, Raskin led museum tours and lectured on art for the Workman's Circle and illustrated *Kundes* cartoons, then served in the thirties as art director for the Ninety-Second Street "Y." In the nineteen-forties and -fifties, he illustrated a series of classic Jewish texts, including *Pirke Avot* (*Ethics of the Fathers*), the Passover *Haggadah,* a book on *Kabbalah,* and several others.

His colleague Zuni Maud is a more obscure figure today, but he was an eclectic, multi-talented, popular character who built a career as illustrator for both satiric and literary publications and Yiddish children's journals. He was also a cocreator of the only Yiddish marionette theater in America, the leftist Modicut Puppet Theatre.[7] Maud's illustrations offer an unusual combination of Jewish cultural and religious references (despite his own secularism) and grotesque scenarios. One typical Maud drawing depicts a gathering of Jewish religious leaders around a banquet table, exchanging words of Torah while they conceal knives behind their backs to stab one another. On the other hand, Maud's love for the working folk of the community is evident, even in his jibes at their absurdities.

The illustrator who had the greatest influence on the tone, political agenda, and legacy of *Der groyser kundes,* however, is a now-obscure artist named Leon Israel, known to readers by his *nom de plume,* LOLA. LOLA exposed the pretensions and corruption of local and federal officeholders and the hypocrisy of financial giants such as J. P. Morgan, Jacob Schiff, and the Rockefellers. He tirelessly reminded his audience about Jewish vulnerability in foreign lands, and urged U.S. in-

---

[7] See Edward Portnoy, "Modicut Puppet Theatre: Modernism, Satire, and Yiddish Culture," *The Drama Review,* 43:3 (1999), 115–134.

„ישראל בין העמים"!
(דער איד צווישען די פעלקער.)

דער בער: — פיין, פיין, מאיעסטעט! אם אזוי... איצם זעהט מען ערשט, אז צוער מאיעסטעט איז א ציוויליזירטע חיה.
דער לייב: — מהענק יו, דושענטעלמען! אבער וזי... וזי מינטסמו דאס, פריינד בער? מיינסטע מיך צו שמייכלען אדער צו בעלײדיגען?...

Figure 1

volvement in protecting Jews at a time when interference in other countries' internal affairs on behalf of oppressed people was a rarity. He exhorted laborers to unite to improve their economic conditions, and he mourned with the immigrant Jewish masses in times of tragedy at home and abroad.[8]

In a LOLA cartoon from the fall of 1911[Figure 1], the predicament of Europe's Jews *vis-à-vis* the world powers is dramatized by one

---

[8] His years as a contributor to *Der groyser kundes* were the highlight of Leon Israel's career. In the nineteen-fifties, a book of his drawings of the Lower East Side, entitled *Di amolike ist side in bilder* (*The East Side of Yesteryear in Pictures*) was published. The tone of the portraits is somber; the subjects, street people and the working poor. These works lack the witty and incisive edge of his cartoons for the periodical, which seem to have resulted from his fortuitous association with a unique forum that fostered the best in him.

of the artist's favorite techniques, the use of animal imagery to denote human bestiality and cunning. A salivating wolf labeled "Austria" hovers behind the proverbial Russian bear, who wears a Tsarist soldier's uniform and is fitted with the trappings of corrupted authority—billy club, handcuffs, and gallows—that oppressed Jews and other undesirables. England is portrayed here as a noble lion wearing a crown, but its massive paw rests on the only human figure in the scene, immobilizing a fist-waving, indignant Jew. The headline reads "Israel Amongst the Nations," in both Hebrew and Yiddish.

By 1914, when the guns of war began to sound in Europe and the Jews' status there became even more precarious, *Kundes* illustrators expressed still greater concern about their coreligionists. In a host of war-related cartoons, they pictured the fighting forces as even more savage than the beasts that LOLA had portrayed three years earlier. The illustrations in *Kundes* during the war years highlight even more dramatically than do its essays and commentaries the terrible circumstances in which the Jews of Europe found themselves. In an October 1914 drawing [Figure 2] by Zuni Maud (who uses an English pseudonym here, M. Sunny), a Jewish family huddles around its holiday table inside a *sukkah*. Legions of soldiers storm the frail structure, jabbing long bayonets through the walls. Simply and poignantly, the message is conveyed by a one-word headline: *"Ushpizin."* The term describes a custom of the *Sukkos* holiday whereby a family invites individuals—usually historical figures like the patriarchs or great rabbis—to be honored guests in their *sukkah*. The note under the cartoon explains that this scene of barbarity is what Europe's Jews can expect in their *sukkahs* that year—bloodletting rather than rejoicing. It appears that Maud's devoutly secular perspective on life and Judaism did not stymie his ability to reach out to his audience with a religious reference. Though he and most of his readers had abandoned the formal practice of religion, it was still a powerful and nostalgic tool around which to rally their forces.

The Jews who had managed to escape Europe's turmoil for America's shores were themselves criticized in a simple tableau from the same period. In a drawing by LOLA from October 1914 [Figure 3], an old, suffering woman, with billowing smoke reaching to the skies behind her head, leans on a section of the globe marked "Europe."

"אושפיזין"

רי (או)שפיזען, וואָס די אידען אין   אייראָפּא זענען ערוואָרטען היינטיגען סכות...   ר ר

Figure 2

Across the ocean in America, a strong young woman stretches out her arms to the mother figure. Rather than bearing food or money for safe passage, the "daughter" extends several rolled-up documents with titles like "Sympathy," "Good Advice," and "Fine Speeches." In the artist's opinion, the American Jewish community was hiding behind expressions of concern instead of providing more concrete aid for their European brothers and sisters.

The journal's contributors were not alone in their criticism of the Great War. The pacifist press in America featured such figures as the cultural idealists Randolph Bourne and Van Wyck Brooks, writing in *The Seven Arts Magazine*. Progressives were not necessarily anti-war in principle, but were often suspicious of the motives of the war's major players. They saw the conflict as an imperialist squabble designed to

שטיצע פון קינדער...

מ אַ כ ט ע ר : וויין ניט, מאַמעניו, זעהסט דאָך, איך פֿערנעם דיר ניט און דיין גרויס אונגליק!

Figure 3

further oppress the workers of the world, a view which was frequently
reflected in the pages of *Der groyser kundes*. The English-language magazine *The Masses,* literary headquarters for many leading radicals, published the work of several non-Jewish artists and writers who also
published in *Der groyser kundes.* One of the foremost illustrators at *The
Masses,* Art Young, was particularly impressed with the work of *Kundes*
artists and by the periodical's dedication to progressive causes. Even
though he was not Jewish and did not speak Yiddish, Young contributed cartoons drawn especially for *Kundes,* which were then fitted
by the editors with appropriate Yiddish captions. In one example from
1920 [Figure 4] Young visually articulated the paper's support for the
presidential bid of Socialist Party leader Eugene V. Debs. As workers
paste a gargantuan poster of Debs over the visages of other contempo-

THE BIG STICK

א זשורנאל פאר הומאר, וויץ און סאטירע

Vol. XII. No. 21.   New York, May 14, 1920.

דעבס איבעראלעם!

דער קאנדידאט וואס פאראקס פאר אונז אלע קאנדידאטען.

Figure 4

rary politicians, the accompanying caption declares its unequivocal political endorsement of Debs *"Uber alles"*—over all other candidates.

A diverse community was certainly developing then, one which valued the concerns of foreign-born, Yiddish-speaking Jews as a political and social barometer, but which also drew on the strengths and connections of more deeply-rooted Americans to challenge the *status quo* on many levels—social, intellectual, and aesthetic. The effort was perceived by some of those involved as no less than a revolution, with words and paintbrushes serving as artillery, and workers of all kinds as its fighting force. As Hutchins Hapgood, journalist and author of *Spirit of the Ghetto* proclaimed, "There seems a vague but real relationship between all the real workers of our day. Whether in literature, plastic art, the labor movement . . . we find an instinct to blow up the old forms and traditions, to dynamite the baked and hardened earth so that fresh flowers can grow."[9]

In *Der groyser kundes,* sympathy for the poverty-stricken masses on New York's Lower East Side and elsewhere resulted in many drawings that lampooned or excoriated capitalists and capitalism. In the realm of labor activism and workers' tribulations, the most dramatic event to confront *Kundes* readers was the tragic fire at the Triangle Shirtwaist Factory on March 25, 1911. In the catastrophe's aftermath, it was revealed—to the public's horror—that exit doors had been locked to prevent workers from leaving on breaks, that fire codes had been ignored, and that the company's owners had escaped by climbing over rooftops. Most of the 146 victims were young Jewish and Italian girls, many of whom were still teenagers, who had submitted to the punishing life of the sweatshop factory to earn subsistence wages for their families.[10] The Yiddish-speaking public, long accustomed to outrages and tales of workers' hardships, was simultaneously overwhelmed by grief and galvanized by fury to rally for changes in working conditions.

---

[9] Hutchins Hapgood, *New York Globe,* January 27, 1913. Quoted in Martin Green, *New York 1913: The Armory Show and the Paterson Strike Pageant* (New York: Charles Scribner's Sons, Macmillan, 1988), 2.

[10] For the most complete account of the tragedy, see David Von Drehle, *Triangle: The Fire That Changed America* (Boston: Atlantic Monthly Press, 2003).

Illustrations published in *Der groyser kundes* at this time, and for years afterwards on the fire's anniversary, captured these twin emotions of mourning and anger and put a face on the tragedy for thousands of readers. In one [Figure 5] of LOLA's many drawings in response to the fire, an elderly Father Time chisels a tombstone for the nearly 150 victims, while an angel hovers overhead attempting to comfort him. In a different frame [Figure 6], two young female figures keen over a grave set aside for the eight victims who were never identified. One woman is labeled "working classes." As she mourns her comrades, she declares that, despite the impossibility of identifying them, they are part of the family of working people: "They are *my* victims. Oh, I know them, I know them!" Significantly, the victims are referred to in the Yiddish text of both cartoons as *korbones*—the traditional Hebrew term for religious sacrifices, especially in the Holy Temple in Jerusalem. Even a largely secular readership could make the connection between their roles as grief-stricken labor activists and as inheritors of generations of Jewish tradition.

A LOLA cartoon [Figure 7] commemorating the third anniversary of the fire depicts the Triangle Factory as a Greek temple far in the distance, with a prominent dollar sign at its entrance. The long road leading to the temple/factory leaves no doubt in the viewer's mind what type of sacrifice is necessary to achieve the factory owners' goals. The pavement is lined with human skulls, and these "stones," according to the caption, cost seventy-five dollars a piece. The implication here is that incidents such as the Triangle fire were inevitable by-products of the capitalist system. Such thinking was in concert with the sentiments of East Side residents and others horrified by the loss of life and the egregious circumstances surrounding the tragedy, and these images were among the most enduring testimonies to this watershed event.[11]

Through such strong visual statements, the popular and outspoken *Kundes* artists influenced the attitudes of their readers toward war, capitalism, and their own participation in the political process. This

---

[11] These illustrations still resonate today. A LOLA cartoon published in *Der groyser kundes* to commemorate the Triangle Factory Fire was featured in a major exhibition in 2004, "From Haven to Home: 350 Years of Jewish Life in America," at the United States Library of Congress.

NEW YORK, MARCH 31, 1911.

פאטער צייט: דורות וועלען קומען, דורות וועלען פערגעהן, אבער די
דיזע אויפשריפט זאל בלייבען ווי א שווארצער פלעק אויף דעם טאוועל פון דער
אייביגקייט...

Figure 5

זי דערקענט די „ניט ־ דערקענטע"...

צרבייטער קלאָס: — פֿון װאַטגען זײ זאָלען ניט קומען און װער זײ זאָלען ניט זײן, זײ זײנען מײנע קרבנות. 8. איך דערקען זײ, איך דערקען זײ !...

Figure 6

political participation is one important way in which these relative new-comers asserted their American identities. Jewish immigrant artists demanded that their adopted land live up to its promise, and they boldly criticized it when it failed to do so. The artists who published in *Der groyser kundes* revealed weaknesses in the American system and its government more candidly than many a yellow journalist. As they had with their nefarious capitalists and noble working girls, the artists developed a repertoire of familiar faces that served as a shorthand to convey their message of immigrant woes and the betrayal of the nation's founding ideals. Chief among their heroes were Washington and Lincoln, considered standard-bearers of American idealism, while most current politicians were presented as bloated villains. Uncle Sam made repeat appearances as a hapless tool of the ruling classes.

75 דאלער אַ קאָפּ...

דער וועג צו פּראָפּיט, איז נעפּלאַסטערט פון דער פירמע: טויט, קאָפּיטאל
און קאָ. מיט "שטיינער", וואָס קאָסטען צי 75 דאָלער אַ שטיק...

Figure 7

In a LOLA front-page cartoon of January 1911 [Figure 8], President Taft is portrayed as a mustachioed, deceptive Delilah, cutting the locks of a sleeping George Washington, who is dressed and coifed as Samson. The founding father's doomed curls are labeled "Righteousness," "Freedom," and "Tolerance," and the caption drums home the message that *this* Samson's strength lies in the free institutions that are America's bedrock.

Even more biting are illustrations that confront specific issues like the controversy surrounding immigration restrictions. The infamous U.S. literacy test is explored, and in particular the extent to which it was applied unevenly, often to the detriment of targeted immigrant groups. LOLA attacks this test in February 1914 in two separate cartoons. The front page illustration [Figure 9] features Uncle

Figure 8

New York, February 13, 1914   Vol. VI. No. 7   יארק, דען 13טען פעברואר, 1914

וועט ער זי קוילען ?...

די גאנז, וואס האט געלייגט די גאלדענע אייער. — וועט אנקעל סעם פאלגען דעם אימיגראנטען פרעסער און זי קוילען ??? ...

Figure 9

Sam next to a "Free Immigration" goose that lays golden eggs marked with many valuable characteristics of the immigrants and the work they did for the benefit of American society. Uncle Sam sits, weighing the decision of whether or not to slaughter the fat goose, while a shifty-eyed anti-immigration advocate tries to hand him a sharp knife designated "Literacy Bill."

A cartoon in the same issue [Figure 10] evokes the giant legacy of Abraham Lincoln, whose imposing specter confronts a diminutive President Woodrow Wilson. With a ghostly hand on Wilson's shoulder, Lincoln peers down at the literacy bill rolled up in Wilson's hand. "Professor," he reminds the little politician in Yiddish, "my father could not write his name." In the caption underneath, Lincoln points out that he started his own career chopping wood—he is portrayed as

דער האָלצהאַקקער און דער פּראָפעסאָר

אי י ב ר א ה א ם ל י נ ק אָ ל ן (צו פּרעזידענט ווילסאָן) : פּראָפעסאָר,
דיר וועט מסתמא באַלד אויסקומען אונטערצושרייבען די "ליטעראַסי בילל". אַלזאָ,
געדענק, אַיידער דו טונקסט אַיין די פּען זאָלסטו וויסען, אַז מיין טאַטע האָט ניט
געקענט אונטערשרייבען זיין נאָמען, און איך אַליין האָב אויך אָנגעפאַנגען מיין
קאַריערע אַלס אַ בעזוגראַמאָטנער האָלצהאַקער . . . .

Figure 10

a working man, from humble origins, just like many of the immigrants who were targeted by the bill.

That latter-day politicians ignored or alienated the immigrant masses at their own peril was made eminently clear by the ubiquitous LOLA. Prior to a local election in November 1911, the artist created a wicked reptilian representation of Charles Francis Murphy, the current boss of Tammany Hall. Murphy was one of the most notorious and powerful bosses of the Democratic Party machine, and his anti-reform stance suffered in the aftermath of the Triangle Fire. The most dramatic moment arrived when many of the 350,000 people at the victims' funeral procession augmented their criticism of the factory's owners by blaming Tammany Hall for its failure to enforce safety regulations. The influence of downtown voters on Murphy's eventual support for certain labor reforms is well documented. With the popularity of *Der groyser kundes*, LOLA's caricature [Figure 11], circulated to thousands of potential voters and may indeed have struck fear into the hearts of Tammany's leaders.

In the cartoon, a strong and classically rendered female figure labeled "The East Side," dressed in the white robes and sandals of a Greek goddess, grips the fleshy neck of a serpent identified as Tammany (on his tail) and Murphy (on his vest). The snake's eyes and tongue bulge in terror as the woman's terrible sword, inscribed with the words "the Jewish vote," is trained on his heart. In this rendering, the immigrant voting bloc has the force to defeat the cruel and corrupt leaders of local government. As if his message was not sufficiently sharp, the artist's caption declares: "If the East Side is in the right mood next Tuesday, the vote will go according to our cartoon!"

The distinctiveness of *Kundes'* cartoons lay not in their political agenda, which at the time was represented elsewhere (in *The Masses* and its successor *The Liberator,* among others), but in their ability to present this agenda in a uniquely and overtly Jewish manner. From its references to Jewish holidays and the weekly Torah reading to its Jewish sense of wit and pathos, *Der groyser kundes* could not be fully understood without some familiarity with Jewish history and culture. Biblical characters were often used to describe various constituencies in New York (Queen Esther from the Purim story is portrayed as an immigrant working girl, bravely confronting an overstuffed "Boss Ahashveros"),

ווען די איסמ־סייד וועט זיין אין א נומער שטימונג!...

אויב די איסמ־סייד וועט נעקסטען דיענסטאאַנ זיין אין דער ריכמינער שמימונג, וועם זי שמימען אַמ אזוי וויא אידוד זעהמ
אויף אונזער קארטון, דאָן וועם עס שוין שמימען!...

Figure 11

and both artists and writers attached modern-day political significance to the Jewish calendar. Some of the work is unabashedly Zionist, despite the opposition of some readers on the far Left. The death of Zionist leader David Wolfson was portrayed by LOLA in a September 1914 front-page drawing as a great tragedy for the entire Jewish people, while on occasion, even the irreverent iconoclast Zuni Maud sympathized with Zionist aspirations in Palestine. Once again evoking a religious tradition, Maud commemorated the holiday of *Shavuos* in 1920 by writing his own "Book of Ruth." The figures in the picture's background [Figure 12], designated "Rumania," "Poland," "Italy," and other European nations, exercise their landed status in order to harvest produce. In the foreground crouches "Ruth the Jewess," gleaning meager stalks of wheat that bear the caption "Jewish rights in the lands of the Exile." As she stoops to retrieve another stalk, a different label catches Ruth's eye: "Balfour Declaration," proclaims the saving grain,

Figure 12

proffering the hope—less than three years old at the time of the cartoon's publication—that a new chapter will yet be written in the story of the Jewish people.[12]

The most common biblical theme to appear in the art of *Der groyser kundes* is that of the Jews leaving Egypt, crossing the Sea of Reeds, and wandering in the desert to the Promised Land. This rich story is mined for elements to make it memorable and relevant for the paper's readers. It highlights the flight from an oppressive regime, the experience of hunger and wandering, and a danger-fraught journey to a golden land. Drawing parallels to the twentieth century, the artists either presented Moses as Karl Marx, with his staff labeled "enlightenment" and his people marching toward a rising sun of "economic freedom," or as a more traditional figure judging his people.[13] The Jews are either noble refugees wading through perils labelled "prostitution," "child labor," "slavery," and "tenement houses," or they are annoying *nudnikim* (pests), badgering their leaders in pursuit of the almighty dollar. As one of the most ecumenical stories to emerge from the Jewish tradition, the Exodus has been adopted by downtrodden groups in various societies over the centuries. It has had resonance in the United States not only for Jews, but also for black Americans and

---

[12] The Balfour Declaration, issued on November 2, 1917, was named for its principal author, British Foreign Secretary Lord Arthur James Balfour, who wrote in a letter to Jewish leader Lord Walter Rothschild that "His Majesty's Government view with favour the establishment in Palestine of a national home for the Jewish people." This was viewed as tremendously significant by Zionists and their supporters, not only because Great Britain was a major power in the region (and ultimately controlled the mandate for Palestine from 1920 to 1948), but because it was the first official recognition of Zionist aspirations by any Western nation.

[13] The Karl Marx as Moses cartoon is by Raskin, 4/11/14, pp. 8–9. The image of Moses as judge is signed by an artist named Chasan, and is unusual in the extent of Judaic knowledge it requires for full comprehension. Under the title "Illustrated *Khumesh* [the Five Books of Moses]," it notes that the Torah reading for the week is *Parashat Yitro*, where Moses sits in judgment on his people in the desert. The caption, which ends with a humorous remark in Yiddish about the tendencies of the Israelites to complain and be argumentative, begins with a quote from the week's Torah reading in Hebrew. 2/17/11, p. 11.

others active in the labor and civil rights movements.[14] The story's repeated appearance in *Der groyser kundes,* therefore, could also be viewed as a strategy to encourage solidarity with other groups in similar economic straits.

By the time communist Jewish papers such as the *Freiheit* were founded, the expectations placed on leftist artists by political groups had intensified and had become more partisan. Instead of producing a gallery of images in general support of the labor movement, freer immigration, and the defense of Jews abroad, the illustrations in the new radical publications of the nineteen-twenties and -thirties were beholden to a specific political platform, which even dictated the preferred colors and style of its art. The clearest example of the marriage between art and dogma on the American Yiddish scene is found on the covers of the monthly journal *Der hamer* and in the pages of the daily *Freiheit,* both of which were sponsored by the umbrella organization *Freiheit farband* (Freiheit Association). This group also organized rallies, study groups, theater companies, and other political and cultural activities.

Founded in 1922 as a Yiddish-language newspaper for the American Communist Party (the CPUSA), the *Freiheit,* in its early years, embodied a singular combination of doctrine and artistic excellence. Though its editors, Moissaye Olgin, Shachna Epstein, and Kalman Marmor, were all "true believers" in communism at the time, many of the essayists, poets, and visual artists who contributed to the paper were attracted more to its reputation for high-quality cultural offerings than to its political platform. William Gropper, however, the *Freiheit*'s most frequent contributor in the realm of fine arts, was both a gifted caricaturist and a dedicated radical. His illustrations in the *Freiheit* and *Der hamer* were vital to conveying the periodicals' ideas to the Yiddish-speaking public.

As befitted a daily newspaper, the *Freiheit's* artwork was more explicitly topical than illustrations featured on the covers of *Der hamer.* Fluid, ink-splattered, and often blatantly enraged, Gropper's *Freiheit*

---

[14] For an extended reflection on various uses of the Exodus story, see Michael Walzer, *Exodus and Revolution* (New York: Basic Books, 1985).

cartoons frequently transmitted the intensity of current events outside the immediate environs of most American Jews to a subset of Yiddish readers. One such issue was the plight of American miners,
whose labor struggles and abysmal health conditions struck a chord
with Jews involved in progressive politics. Jewish artists were prominent among the activists who visited mines in the nineteen-thirties,
sponsored both by the radical John Reed Clubs and by the federal
government's WPA relief programs. (Even those on government-
sanctioned trips often had to resort to subterfuge to gain access to the
mines, since the powerful mining companies did their utmost to prevent eyewitness accounts of conditions underground.) Jewish artists
such as Harry Sternberg, Riva Helfond, Minna Citron, and Frank Kirk
spent significant time in mining regions getting to know the miners
and their families, and their lithographs and paintings reflect the in-
habitants' dignity and determination. Likewise, sculptors Minna
Harkavy and Berta Margoulies executed fine works focusing on the
miners' hardships, which were featured in art shows and purchased
by major museums.[15]

But even these outlets could not provide the large audience that
the mass media afforded the artists. On March 19, 1929, Gropper's *Freiheit* cartoon *"Dem miners freeling"* ("The Miner's Spring") [Figure 13]
translated the misery of life underground to thousands of newspaper
readers. The illustration's entire frame is darkened, spotted with the
same ash that blackens the miner's face, clothes, and lungs. Even the
weak light from the man's headlamp is unable to brighten his surroundings. He toils in a perpetual night and winter; to him and his
comrades, spring is a cruel taunt never to be realized.

In other cartoons, Gropper dramatized an issue that did not af-
fect *Freiheit* readers directly, but which had a great impact on American Jews generally—the status of black Americans, particularly those
in the southern states. As historian Hasia Diner has noted, America's
Jews were disproportionately attuned to anti-black discrimination at

---

[15] Harkavy's bronze five-person bust, "American Miner's Family" (1931), was
purchased by the Museum of Modern Art in New York by the Abby Aldrich
Rockefeller Fund. Margoulies' bronze, "Mine Disaster" (1942), is in the collection of the Whitney Museum of American Art.

Figure 13

the beginning of the twentieth century. This was reflected in their rhetoric, in the depiction of blacks in fiction by Jews, and in Jewish attention to lynching and *causes célèbre* like the Scottsboro Boys trials in the 1930s.[16] The Yiddish press in America placed such stories on their front pages far more often than other newspapers, except for those specifically geared toward the black community. Gropper was among the many Jewish artists who addressed these topics.[17] On March 20,1929, he published a cartoon [Figure 14] in the *Freiheit* entitled "One May Not Rescue a Negro." Echoing the widely-held belief that authorities had shown egregious racial discrimination in responding to the Mississippi Delta floods of 1927 and 1929, Gropper relates this situation to the flood of racial hatred engulfing the black population of Alabama—the leading state in the number of lynchings of black men. His caption declares, "In the flood taking place now in Alabama, it has been decided that Negroes are the last to be rescued."[18] The words are harsh, but they pale in comparison to the image of two snarling white men in a boat, brandishing an oar and a whip to fend

---

[16] Hasia R. Diner, *In the Almost Promised Land: American Jews and Blacks, 1915–1935* (Westport, CT: Greenwood Press, 1977), 51 and 59.

[17] There is substantial documentation on the involvement of twentieth-century American Jewish artists in issues relating to black Americans. The most comprehensive treatment is by art historian Milly Heyd, *Mutual Reflections: Jews and Blacks in American Art* (New Brunswick, NJ: Rutgers University Press, 1999). Also see Helen Langa, "Two Antilynching Art Exhibitions: Politicized Viewpoints, Racial Perspectives, Gendered Constraints," *American Art,* 13 (Spring 1999): 10–39, and my own dissertation, "Painting the Town Red: Jewish Visual Artists, Yiddish Culture, and Progressive Politics in New York: 1917–1939" (UMI Dissertation Services, 2004), 272–280 and *passim.*

[18] In the floods—which ruined coastal towns and farmlands, stranded and drowned residents (most of whom were African Americans), and further crippled the economy of an already-impoverished region—state, federal, and local authorities, including local offices of the Red Cross, were accused of being much slower to respond to the poor, black population than to white residents of other flooded areas. A commission headed by Robert Moton and convened in 1928 by the Tuskegee Institute found evidence to support many of these claims for the 1927 flood. Even greater floods swamped the area the following year, when Gropper's cartoon was published.

Figure 14

off the drowning black figure, with a pleading expression on his face, and the outstretched hands of several more victims.

The covers of the monthly journal *Der hamer* were more general—though no less ardent—in their advocacy of a political program. Rather than addressing specific events, the magazine's covers, drawn by such artists as Gropper, Louis Lozowick, Hugo Gellert, and Yosl Cutler, usually promoted the same themes of progress, equality, and general contentedness under communism that were found in other pro-Soviet organs at the time.[19] In one cover from May 1926 [Figure 15], an overall-clad worker sporting revolutionary colors of red and black stretches across the frame, smiling as he celebrates the accomplishments of the young Soviet state. On one side, a glistening new factory rises as a sign of progress, and on the other, the presence of an interlocked hammer and sickle erases any doubt about the allegiance of the journal and its supporters.

Another radical artist, the Hungarian-born Hugo Gellert (who was only minimally involved in ventures related to the Jewish community), contributed a cover [Figure 16] with similar themes, but which offers an even more intricate view of the Soviet state. His two workers—rendered again in a black and red palette, as were many *Der hamer* covers—stand back to back, defending their respective territories. One is an agricultural worker with traditional lace-up boots and cap, who gazes at fields and a tractor as he guards the lush lands of the Russian countryside. The other man is an industrial worker, who faces his factory's towers and the houses inhabited by his fellow laborers. By placing the tools of their respective trades—a sickle for the farmer and a hammer for the factory worker—in an interlocking position, Gellert emphasizes the point that one cannot stand securely without the other. Neither the nation's people nor their symbols can stand alone; all of its components—including a small, Yiddish-language journal

---

[19] Several covers by Lozowick, however, were semi-abstractions of city skylines and technology, reflecting his belief in the power of the "Machine Age" to bring about great social advances. During the late twenties and the thirties, he was roundly criticized by certain Party observers for his perceived lack of attention to the figure of the worker. See Pauline Zutringer, "Machine Art Is Bourgeois," *New Masses*, 4 (February 1929), 31.

Figure 15

Figure 16

thousands of miles from the Soviet Union—were necessary for the great communist experiment to succeed. In this way, readers of *Der hamer* and participants in other *Freiheit farband* activities were drawn into a world-wide circle of ideological compatriots who may not have spoken the same languages, but who could see themselves reflected in the popular images generated by artists in their camp.

The range of issues addressed by Yiddish periodical illustrators in the early twentieth century is too exhaustive to encapsulate in a single study. Yet, even a relatively brief exploration suggests the breadth of subjects that interested Yiddish-speaking, progressive immigrant artists in this period. It also testifies to the agility of the artists who labored to convince their community of the justness of their positions. From the working-class and immigrant sympathies of *Der groyser kundes,* to the ideological platforms and formal group loyalties of *Freiheit* and *Der hamer* illustrators, a significant cross section of Jewish communal concerns were portrayed. By visually articulating Jewish support for the labor movement and free immigration, by highlighting injustices that affected groups outside the parameters of urban Jewish life, and by giving a face to the communists' utopian dreams, the artists who illustrated these left-wing Yiddish periodicals helped to forge a dynamic culture and a political consensus among progressive Jews in early-twentieth-century America.

Yiddish Scholars Meet the Yiddish-Speaking Masses: Language, the Americanization of YIVO, and the Autobiography Contest of 1942

Daniel Soyer

In May 1942, the Yiddish Scientific Institute (YIVO) called upon Jewish immigrants to write their autobiographies and submit them for a contest on the theme, "Why I Left Europe and What I Have Accomplished in America" (*Far vos bin ikh avek fun der alter heym un vos hob ikh dergreykht in Amerike*). The institute was itself a newcomer to America, having officially transferred its headquarters from Vilna, then part of recently sovietized Lithuania, to New York in the fall of 1940. For the institute, the contest, which resembled several similar projects that it had undertaken with Jewish youth in Poland in the 1930s, represented an opportunity not only to collect material for the archive that it was reconstructing in its new home, but also to reach out to a new constituency and establish the relevance to American Jewry of its particular brand of Jewish social scientific research. For the writers, the contest provided a chance to take stock of their lives, pour out their hearts to a group of sympathetic readers, and perhaps, if they believed what YIVO told them, to demonstrate the importance of their stories for "science."

The Yiddish language was central to YIVO's work, both as an object of study and as a medium of expression, and issues relating to this language were very much in evidence during the 1942 contest. As Yiddishists, the scholars at YIVO believed that language was an essential carrier of national identity, and that Yiddish embodied the Jewish character, values, and historical experience. In this regard, they could point to the autobiographies as evidence of the language's broad range of social and cultural expression. Some writers, for example, demonstrated their traditional educational attainments through the liberal admixture of Hebrew/Aramaic citations and quotes in their prose, while others demonstrated fluency in the terminology of modern national and political movements, and still others resorted to English picked up in the immigrant neighborhoods in America. Quite apart from the stories themselves, the language that the writers chose to use was an expression of the modern Eastern-European Jewish experience in both Europe and America.

At the same time, the contest revealed a fundamental tension between two aspects of YIVO's brand of scholarly Yiddishism. On the one hand, YIVO shared the movement's democratic ethos, admiring Yiddish precisely because it was the everyday tongue of the Jewish masses—in whom the true spirit of the folk was presumed to reside. YIVO joined with other Yiddishists in believing that raising the status of the people's language went hand in hand with raising the status of the people themselves. On the other hand, if Yiddish was to gain stature as a full-fledged *kulturshprakh,* with all of the rights to which such languages were entitled, YIVO's collaborators believed it needed to function as a means of communication on all sorts of levels, from the most simple and mundane to the most complex and rarified. YIVO therefore set out consciously to develop a modern, secular, academic Yiddish that would necessarily be unfamiliar and, often, barely intelligible to the masses of Yiddish speakers. In its Vilna period, YIVO had often involved the Yiddish-speaking public in its work, and the 1942 contest was a continuation of this innovative approach. But despite their shared use of Yiddish, their many common points of cultural reference, and their similar Eastern-European roots and immigrant experiences, the scholars and their public sometimes had a hard time communicating.

YIVO arose from the highly politicized cultural struggle, within the Jewish community in the late nineteenth and early twentieth centuries, over the nature and future of the Jewish people. The role of Yiddish in Jewish life was at the center of the debate. Traditionally, Yiddish served as Eastern-European Jewry's vernacular, while Hebrew and Aramaic served as the languages of prayer, of the sacred texts, and of traditional learning and scholarly discourse. While virtually all Jews spoke Yiddish, fewer, mostly men, could read Hebrew with any fluency, and fewer still could read the Talmud in Aramaic or write in either of the sacred languages. Many Yiddish speakers also spoke, with varying degrees of fluency, the languages of the local populations and the governing authorities: Polish, Russian, Ukrainian, German, etc. The linguistic palette that average Yiddish speakers had to work with was thus varied, and they could easily borrow words and whole phrases from other languages without disrupting the essentially Yiddish character of their speech and writing. In this way, Yiddish was an *open* language, readily absorbing elements from its surroundings. The mix depended on many factors, including the user's embeddedness in the worlds of traditional Judaism, a modernizing Eastern Europe, and emigrant communities.[1]

Partly because of this openness, Yiddish had a low social status in comparison with the languages that surrounded it. Within the traditional Jewish world, Hebrew and Aramaic—considered as one unit and collectively known as *the Holy Tongue*—enjoyed much more prestige. But Russian, Polish, and German, as the cultural languages of the ruling states and urban elites, were held in high regard as well, especially in the nineteenth century, when many Jews began to seek integration into European society. At the same time, some *maskilim*—and later, many Zionists—sought to revive Hebrew as the Jews' living national language. Both assimilationists and Jewish nationalists held Yiddish in contempt as a deformed and chaotic symptom of exile, incapable of fine or complex expression.

This widespread contempt for Yiddish became a matter of contention at the turn of the twentieth century, when the new Yiddishist movement sought to improve the status of the language of the folk. Often associated with the Left, Yiddishism constituted a form of Diaspora nationalism that viewed the Jews as a nation with the right, the ability, and even the need to develop their national culture in the

---

[1] Benjamin Harshav, *The Meaning of Yiddish* (Berkeley: University of California Press, 1990), 61–73. On the history of the Yiddish language, see also Dovid Katz, *Words on Fire: The Unfinished Story of Yiddish* (New York: Basic Books, 2004); Max Weinreich, *Geshikhte fun der yidisher shprakh* (New York: YIVO Institute for Jewish Research, 1973).

countries where they lived. In addition to being the prime expression of Jewish culture, Yiddish was the glue that would hold together this peculiar nation without its own territory, dispersed over a number of states. In the modern period, many Yiddishists believed that language would need to take the place of religion as the main unifying element in Jewish life, binding together intellectuals and masses.[2] Clearly most relevant to the Jewish heartland of Eastern Europe (in the Russian census of 1897, 98 percent of Jews in the Pale of Settlement listed Yiddish as their mother tongue), Yiddishism also influenced emerging immigrant communities abroad.[3]

Paradoxically, even as they extolled Yiddish as the natural expression of the soul of the common people, Yiddishists sought to create something that had not existed before—a modern, secular, and high culture in Yiddish. This process began in the nineteenth century, before the rise of Yiddishism, as writers such as Mendele Moykher Sforim, Sholem Aleichem, and I. L. Peretz started to develop a modern Yiddish literary language, just as newspaper editors in Europe and America were creating a modern Yiddish journalistic language, and political movements on both sides of the Atlantic were devising ways of discussing current issues and social theory in Yiddish. Eventually, Jewish social welfare organizations such as the Hebrew Immigrant Aid Society (HIAS), the American Jewish Joint Distribution Committee, and the Society for the Protection of the Health of the Jews (OZE,

---

[2] David Weinberg, *Between Tradition and Modernity: Haim Zhitlowski, Simon Dubnow, Ahad Ha-am, and the Shaping of Modern Jewish Identity* (New York: Holmes and Meier, 1996), 138–142; Emanuel Goldsmith, *Modern Yiddish Culture: The Story of the Yiddish Language Movement* (New York: Shapolsky, 1987); Itzik Nakhmen Gottesman, *Defining the Yiddish Nation: The Jewish Folklorists of Poland* (Detroit: Wayne State University Press, 2003), xi–xvi; Cecile Esther Kuznitz, "The Origins of Yiddish Scholarship and the YIVO Institute for Jewish Research (Lithuania)" (Ph.D. dissertation, Stanford University, 2000), 6–10. On Jewish language politics, see also, Benjamin Harshav, *Language in the Time of Revolution* (Berkeley: University of California Press, 1993).

[3] Evyatar Friesel, *Atlas of Modern Jewish History* (New York: Oxford University Press, 1990), 64.

from its Russian name, *Obshchestvo Zdravookhraneniya Yevreyev*) also created a bureaucratic/professional Yiddish jargon.[4]

In addition to remaining the language of the simple folk, Yiddish thus also emerged as the medium of a democratically-inclined and Diaspora-centered high culture. In its rise from *folksshprakh* to *kulturshprakh,* Yiddish was not unique. Unlike other emerging languages and dialects, however, Yiddish was a minority language everywhere, even in its densest strongholds, and its supporters fought to create a modern literary and scholarly language—for the most part without the benefit of state support.[5] This struggle took on increased urgency after World War I in the successor states of East and East-Central Europe, where Jews and other minorities fought for the official recognition of their cultures, including the right to maintain their own school systems. Most political theorists and leaders, even those who favored minority rights, assumed that only fully-developed languages, as opposed to regional or ethnic dialects, would or should have these rights.[6]

Without a central body to guide the development of the modern language, however, a variety of orthographies, sets of grammatical rules, and methods of lexical innovation were pressed into use. Standardization of spelling, grammar, and vocabulary was thus an important goal of the Yiddishist movement, not only because the rise of Yiddish-language schools made it necessary to settle on clear standards, but also because such norms were considered an important part of a true *kulturshprakh* worthy of respect from insiders and outsiders alike. The issue of standardization occupied a prominent place on the proposed agenda of the famous 1908 Czernowitz Language Conference, called by an *ad hoc* committee of Yiddish writers and cultural figures, which proclaimed Yiddish a national language of the Jewish people and marked the coming of age of the Yiddishist movement.

---

[4] Goldsmith, *Modern Yiddish Culture,* 267; Kuznitz, "Origins of Yiddish Scholarship," 168–169.

[5] The Soviet Union was a partial exception in the early years.

[6] Kuznitz, "Origins of Yiddish Scholarship," 17–18; Goldsmith, *Modern Yiddish Culture,* 224.

Representatives of a wide range of Jewish political tendencies attended
the conference and quickly became caught up in theoretical and political debates concerning the respective roles of Yiddish and Hebrew
in Jewish life and national identity. They never did get around to the
problems of spelling and grammar. However, these practical issues remained uppermost in the minds of leading Yiddishists, who continued
to call for a central authoritative body to regulate the language.[7]

It was in this context that the *Yidisher visnshaftlekher institut* (the
Yiddish Scientific Institute—now called the YIVO Institute for Jewish
Research) came into being in 1925. An outgrowth partly of the Yiddishist desire for a normative language academy, YIVO also represented a culmination of other trends in the growth of Eastern-
European Jewish scholarship, most importantly the movement for historical documentation sparked by the pioneering Jewish historian and
social thinker Simon Dubnov and the drive to collect and study Jewish folklore. The institute's founders, led by linguist Nokhem Shtif
and historian Elias Tcherikower in Berlin, and linguist Max Weinreich
and philologist Zalmen Reisen in Vilna, were a dedicated group of
mainly self-trained scholars who worked not only *on* Yiddish, but also
in Yiddish.[8] Supportive of several varieties of Diaspora nationalism,
YIVO's leaders were committed to a form of scholarship passionately
engaged with the political, social, and cultural issues of the time. They
intended for the institute to have high scholarly standards, but also
believed that research should help the Jewish people in its quest for
self-understanding and national self-determination. *Visnshaft* was
"science," as historian Lucy Dawidowicz put it, "in the German sense
of critical scholarship."[9] But as Max Weinreich—YIVO's guiding
light—later punned, *visnshaft* (science, research, scholarship) was *visn*

[7] Goldsmith, *Modern Yiddish Culture,* 183–184; Kuznitz, "Origins of Yiddish
Scholarship," 7, 27; Mordkhe Schaechter, "Fun folkshprakh tsu kulturshprakh," in Schaechter, *Der eynhaytlekher yiddisher oysleyg* (New York:
YIVO/League for Yiddish, 2000), 53–55; Katz, *Words on Fire,* 276–277.
[8] In addition to Kuznitz, "The Origins of Yiddish Scholarship," see Lucy S.
Dawidowicz, *From That Place and Time: A Memoir, 1938–1947* (New York, 1989).
[9] Dawidowicz, *From That Place and Time,* 81.

vos shaft (knowledge that creates).[10] YIVO would fulfill its Yiddishist mission by standardizing the language, by serving as the institute of higher learning for the Yiddish-speaking Jewish nation, and by developing Yiddish as a modern scholarly language as rarified as any other academic medium.[11]

The initiative for YIVO's establishment came from Berlin, where some of the founders lived and where Shtif had made the original call for a Yiddish academy of higher learning, and from Vilna (*Wilno,* in Polish), where Weinreich, Reisen, and others had responded enthusiastically to Shtif's appeal. It should not have been surprising, however, that Vilna quickly became the institute's true home. The city boasted a long history as a center of traditional Jewish scholarship, as well as of modern Jewish radical and nationalist movements. Most importantly, its multiethnic character in the cultural, linguistic, and political borderlands between Poland, Lithuania, and Russia discouraged assimilation and encouraged Jewish national consciousness. In Vilna, the intelligentsia, communal leadership, and upper classes, which elsewhere were making a transition to Polish, continued to speak Yiddish even in their public and official utterances. By the time YIVO was founded, Vilna already had an impressive infrastructure of Yiddish educational and cultural institutions. YIVO helped solidify its status as "the capital of Yiddishland."[12]

---

[10] Max Weinreich, *Der YIVO in a yor fun umkum* (New York: Yiddish Scientific Institute, 1943), 5.

[11] Nokhem Shtif, YIVO's initiator, noted the need to develop Yiddish as a vehicle for "serious thought," as it had already been made suitable for "deep, fine feeling." Kuznitz, "The Origins of Yiddish Scholarship," 53.

[12] For Vilna as the "capital of Yiddishland," see Cecile Kuznitz, "On the Jewish Street: Yiddish Culture and Urban Landscape in Interwar Vilna," in Leonard Jay Greenspoon, ed., *Yiddish Language and Culture Then and Now* (Omaha: Creighton University Press, 1998), 66. See also Ezra Mendelsohn, *The Jews of East Central Europe between the Wars* (Bloomington: Indiana University Press, 1983), 21–22; Gennady Estraikh, "The Vilna Yiddishist Quest for Modernity," in Marina Dmitrievna and Heidemarie Petersen, eds., *Jüdische Kultur(en) im Neuen Europa: Wilna 1918–1939* (Wiesbaden: Harrassowitz Verlag, 2004), 101–116; Dawidowicz, *From That Place and Time.*

YIVO immediately took it upon itself to become the authoritative
Yiddish-language academy. Its descriptive linguistic work included the
analysis of Yiddish dialects and the compilation of vocabularies for
various trades. Its normative activities included working with Yiddish
schools to develop a standard grammar and judging the admissibility
of words to the standard language. For many years, it debated a standard orthography, finally issuing a set of rules in 1936. Since part of
YIVO's charge was to ensure that Yiddish had all the tools necessary to
cover every field of endeavor, and its nationalist bias discouraged bor-
rowing too many words from other languages, especially from German, it often invented vocabulary when it seemed necessary. Max
Weinreich commented on the "intensive, sometimes feverish fashion-
ing of words" necessary for Jewish cultural autonomy in education,
government, social welfare, and so on. YIVO took the lead, especially
in developing scientific terminology.[13]

Besides the study of language, YIVO scholars examined Jewish
life from a number of perspectives. They especially saw social science
as key to creating a viable modern Jewish culture. The institute would
serve the Jewish people by giving them knowledge about themselves—
their history and folklore, their emerging modern literature, their
economic and demographic condition, and their social psychology.
Dr. Max Weinreich, who emerged as YIVO's guiding intellectual light
by 1930, began as a linguist, but soon developed much broader interests.[14] He believed that members of minority groups, including Jews,
faced powerful social pressures that threatened to undermine their

[13] Leybl Kahan, "Der terminologisher oyftu fun YIVO," *YIVO bleter,* 46 (1980),
229–241, quote on 235; Schaechter, "Fun folkshprakh tsu kulturshprakh," 62;
Kuznitz, "The Origins of Yiddish Scholarship," 167–169; Mordkhe Schaechter,
"Dem YIVOs yidish-oyftu: Roshe-protimdike observatsies un sakh-haklen tsu
a yoyvl-date," *YIVO bleter,* 46 (1980), 192–193; Estraikh, "The Vilna Yiddishist
Quest for Modernity," 110.
[14] Barbara Kirshenblat-Gimblett, "Coming of Age in the Thirties: Max Weinreich, Eduard Sapir, and Jewish Social Science," *YIVO Annual,* 23 (1996);
Dovid-Eliohu Fishman, "Bamerkungen vegn Vaynraykhs role in der antviklung
fun der yidisher visnshaft," and Dovid-Hirsh Roskies, "Maks Vaynraykh: oyf
di shpurn fun a lebedikn over," both in *YIVO bleter,* n.s.3 (1997); 298–307,
308–318 respectively.

sense of self. The antidote consisted of a positive affiliation with the group, a conscious appreciation of its culture, and a sense of continuity with its past. Unfortunately, Weinreich believed, traditional Jewish culture was unable to provide these things in the modern era. Its outmoded religious beliefs and practices, which served well as long as Jews remained isolated from the surrounding cultures, would no longer appeal to the masses of Jews more and more integrated into the Western world. Research was therefore needed to uncover those aspects of Jewish culture—especially its language and folk life—that could be salvaged for the present and future generations. Under Weinreich's leadership, YIVO developed a particular interest in the problems of Jewish youth and created a Division of Youth Research in 1934.[15]

Another hallmark of YIVO's work was the innovative collaboration it fostered between its own scholarly elite and the broader Yiddish-speaking public. Implicit in YIVO's mission was the belief that the Jewish masses not only needed the fruits of high-level scholarship, but would also appreciate them. As YIVO's initiator, Nokhem Shtif, once commented, "There is nothing to fear from the people of the masses, that they will not understand. The most important thing, the kernel, that a folk culture must have a scholarly base, they will grasp."[16] And beyond seeking the support of the people of the masses, YIVO sought to enlist them in active collaboration, especially as collectors (*zamlers*) in its lexicographical, folkloric, historical, and other documentary efforts. What emerged, according to Yiddish folklore historian Itsik Gottesman, was a "true dialogue . . . between field collectors who gathered the folk texts and academic scholars who analyzed those texts."[17] YIVO soon had a widespread network of active collaborators throughout Poland and, to a much more limited extent, abroad. This collaboration was not always easy, as the institute had to instruct its lay workers on the needs of science and assure them frequently of the importance of their work for the scientific enterprise. For the most part, though,

---

[15] Kuznitz, "Origins of Yiddish Scholarship," 243–247. For Weinreich's ideas on youth research see Max Weinreich, *Der veg tsu undzer yugnt: yesoydes, metodn, problemen fun yidisher yugnt-forshung* (Vilna: Yiddish Scientific Institute, 1935).
[16] Kuznitz, "Origins of Yiddish Scholarship," 76.
[17] Gottesman, *Defining the Yiddish Nation,* 132.

both sides benefited from the relationship: the YIVO scholars from the material the *zamlers* collected and from their closes ties with the people they sought to serve, and the *zamlers* from the satisfaction of contributing to an important national undertaking.[18]

All of YIVO's, and especially Weinreich's, interests came together in three autobiography contests that YIVO sponsored in 1932, 1934, and 1938–39 for Jewish youth in Poland. Weinreich had come to believe that life stories were the most useful kind of primary source. He drew especially on the work of the Chicago School of Social Science, and in particular that of William I. Thomas and Florian Znaniecki, who pioneered the use of personal documents, such as letters, diaries, and autobiographies, to understand their subject's point of view. Likewise, Weinreich learned from Viennese social psychologist Charlotte Buehler's *jugendforschung* the importance of life stages and especially of youth in social analysis. Collecting autobiographies also allowed Weinreich and his colleagues to listen to the people, as they had promised to do, and to express their special concern for the problems of young people. Finally, by connecting participants with YIVO, the contests exposed them to the sort of modern, sophisticated, secular Jewish cultural milieu that could compensate for the difficulties they faced as members of a despised minority group. Once again, YIVO assured participants in the autobiography contests that their efforts would contribute to science and thereby help to ameliorate the catastrophic conditions under which Jewish youth lived in 1930s Poland.[19]

YIVO had intended to announce the results of its latest youth autobiography contest on September 1, 1939, but on that day Germany invaded Poland and World War II began. The war spelled the end of YIVO's independent existence in Europe, as Vilna fell into the hands

[18] Kuznitz, "Origins of Yiddish Scholarship," 167–169, 174–183; Gottesman, *Defining the Yiddish Nation*, 118, 137–138, 147–148, 169–170.
[19] Marcus Moseley, "Life, Literature: Autobiographies of Jewish Youth in Interwar Poland," *Jewish Social Studies*, 7 (Spring/Summer 2001), 1–51; Jeffrey Shandler, *Awakening Lives: Autobiographies of Jewish Youth in Poland before the Holocaust* (New Haven: Yale University Press, 2002); Max Weinreich, *Der veg tsu undzer yugnt*; Kuznitz, "Origins of Yiddish Scholarship," 245–247.

first of the Soviets, then the Lithuanian Republic, the Soviets again, and finally, the Germans. Weinreich, who had been in Copenhagen on his way to a linguistics conference when the war broke out, made his way to the United States, arriving in March 1940. There he joined YIVO founders Elias Tcherikower and Jacob Lestchinsky, as well as other refugee scholars such as the historian Raphael Mahler and the linguist Yudl Mark.[20] These émigrés, together with Yiddish scholars already settled in America, moved YIVO's headquarters to New York.

The American Section of YIVO, known as *Amopteyl* (short for *Amerikaner opteyl*—American Section), had in fact existed since 1925. Led by the historian Jacob Shatzky, folklorist Judah Leib Cahan, and pedagogue Leybush Lehrer, *Amopteyl* raised money in America for the Vilna institute and sought, in Lehrer's words, to create a "bit of a scholarly (*visnshaftlekhe*) atmosphere" in New York.[21] The American Section found it difficult, not only because the number of American Yiddish intellectuals interested in academic research was quite small, but also because of the limited interest in such pursuits on the part of the broader Yiddish-speaking public. Nevertheless, over the years, *Amopteyl* succeeded in issuing several volumes of scholarly articles, and Shatzky, Cahan, and Lehrer collaborated with the work in Vilna, contributing to the institute's publications, corresponding with its committees to set research agendas, and occasionally speaking at its conferences. In addition, Cahan and Shatzky joined with several other supporters of YIVO to found the Central Jewish Library and Press Archives in 1935. By the time the library merged with YIVO in 1940, it possessed more than five thousand books and a number of important archival collections.[22]

[20] Kuznitz, "Origins of Yiddish Scholarship," 271; Dawidowicz, *From That Place and Time*, 213.
[21] Zosa Szajkowski, "Der YIVO un zayne grinders," *YIVO bleter,* 46 (1980), 42.
[22] Szajkowski, "Der YIVO un zayne grinders," 41–43; Zachary Baker, "Die Amerikanisierung der jiddischen Wissenschaft," *Judaica,* 51 (December 1995): 222–226; Jacob Shatzky, "Finf un tsvantsik yor YIVO," in Y. Lifshitz, ed., *Shatzky-bukh* (New York: YIVO Institute for Jewish Research, 1958), 313; Kuznitz, "Origins of Yiddish Scholarship," 109. On Shatzky, see Irving Howe, *World of Our Fathers* (New York: Harcourt Brace Jovanovich, 1976), 513–514.

When YIVO proclaimed the New York branch its center in October 1940, it thus possessed a head start in reconstructing its collections. Nevertheless, America in 1940 was a far cry from Vilna and, in many ways, much less fertile ground for striking roots. Difficulties came from several corners. In general, the culture in New York was much more *farbiznevet* (caught up in business), as the Vilners had complained even before they arrived in the United States.[23] In America, YIVO simply lacked the authority it had in Europe. Few American Jews had ever heard of the institute and, even to many of those who had, it must have seemed marginal (if not counterproductive) to the vital business of integration and advancement in American society.[24] And although most of American Jewry derived from the wave of Yiddish-speaking immigrants of the 1880s to the early 1920s, the use of Yiddish was rapidly waning among the second generation, which by 1940 already formed the majority of the community.

Even those who did use Yiddish regularly were not necessarily receptive to YIVO's mission of standardization and linguistic uplift. As socio-linguist Joshua Fishman has written, "Most East European Jews coming to America . . . were either untouched or only superficially touched by modern Jewish 'nationalist'-secular thinking. Subsequently, when secular-'nationalist' ideologies found little basic environmental encouragement in America, it was all the more natural for most American Jews to gravitate toward less conscious and less prestigeful roles for Yiddish and toward less retentivist behavior in connection with it."[25] Most of the immigrants had left Europe prior to the widespread availability of modern Yiddish education and before the Yiddishists' success in spreading their modern linguistic consciousness among the public. Yiddish-speaking immigrants therefore mostly retained older, less respectful attitudes toward their vernacular and had no interest in guarding its purity against the intrusion of Anglicisms. Indeed, they often shifted at least partly to English when they could.

---

[23] Kuznitz, "Origins of Yiddish Scholarship," 224–225.
[24] Shatzky, "Finf un tsvantsik yor YIVO," 313; Joshua Fishman, *Yiddish in America: Socio-Linguistic Description and Analysis* (Bloomington: Indiana University Press/The Hague: Mouton, 1965), 43–45.
[25] Fishman, *Yiddish in America,* 10.

The Yiddish of the second generation, when it existed at all, was even worse than that of the first. Weinreich complained that it was not even authentic enough to be held up as an example of the folk's speech or used as raw material in constructing a linguistic standard.[26]

Even the Yiddish intelligentsia was not as supportive of Yiddishism in America as in Europe, and the press was downright hostile toward efforts at standardization. This was partly because the American Yiddish press had proceeded along a track parallel to the Europeans in the process of linguistic modernization in the late nineteenth century. The Americans had developed their own orthographic and lexical standards, but these often drew on the German model rejected by YIVO and other Yiddishists. Moreover, American Yiddish journalists retained the nineteenth-century disdain for Yiddish even as they adopted it as a practical means to speak to the Jewish masses. Abraham Cahan, the powerful editor of the *Forward,* made a particular point of using simple Yiddish that his broad base of readers would understand. He also resisted surrendering any of his own authority to another institution. He therefore not only rejected standardization of orthography, but also was overtly hostile toward the project of developing a refined, and necessarily somewhat obscure, scholarly Yiddish. While YIVO favored neologisms drawn from internal resources, Cahan borrowed liberally from English and German. In one famous incident, Cahan rejected an article that one of his editors had written on a series of World War I battles because it included the word *kilometers.* Cahan demanded that the man rewrite the piece so that his illiterate mother would understand it. Although Cahan was the acknowledged master of this sort of journalistic writing, he was not far from the general attitude of the Yiddish press.[27]

In this context, YIVO struggled to find a role for itself in its new home. Weinreich was convinced that American Jewry needed YIVO

[26] Max Weinreich, "Vegn englishe elementn in undzere kulturshprakh," *Yidishe shprakh,* 1 (March–April 1941), 33–46.

[27] Schaechter, "Dem YIVOs yidish oyftu," 216; Schaechter, "Fun folkshprakh tsu kulturshprakh," 34; Milton Doroshkin, *Yiddish in America: Social and Cultural Foundations* (Rutherford, New Jersey: Farleigh Dickenson University Press, 1969), 100–103; Howe, *World of Our Fathers,* 522–531.

and its brand of Jewish social science just as much as European Jews did. No other institution was carrying out the serious research needed to properly understand the community and communal needs. As an ethnic minority, American Jews suffered from the same dilemmas of identity that Polish Jews had faced, perhaps more acutely, since American Jews were even more unmoored from their past than were their European cousins. A healthy individual and communal life were dependent on each other and on a positive relationship to the Jewish cultural heritage, including language, even when many elements of traditional Jewish practice were no longer applicable to the modern world. In Weinreich's view, research was needed to weld American Jews into a healthy collective: "From the atomization of millions of individual 'Americans of Jewish faith' we must arrive at a consciousness of a community [*klal*] of American Jews. To do this we must first of all recognize the elements that make up the essence of this community [*klalishkayt*]. . . . Recognition means research."[28]

Weinreich wanted to continue his work with youth, but YIVO proved unable to reach English-speaking American Jews in great numbers. Instead, YIVO turned to immigrants of the older generation, with whom it shared a language, the experience of migration, and a broader set of common cultural referents. Weinreich believed that the Yiddish-speaking immigrants would be open to YIVO's appeal in ways that the American-born might not be. As he put it, "Among those elements with a connection to Yiddish, we do not find, perhaps, a clear understanding of the meaning of research (*forshung*). But neither is there fear of it. On the contrary, the respect for learning lives on, a respect that combines the old Jewish reverence for Torah study with the Socialist labor movement's faith in science (*visnshaft*) as a bearer of progress."[29] Perhaps the Yiddish-speaking immigrants would enlist in YIVO's cause with something like the enthusiasm with which the Yiddish-speaking public in Poland had carried out the institute's work in the 1920s and 1930s.

---

[28] Max Weinreich, *Der YIVO in a yor fun umkum*, 9–10.
[29] Max Weinreich, *Der yidisher visnshaft in der hayntiker tsayt* (New York: YIVO, 1941), 11.

With this in mind, YIVO issued the call in May 1942 for a new autobiography contest on the theme, "Why I Left Europe and What I Have Accomplished in America."[30] As incentive to contribute, the institute offered six monetary prizes (of up to one hundred dollars) and nineteen book prizes. The results were gratifying to the organizers. By the end of the contest, 223 autobiographies had been assembled, with some 25,000 pages of material, including correspondence and other personal documents, in addition to the autobiographies. Analyzing the returns, the YIVO staff found that 176 of the works had been written by men and 47 by women; just over half had come from New York, while the others had arrived from other places in the United States, Canada, Mexico, Argentina, and Cuba; and the majority of the writers were between 51 and 70 years of age. The writers came from all over Eastern Europe, as well as from Germany and Palestine, and they had arrived in America in every decade from the 1880s to the 1940s, though most had come during the years of mass migration between 1882 and 1924. Ninety percent of the works were written in Yiddish, with the rest in English, German, and Hebrew.[31]

Weinreich noted that the social scientists who sponsored the contest had much in common, linguistically and culturally, with the other "ordinary" immigrants who participated in it. This close affinity influenced how the autobiographers wrote and what they wrote about. Indeed, in other contexts, literary scholars have found that the

---

[30] "A konkurs af oytobiografies fun imigrantn," *YIVO bleter,* 19:2 (March–April 1942), 281–282. See also the draft English-language version, American-Jewish Autobiographies Collection, unsorted materials, RG 102, YIVO. For more on the autobiography contest see Jocelyn Cohen, "Discourses of Acculturation: Gender and Class in East European Jewish Immigrant Autobiography, 1942" (Ph.D. dissertation, University of Minnesota, 2000); Daniel Soyer, "Documenting Immigrant Lives at an Immigrant Institution: The YIVO Autobiography Contest of 1942," *Jewish Social Studies,* 5 (1999), 218–243.

[31] "Der kontest af oytobiografies fun yidishe imigrantn in Amerike," and "The YIVO Contest for the Best Autobiographies of Jewish Immigrants to America," *Yedies fun YIVO/Newsletter of the YIVO,* 1 (September 1943), 3 (Yiddish section), 4 (English section).

English-language work of bilingual immigrant writers differs significantly from the same writers' work in their native languages. Aviva
Taubenfeld argues, for example, that in Abraham Cahan's Yiddish stories, the bilingual writer "could follow his heart, write as he pleased,
and trust his own insights into his audience's taste" because author
and reader inhabited "the same cultural and linguistic space." Cahan's
Yiddish stories contain dense and meaningful cultural references—including English words and expressions—that would have been missed
by an English-language reader. They also exhibit fewer constraints on
language and subject matter than the English versions of the same stories—which were designed to interpret Jewish culture to outsiders,
and therefore reveal some anxiety about Anglo-American acceptance
of Jewish immigrants.[32]

Since each of the YIVO autobiographers wrote in only one language, it is impossible to make such comparisons of their work. Nevertheless, the Yiddish manuscripts clearly contrast sharply with at least
some of the most widely-read English-language immigrant memoir literature in a number of ways. Most of the YIVO autobiographers were
adults when they arrived in the United States, and their perspectives
and experiences differed from those of writers who came as children.
Perhaps most significantly, the YIVO collection includes the life stories
of a number of immigrant mothers—women who had already married
and given birth to children in the old country. These women could not
write in English (indeed it is not clear how many of them could write
fluently in Yiddish) and were not as conspicuous in the public sphere
as were young, unmarried women. When Jewish immigrant women's
voices have found their way into the historical record—either through
published autobiographies or later through oral history projects—
they have usually been those of the immigrant daughters who had ar-

---

[32] Aviva Taubenfeld, "'Only an 'L'": Linguistic Borders and the Immigrant Author in Abraham Cahan's Yekl and Yankel der Yankee," in Werner Sollors,
ed., *Multilingual America: Transnationalism, Ethnicity, and the Languages of American Literature* (New York: New York University Press, 1998), 144–165, quotes
on 148–149. See also Xiao-huang Yin, "Worlds of Difference: Lin Yutang, Lao
She, and the Significance of Chinese-Language Writing in America," in the
same volume, 176–187.

rived in the United States as young girls and subsequently mastered the English language.[33]

Perhaps most importantly, the YIVO autobiographers implicitly rejected the assimilationist message evident in the works of Mary Antin and others who wrote in English and who appealed to a potentially hostile Anglo-American audience. Antin's autobiography, in particular, was in itself an argument against immigration restriction, very much on the agenda, though not yet enacted when the autobiography appeared in 1912. Not only did the YIVO writers feel free to describe unseemly aspects of Jewish life, but they often asserted continuity between past and present within their own lives. They would never have proclaimed, as Antin did in the foreword to her autobiography, that their past selves had died to enable them to be born anew in the United States. Besides being a function of audience, this search for continuity arises from the YIVO writers having been adults when they emigrated. Moreover, for those politicized in Eastern Europe, radicalization in the social movements of the old country rivaled emigration itself as the most significant transformative experience of a lifetime. For these reasons, the autobiographers may have been less willing to relinquish ties to home.

This is not to argue that the writers did not in fact change fundamentally. Rather, they took it as their task to weave their lives into a coherent whole in the face of the reality of a profound disjuncture between past and present. Among the many types of stories in the collection, a common theme is the writer's rise to modernity *through* Yiddish culture, not in opposition to it. Some writers had joined the Bund (the largest Jewish Socialist party in Eastern Europe), others the Zionist or Labor Zionist Movement. Many had been avid readers of modern secular Yiddish literature and world literature in Yiddish translation. They had acquainted themselves with the most progressive theories of political economy in Yiddish. As far as the YIVO writers were concerned, there was nothing old-fashioned or backward

---

[33] See Daniel Soyer, "The Voices of Jewish Immigrant Mothers in the YIVO American Jewish Autobiography Collection," *Journal of American Ethnic History*, 17 (Summer 1998), 87–94.

about Yiddish. If anything, the nationalistic intent of the sponsors influenced some authors to apologize for not giving their American children a proper Jewish or Yiddish education.

Language itself played an important role in the writers' lives and their transformation from traditional to modern Jews. The writers' own language reflected the variety of their experiences. Those men who had gone through the institutions of traditional learning studded their Yiddish with quotes from the sacred texts in Hebrew and Aramaic. Contest winner Ben Reisman, a Pittsburgh roofer and tinsmith, followed the custom of those who had received a good traditional education by quoting, in the original, from the Talmud and the Bible, thus demonstrating his status as an educated Jew. To Reisman's everlasting dismay, his traditional education was cut short so that he could apprentice at a trade and contribute to his family's income. More than half a century later, he still remembered his moment of triumph in *heder,* the traditional Jewish elementary school, when he correctly parsed a passage in the Gemara after a classmate had failed ridiculously. As a matter of course, Reisman relates the episode in Yiddish and the original Aramaic of the Talmud. Indeed, the classmate's error is a very comic one, but only in the original language:

> Once I was sitting and reading the mishna that starts out, "If a man sells a house . . . ,"[34] and the teacher was studying the chapter, "A Presumptive Title to Houses," with another youth—*the Innkeeper's Zekharye,* he was called. Zekharye says, "*Omar Robo shato,* he drank. . . ." The teacher was dozing off. Suddenly he sat up and said, "Wait. Don't rush, Zekharye. Say it again." So he began, "*Omar robo,* Rabba said, *shato,* he drank." Here the teacher said, "*komayso,* he got drunk." Zekharye repeated. "*Mokhil,* he lay in the mud. *Inish,* he made a *tsimes.*" I could no longer hold it in and I burst out laughing. The teacher addressed me, "Binyomen, what are you laughing at? Let's hear how you would interpret the passage." I read, "*Shato komayso mokhil inish.* The issue has to do with title over land and fruit when one has held it for two or three years." After I had interpreted the pas-

---

[34] First mishna of chapter 4 of Bava Batra.

sage the teacher addressed Zekharye, "Tell your father that I want to see him tomorrow in the small study house."[35]

The joke—utterly lost when translated—is that when Zekharye mistranslated *shato,* year, as "he drank," which sounds similar in the original, the teacher started leading him to ever greater absurdities. This incident was so important to Reisman that he returned to it twice in his autobiography.[36] In some ways it sums up who he felt himself to be—an educated, intelligent man, literate in the sources. Nevertheless, when he decided to go into business for himself after years as a worker, he resorted to English, writing out what he calls his "Declaration of Independence."[37]

On the other hand, a disproportionate number of the participants in the YIVO contest were socialists, and political rhetoric, whether delivered orally or in print, had had a profound impact on their young lives, altering their perspective on the world—sometimes dramatically, in a single instant, other times gradually, over a period of time. Political oratory of all kinds occupies a central place in nearly all of the stories in the collection, as does the reading and distribution of literature, most of it forbidden. The socialist catchwords—unity, equality, freedom—spoke directly to the writers' experiences.

An example in the autobiography of Aaron Cohn, who was a young weaver in the industrial city of Lodz, Poland, is when he came across a flyer published by the Bund:

> Remarkably, I was so seized with every word, I practically wanted to scream, shout, fly, to share my feelings with someone. . . . "This, father," I shouted in my loudest voice, "This is it, right here! Yes, yes,

---

[35] The full passage reads: "Rabba said, for the first year a man will forgo [his rights to the produce], for two years a man will forgo [his rights], but for a third year no man will forgo his rights." Bava Batra, Chapter 3, first mishna, folio 29a. Translation from *The Babylonian Talmud: Seder Nizikin,* vol. 2, trans. and ed. I. Epstein (London: Soncino, 1935), 142.

[36] Autobiography of Ben Reisman, Autobiography no. 38, American Jewish Autobiographies Collection, RG 102, YIVO Institute for Jewish Research, 9, 139–140.

[37] Reisman, 104.

this is it! I have searched for this the entire time. Unity, unity with each other. Oh, God, all workers must unite and raise themselves to a higher level of humanity." The words of that Bundist proclamation went into the deepest depths of my heart. A distinct joy embraced me. . . . It did not stop ringing in my ears: "Only through unity, only through unifying can we attain a better life."[38]

The experience was so deeply felt and remembered that even later, as a silk manufacturer in Paterson, New Jersey, Cohn remained true to his Bundist socialist principles. His was a trajectory not uncommon in the autobiographies.

Another way that language impacted many of the writers' lives was in their struggle to achieve basic literacy, especially in the case of some of the women, or to acquire worldly knowledge and understanding, as in the case of some of the men who had been deeply involved in the traditional world of the *yeshiva*. One of the most moving stories in the collection is that of Minnie Goldstein—a housewife and "landlady" (as she writes, using the English word) in Providence, Rhode Island—whose written Yiddish is among the most labored in the collection. Indeed, the narrative of her rise to literacy is highlighted by the visual effect of her script, her phonetic rendition of her dialect, and her use of English words. Never having received any formal education in her native Warsaw, nor in New York, where she moved with her family in 1894 at the age of twelve, Goldstein taught herself to read Yiddish as an adult using the *Forward*'s famous advice column, *Bintel brief* (Bundle of Letters). She learned to read and write English at a course offered by the New Deal's Works Progress Administration (WPA). Her knowledge of English remained imperfect; she described her son, for example, as a young "loklok" (law clerk) who was not yet established well enough to marry. But she appreciated the columns of Eleanor Roosevelt and Dorothy Thompson, and she reported that she was currently reading *Mein Kampf* in order to understand the enemy.

---

[38] Autobiography of Aaron Cohn, Autobiography no. 108, American Jewish Autobiographies Collection, RG 102, YIVO, 4–15.

Her pride—mixed with surprise—in having won a prize in an "S.A." (written out in Roman characters, meaning *essay*) contest testifies movingly to the strength of her desire for both literacy and recognition.[39]

The writers' varied use of Yiddish and other languages offered the YIVO scholars plenty of raw material for study, but the writers' lack of Yiddishist consciousness, and sometimes even shaky literacy, differentiated them sharply from the scholars at YIVO. Indeed, while the contest organizers and participants had much in common, there was also much that divided them.[40] Ironically, while the scholars and writers shared the Yiddish language, YIVO's "special brand of discursive, highly conceptualized" Yiddish was one of the things that separated the scholars from their new constituency.[41] The American immigrants were in this way more distanced from the scholars than the Polish Jewish youth had been, even though the young writers had been less likely to write their stories in Yiddish. While the young people in Poland had been primed for YIVO's work by their experiences in the Yiddish secular schools and youth movements, the immigrants had arrived from Eastern Europe before those schools had developed. Most had only had a few years of traditional education. As historian Jocelyn Cohen has noted, even when discussing the basics of the contest, the YIVO scholars and the participants sometimes seemed to speak past each other. While YIVO termed the project a *konkurs,* for example, the autobiographers preferred the English-influenced *kontest.* While YIVO referred to the *premie* (prize) each winner would be given, the contestants preferred *prayz.* This latter example was particularly problematic since, according to YIVO norms, *prayz* meant price.[42] Even American-born Chana Gordin (Mlotek), who had studied in a Sholem Aleichem school and had spoken Yiddish at home, reported that she "learned a

---

[39] Autobiography of Minnie Goldstein, Autobiography no. 155, American Jewish Autobiographies Collection, RG 102, YIVO, 18, 21–22.
[40] See Cohen, "Discourses of Acculturation," 53–85.
[41] Dan Miron, "Between Science and Faith: Sixty Years of the YIVO Institute," *YIVO Annual,* 19 (1990), 1–15.
[42] Cohen, "Discourses of Acculturation," 61.

new language—"YIVO Yiddish" when she went to work at the institute in the mid-1940s.[43]

The word *science* (*visnshaft*), one of YIVO's key concepts, is also an example of how, even though they spoke the same language on one level, the scholars and the autobiographers did not always understand each other.[44] Of course, science—actually social science or research—was central to the mission of YIVO, the Yiddish *Scientific* Institute. The systematic, objective study of social phenomena was a prerequisite for the fulfillment of the institute's vision of a healthy Jewish social life in the Diaspora. But what did the writers, many of whom had had only a few years of traditional education, make of Weinreich's repeated invocation of the word *science?*

Many of the writers were anxious about their undertaking, and Weinreich responded patiently to the many inquiries about technical matters. In encouraging the contestants to persevere, he reassured them that their lives really did matter and that they had much to contribute to scholarship. He frequently resorted to an appeal to science as the highest value. "There is no human life," he told one nervous autobiographer, "that is not interesting to science."[45] "You should not think that we're just reading the material," he told another, "We are studying everything with utmost diligence and exactness—scientific work cannot be done otherwise."[46]

To some extent, as Weinreich knew, those who had been exposed to socialist literature had come across the word *science* before—if not exactly in the same sense as YIVO used it, then at least close enough.[47] But many seemed uncertain as to what Weinreich meant. One writer questioned Weinreich about the word: "You spoke of science, so I ask

---

[43] Chana Gordin-Mlotek, "Zikhroynes vegn der Maks Vaynraykh," *YIVO bleter,* n.s. 3 (1997), 337, 339.

[44] Joshua Fishman, "YIVO in Amerike," *YIVO bleter,* 46 (1985), 98–101.

[45] Max Weinreich to Harry Sprecher, July 4, 1942, letter accompanying autobiography no. 20.

[46] Cohen, "Discourses of Acculturation," 68.

[47] On the concept of *visnshaft* in the Jewish socialist press, see Tony Michels, *Socialist Politics and the Making of Yiddish Culture in New York City, 1890–1923* (Ph.D. dissertation, Stanford University, 1998), 57–58.

whether according to science one may write in an unwriterly way, like in the newspapers with their mixture of Hebrew and English words. And may one write as one speaks, whether in a Galician language or a Polish-Yiddish language, as long as that language can be understood? And is there science among cattle or poultry? As an experienced farmer, I have gotten to know cattle and poultry very well, and I think that they understand science."[48] Weinreich's response is not preserved.

Weinreich showed tremendous patience when dealing with the participants in the contest. But contest secretary Moses Kligsberg later complained of the writers' apparent inability to follow—or perhaps to understand—what, to the organizers, seemed a simple set of technical directions.[49] He noted that the call for the contest had been "edited with great care" and "submitted for approval to outstanding American authorities in the field." But despite all efforts to make the instructions clear and simple, many contestants had misinterpreted or simply ignored the rules. "All this," wrote Kligsberg with ill-disguised pique, "leads to the conclusion that what one writes or says, no matter how clearly, and what the other one understands or reads into it, may be two different things." Most significantly, Kligsberg complained that the autobiographers lacked a clear understanding of the needs of science: "Science seeks to discover laws, principles, and general tendencies. Our correspondents believe to the contrary that science is in pursuit only of the unusual, the rare; and that the common, the average, is not important, 'not interesting.' One contestant expresses her misgivings thus: 'What sort of science could it be if I should narrate how I came to America and what I have accomplished here?'"

The 1942 contest thus reveals both the promises and pitfalls of using YIVO's brand of Jewish social science in America. Certainly, the contest was a success, acquiring for the institute a wealth of material for studying Jewish history, folklore, language, and other conventional fields, as well as for Weinreich's interdisciplinary science of self and culture. It was an example of the kind of scholarly collaboration with the

---

[48] Sam Langer to Max Weinreich, January 10, 1943, letter accompanying autobiography no. 57.
[49] Moses Kligsberg, "Socio-Psychological Problems Reflected in the YIVO Autobiography Contest," *YIVO Annual of Jewish Social Science* 1 (1946), 241–249.

public for which YIVO had become famous in Europe. Still, the problems of communication between the institute and the autobiographers also reveal YIVO's difficulties in building a constituency for its work. The miscommunications point out the contradictions between the democratic aspiration of Yiddishism to raise the status of the people through raising the status of their language, and the effort to do so by creating an academic Yiddish that, ironically, the folk found difficult to understand.

YIVO did succeed in striking roots in America, but in so doing it inevitably changed its mission.[50] Indeed, Dan Miron points out that the institute's mission took on even more urgency in the wake of the Holocaust, when American Jewry was left as the main inheritor of the cultural legacy of Ashkenazi Jewry.[51] While Weinreich and others tried to maintain YIVO's tradition of Yiddish scholarship in Yiddish, this became harder and harder to maintain as time went on. Although the institute continued to publish scholarly journals and other publications in Yiddish into the twenty-first century, more of its resources went toward teaching Yiddish to young English-speaking American scholars and others, who could then interpret the Eastern-European Jewish cultural heritage for primarily English-speaking audiences. Among its most important accomplishments were *College Yiddish* (1949), a textbook by Max Weinreich's son, the brilliant linguist Uriel Weinreich, and the *Modern English-Yiddish Yiddish-English Dictionary* (1968), also by Uriel Weinreich. In 1968, the Uriel Weinreich Summer Program in Yiddish Language, Literature, and Culture was established after the linguist's untimely death. Several generations of scholars and Yiddish enthusiasts have learned their Yiddish—YIVO Yiddish—from these sources.

The 1942 autobiography contest revealed both the virtues and the tensions inherent in the YIVO approach to Jewish social science. On the one hand, the contest continued a remarkable tradition of collaboration between scholars and masses that YIVO had established in Poland. In organizing the contest, YIVO reaffirmed its abiding faith

---

[50] In the mid-1950s, it also changed its English-language name to YIVO Institute for Jewish Research.

[51] Miron, "Between Science and Faith," 10.

that high scholarly standards could be put to the service of the people. On the other hand, the difficulty that YIVO sometimes had in communicating with its constituency was a symptom of a contradiction in the institute's brand of Yiddishism. Namely, while YIVO extolled Yiddish precisely because it was the language of the folk, the institute had, in order to carry out its own scholarly mission, to develop an academic Yiddish that was often incomprehensible to that folk.

The contest also indicated some problems inherent in YIVO's use of Yiddish as a means of integrating itself into American Jewish life in 1942. Even within the Yiddish-speaking sector of the Jewish community, YIVO had to struggle with the American Yiddish establishment, which had developed its own very different linguistic standards over the course of decades, based on a very different sort of populism from that of YIVO. Neither the Yiddish press nor the Yiddish-speaking masses shared the institute's belief in the importance of maintaining a pure language. In any case, the number of Yiddish speakers—still a major constituency—was declining. YIVO only settled on a contest for *immigrant* autobiographies when it realized that it had little access to American Jewish youth. And a focus on immigrants necessarily meant a focus on older people, since most immigrants had come to the United States in the years prior to World War I.

YIVO did ultimately find a niche in America. To do so, it had to adjust its mission. To the extent that it worked to reacquaint modern American Jews with the cultural legacy of Eastern-European Jewish civilization, its new mission was consistent with the old. But as its Yiddish-speaking constituency declined in number, YIVO was forced to educate English-speaking Jews in the basics of the Yiddish language and culture.[52] An important new constituency consisted of American-born scholars who pursued more conventional careers in the academy than had been possible for YIVO's founders. No longer the institute of higher learning for a Yiddish-speaking nation, YIVO still maintains a major role in keeping the legacy of that nation alive.

---

[52] YIVO's Yiddish-speaking public declined slowly because a new influx of Yiddish-speaking Jews arrived after the Holocaust, some of whom were familiar with YIVO's work before the war.

THE YIDDISH CINEMA IN AMERICA: A CELEBRATION OF JEWISH LIFE

Eric A. Goldman

Yiddish cinema in America was the product of a changing world and a desire to hold onto traditions and ideals that were being questioned by the majority of Jews. While Hollywood's Jewish filmmakers presented a picture of the American melting pot that illustrated their own desire to assimilate into American society, the Yiddish filmmakers celebrated the beauty and particularity of Jewish life and culture.

THE SILENT FILMS

Jewish-subject pictures had been popular in the United States since the beginning of the twentieth century. The early pictures were often slapstick comedies or melodramas with Jewish protagonists. They rarely tackled Jewish issues of import, with one exception—the oppression of Russia's Jews. Early on, producers realized that this subject spoke to the great masses who had sought refuge from the tyranny inflicted on Jews in Eastern Europe. In 1911, this new genre of Jewish filmmaking became all the more popular when Mendel Beilis, a Jewish factory worker in Russia, was accused of the blood-libel murder—for ritual purposes—of a gentile youth.

Leading the way was film director Sidney M. Goldin, who began his career directing gangster movies. With the Beilis case and pogroms in Russia, he was not only moved as a Jew to react to Jewish persecution, he also saw potentially profitable material for his films. Between 1910 and 1914, he unleashed a series of films including *The Sorrows of Israel, Bleeding Hearts: Jewish Freedom under King Casimir of Poland, The Terrors of Russia,* and *Escaped from Siberia,* depicting Jewish persecution.

Though these were not Yiddish pictures, they showed that Jewish-subject films could have great appeal to the immigrant Jewish audience.

In the summer of 1914, Sidney Goldin decided to make a different kind of Jewish movie, one more closely geared to the Jewish audience struggling with issues of Jewish identity and peoplehood. His was the first American Yiddish movie, defined as a Jewish cultural expression on film, aimed primarily at Yiddish-speaking audiences, which works toward strengthening Jewish identity and survival. Goldin's previous films were made for the mass market immigrant population, the primary customers for movies at the time. This time he deviated by tackling a Jewish story adapted from the Yiddish stage. It was *Uriel Acosta,* based on the Karl Gutskov play about the seventeenth-century apostate. Acosta was a Portuguese-born Jew who converted with his family to Roman Catholicism and then returned to Judaism, only to be excommunicated by the Jewish community for his free-thinking rationalism. Goldin's choice of the Acosta story was an interesting one in that it focused on a Jew who challenged the intolerance of his own religious community. This theme was common in European Yiddish literature and theater, as secular Jewish writers often attacked the perceived rigidity of their religious leaders. Yet, for America, it was a novel theme, and Goldin must have been eyeing the European market, where the subject evoked greater interest. With the outbreak of World War I in August, the European market for Goldin's films closed, and he was forced to stop his Yiddish movie production. He reemerged in 1921 in Vienna, where he made *Mizrekh un Mayrev* (released in the United States as *Mazel Tov*) with Molly Picon, and *Yisker* with Maurice Schwartz. Eventually, Sidney M. Goldin would lay claim to the title of "grandfather" of the Yiddish cinema.

After the war, the American film industry continued to make pictures geared for universal consumption, and despite the complete dominance of Jews in film production, the film business was uninterested in making pictures aimed solely at any one ethnic group. Some Jewish-subject films with Jewish characters were produced during this period. Most often, these told stories of Jews who sought intermarriage and assimilation and, upon achieving the American Dream, left their Jewishness behind. This type of story appealed to a broad audience. Yet, for many Jews, these films were objectionable, especially when the intermarriage of Jew and Gentile was suggested. Other Jews found no problem with these Jewish-subject pictures. They were integrated into American society, English was their language, and intermarriage was a fact of life. But for the majority of Jews, Yiddish was still their *mame-loshn* (mother tongue), English something only learned. They maintained a tradition that encouraged education, upward mobility, and acceptance into society, while still remaining Jews and passing their heritage to their children. They could not accept the Hollywood product.

It was not surprising that in response to the Jewish-subject picture, there was growing interest in turning out another form of cinema. With the success in America, in the early 1920s, of such Goldin-directed European Yiddish pictures as *Mizrekh un Mayrev* and *Yisker,* there was hope for a new Yiddish film entertainment industry geared specifically toward the Jewish audience. Maurice Schwartz, director of the Yiddish Art Theater, decided to be the first to try. In the early twenties, Schwartz had become the master of the Yiddish stage and Second Avenue. The Yiddish Art Theater, under his tutelage, had attracted many of the great Yiddish actors. It quickly became a New York institution that would last for over thirty years, a central meeting place for the theatrical elite—Jew and non-Jew alike. His company toured the capitals of Europe, playing everything from Sholom Aleichem to Molière. Within a short number of years, Schwartz had proven himself an extremely talented actor, director, and producer.

Maurice Schwartz had always shown great interest in the cinema and was excited by its power to reach the masses. He first fell in love with film when he starred in Sidney Goldin's *Yisker* (1924). Schwartz also spent part of 1925–1926, along with fellow actors from the Yiddish theater, under contract to MGM in Hollywood, learning film technique. Schwartz badly wanted to direct film and, with Jewish subject pictures that endorsed assimilation and intermarriage being released in Hollywood, it seemed to him that there was no better time. He reasoned that with his knowledge of Yiddish literature, Jewish life, acting, directing, and film, he could create a Yiddish film form. It was a determined effort, but an unsuccessful one.

In 1926, Schwartz chose, as his entree into motion pictures, a play in which he had both starred on stage and directed. It was Z. Libin's

Tsebrokhene Hertser (*Broken Hearts*), a starkly realistic portrait of Jewish life in New York's Lower East Side. Writer David Denk, who was at the New York City studio where the film was being made, was on the set.[1] According to him, Schwartz might have seemed to be in charge, but the filmmaking overwhelmed him. Not yet completely comfortable behind the camera, Schwartz had trouble setting the pace and angles for his technicians. Schwartz also found differences between the direction he was used to giving his actors on the stage and that required for the camera. To further complicate matters, Schwartz played the lead role, hindering his ability to take full control. Though his actors were supportive, many of them players from his Yiddish Art Theater, they could not save the film. The film failed to garner good reviews and suffered financially, largely due to Schwartz's inexperience. There had been several Yiddish silent film successes in both Poland and Russia, but Schwartz's film was the only American post-war attempt at making a Yiddish silent picture. Within a year, sound captured the hearts of the American viewer, bringing to a close a brief chapter in Yiddish filmmaking. It was no longer a question of what you saw on the screen; of great concern now was what you heard and whether you understood the language spoken—Yiddish talking pictures were not far off.

THE AMERICAN YIDDISH SOUND PICTURE, 1929–1937

Talking pictures had been a technical possibility since the turn of the century, but the technological changes required before a movie theater could show sound films made it, at first, an undesirable medium. Motion picture companies experimented with it, but Warner Brothers, in search of a novelty to turn around its financial woes, was the first studio to exploit sound. Once theaters became equipped with sound systems, people began to queue up outside the talkies, no matter the quality of the picture. As the Depression hit America in 1929, the motion picture industry experienced growth and great profit in contrast to the economic disaster which the rest of the country was encounter-

[1] David Denk, *Shvarts Oyf Vays* (New York: Greenwich Press, 1963), 108.

ing. In 1930, theater attendance was better than the year before. However, motion pictures were failing to respond to the needs of the immigrant urban populations who thronged to witness the miracle of sound on film. Immigrants found themselves watching films often unaware of what was happening on the screen. Unable to fully comprehend English, they stopped going to the movies.

Jewish immigrant filmgoers faced the same problem. For many of them, English was a mystery and Yiddish a way of life. A number of Jewish filmmakers, sensitive to this issue, sought to meet this need by producing sound pictures in Yiddish. In 1928, writer Abraham Schomer took the lead by announcing that he would film his play *The Green Millionaire* in Yiddish, but the project was never realized. Then, producer Max Cohen, at New York's Metropolitan Studios, began preparations in 1929 for a Yiddish sound film. He enlisted the aid of Sidney Goldin, who was acquainted with the material, the language, and many of the actors. Having just completed *East Side Sadie* for Worldart Film, a picture which included talking segments, he had experience, albeit limited, with talking pictures. For this picture, Goldin pulled together many of the well-known talents of the Yiddish stage, including Lucy Levine, Lazar Freed, Anna Appel, and Mark Schweid. He also used Samuel Kelemer, a youth known as "Shmulikel, the boy *khazn* (cantor)" to chant Jewish tunes and prayers. The Cohen/Goldin film, *Ad Mosay* (*Until When*), also released as *The Eternal Prayer,* was about a youth who finds out that his father has been killed in Palestine during the Hebron riots of 1929. The film work was quite primitive and drew terrible reviews. Yet, it showed that a Yiddish sound film could be made and that such films had potential.

Though the first Yiddish talkie was feeble, it was well received by an audience hungry for Yiddish on the screen. Goldin proved that Yiddish sound pictures had a market. In late 1929 Joseph Seiden, owner of a motion picture sound equipment rental outfit, brought together a few movie house owners and created Judea Pictures. Seiden produced the pictures, and his associates, Sam Berliner and Moe Goldman, guaranteed their exhibition. Sidney Goldin, who was established as the "dean" of Yiddish-language cinema and the only person immediately capable of directing in the medium, was hired as director. Judea's immediate goal was to make two short films, two-reelers of about twenty minutes each, which could be exhibited between live stage performances in Jewish neighborhood theaters. If the films were successful, then further production would ensue, including feature-length films. *Variety* claimed that the premier pictures were budgeted at $15,000 apiece.[2] In truth, the pictures were made for less than $3,000 each, as actors worked largely on a deferred-percentage basis and little cost was incurred for equipment rental.[3]

In February of 1929, filmmakers began production on the first of the Judea pictures, *Style and Class*. It was a filmed recording of a musical revue, featuring Marty Baratz and Goldie Eisman, which was being presented at Gabel's Public Theater in New York. The following week, Judea made *Shuster Libe* (alternately titled *Shoemaker's Romance* or *Cobbler Love*), a comical story of Jewish life in Eastern Europe. The twenty-one-minute film featured members of the Vilna Troupe—Joseph Buloff, Liuba Kadison, Leah Noemi, and Leon Kadison. The pictures were made in Manhattan and released the following month in Brooklyn and the Bronx. Response to the two short films was most favorable and, almost immediately, plans were readied for the next production. Judea signed Jennie Goldstein, noted for her tear-jerking portrayals on the Yiddish stage, to star in a series of pictures. However, after several disagreements with the company, Goldstein backed out of her contract and was not seen on the Yiddish screen until *Tsvey Shvester* (*Two Sisters*) in 1938. This setback notwithstanding, Judea quickly went to work on its first feature picture, *Mayne Yidishe Mame* (*My Jewish Mother*) with Mae Simon. Simon, enthusiastic about the new technology she had witnessed at the RCA Sound Studios in Manhattan, described her experience: "The thrill of grinding cameras, glaring batteries of lights, cameramen inside soundproof booths, sound engineers, and many other workers standing around during our performance was surely most novel, and I am looking forward to seeing and hearing myself on the screen."[4]

[2] "Jewish Films in Own Tongue," *Variety*, January 22, 1930.
[3] Morris Freedman, "Contemporary of William Fox Still Making Yiddish Pictures," *New York Herald-Tribune*, November 14, 1948.
[4] "A Yiddish Talkie," *Jewish Outlet*, April 17, 1930.

With *Mayne Yidishe Mame* ready for release, Judea considered expanding its distribution by creating a national chain of theaters devoted to exhibiting Yiddish talking pictures. By late May, three New York theaters, one in Brooklyn's Brighton Beach, another in the Bronx, and a third on the Lower East Side of Manhattan, had contracted to serve as the anchor for this national chain. According to several accounts in the Jewish press, there was a favorable response in New York's Jewish neighborhoods. Judea reasoned that they could successfully take the pictures to other Jewish enclaves around the country.

As soon as distribution plans were finalized, Seiden directed Judea to produce a number of one- and two-reel pictures for national consumption. Plays and skits presented at that time on the Yiddish stage were major sources of material for these early pictures. Judea produced four short films in June 1930: *The Broken Doll* with Sadie Banks and Celia Person, *The Jewish Gypsy,* with Hymie Jacobson and Miriam Kressyn, *Oy Doctor* with Menashe Skulnick, and (Abraham Reisen's) *Mai-Ko-Mashma-Lon?* (*What Does It Mean?*) with Harry Peld. Upon screening a surviving piece of *Oy Doctor,* I watched a playful and talented Skulnick performing his Yiddish vaudeville act, which was soon to be sent around the country. With the static camera, there was only one take, with segments limited to a maximum of ten minutes—the amount of time the sixteen-inch sound disk was capable of recording. (When Skulnick made a mistake, it was captured on sound film for posterity.)

Judea also filmed some of the great cantors of the day. Two separate renditions (by the cantors Shmulikel and Leibele Waldman) were made of the moving Yom Kippur plea for the annulment of vows, *Kol Nidre.* Waldman was also filmed in the ten-minute picture, *Yidishe Nign* (*Jewish Melody*), in which he sang liturgical music composed by Sholom Secunda. Judea's films were making money, so the company expanded production. In mid-June, it was announced that thirty-six Yiddish sound films—twelve feature-length and twenty-four short films—would be completed by the end of 1930. Yiddish cinema had finally taken its place in the American Jewish entertainment landscape.

This new group of American Yiddish moviemakers enjoyed a tenuous relationship with their Yiddish theater colleagues. In Europe, film plots were largely drawn from Yiddish literature and theater. Most of the European directors, producers, and actors who appeared in Yiddish movies were also involved in the Yiddish theater world. In contrast, most of the American Yiddish moviemakers came from the non-Jewish cinema, and their scripts were not as closely tied to the long tradition of Yiddish literature. Within a short time, animosity grew between this new group of Yiddish moviemakers and their counterparts in the Yiddish theater. Things grew tenser as the filmmakers increasingly drew actors from the Yiddish stage in order to capitalize on the name value and popularity of the Yiddish actors, while producing mediocre films with bad performances. The Yiddish films embarrassed the Yiddish theater establishment. This came to a head in mid-June 1930, when the Yiddish press reported that Judea Films was planning to film some of the great Yiddish classics, including S. Anski's *Dybbuk* and H. Leivick's *Golem*. On June 25, the Yiddish Actors' Union adopted a resolution prohibiting members of the union from appearing in Yiddish talkies. The union claimed the reputation of Yiddish theater was being injured by the low-caliber films produced by Judea Pictures. The union further claimed that "the Jewish public was being misled into believing that actors would personally appear in the theaters where the films were being shown."[5] The Yiddish Actors' Union was powerful, and film production was shut down for nearly two months. Finally, an agreement was reached between Seiden and the Yiddish Actors' Union manager, Reuben Guskin, requiring compensation to the union when non-union actors were used. Film production began anew in late August with the expectation that Yiddish movies would be of a higher quality from that time on.

With Joseph Seiden as producer and Sidney Goldin as director, Judea Films produced several short-subject films over the following months: Seymour Rechtzeit's *Land of Freedom; Sailor's Sweetheart* with Hymie Jacobson and Miriam Kressyn; *Natasha* with Pinchus Lavenda and Mildred Block; *An Evening in a Jewish Camp* with music by Sholom Secunda; *Ets Khaim* (*Tree of Life*); Z. Rubinstein's *Jewish Day Hour;* and Cantor Leibele Waldman chanting the Yom Kippur prayer "*Unsane-*

[5] "Yiddish Actors' Union Condemns Yiddish 'Talkies,'" *Tsayt* (London), June 30, 1930.

Toykef." Seiden finally had a collection of quality pictures available for exhibition.

Judea then began producing its second Goldin-directed feature film, *Eybike Naronim* (*Eternal Fools*), based on a story by H. Kalmonowitz starring Yudel Dubinsky, Yehuda Bleich, and Seymour Rechtzeit. It was the first all-talking Yiddish film (using sound on film, rather than discs). Its story centered on the tragedy of a traditional Jewish family trying to cope with contemporary society. *Eybike Naronim* was representative of the type of picture that became Seiden's trademark—a quickly made, overly sentimental, melodramatic film. These films attempted to speak to the immigrant audience by portraying dilemmas experienced by the American immigrant population. In 1931, Seiden produced a few more low-budget short films: *Eli, Eli* (*My God, My God*) and Abraham Goldfaden's *Shulamis*. But the novelty of Yiddish sound film was wearing off, and theaters were less inclined to exhibit this product. Audiences wanted quality films and refused to spend their money just to hear Yiddish on the screen. Judea released one more picture in 1931, *The Voice of Israel,* a film recording of cantorial renditions by great cantors like Zeidl Rovner, David Roitman, Adolf Katchko, Leibele Waldman, and Yossele Rosenblatt. This is now one of the few remaining film recordings of the great cantors of the day.

ONE-TIME INDEPENDENT COMPANIES

There were short films made by other newly formed companies in 1931, like the two Yiddish-language cantorial shorts *A Cantor on Trial* and *The Feast of Passover.* But the most exciting development in 1931 was the creation of High Arts Pictures Corporation. This new company announced it would make Yiddish movies based on Yiddish-theater productions of the day and began by filming *Zayn Vaybs Lubovnik* (*His Wife's Lover*). The play, written by Sheyne Rokhl Semkoff and loosely based on Ferenc Molnar's *The Guardsman,* had played Second Avenue successfully the previous two seasons. Directed by Goldin, it was the most expensive Yiddish film production to date. But Goldin failed to use the new medium of cinema to his advantage, creating a largely staged theater film. Better camerawork might have covered up over-theatrical acting, but long sequences with one static shot made these stagy performances all the more glaring. Had more production money been available, covering shots and a variety of camera setups would have been possible. Extensive rehearsals and second takes were other luxuries infrequently available to Yiddish cinema of this period. The real problem of this film, and many other Yiddish pictures that followed, was the low budget. Still, strangely enough, the film enjoyed great success—due in large part to the fine performance of comedian and actor, Ludwig Satz.

By 1932, Goldin had directed every American Yiddish narrative talking picture to date. Next, he adapted Sholom Asch's *Uncle Moses,* and this time he was joined by Aubrey Scotto, an established film director brought in primarily to enhance film technique. *Uncle Moses* opens with a camera pan across Orchard Street on New York's Lower East Side, with the camera jerking as it moves from person to person. The star of the film was one of the great talents of Yiddish theater, Maurice Schwartz—at his best as the despot, the same role he played on Second Avenue. The film is remarkable despite being highly theatrical in style, with mediocre camerawork and often crude editing. Schwartz gave one of the great performances of his career. Supported by the talented Judith Abarbanel, Mark Schweid, and Zvee Scooler, the sweatshop scenes conveyed the tensions that were so close to the audience. The picture was the first Yiddish sound picture to deal with a difficult contemporary social theme—in this case, the sweatshop and labor abuse.

ATTEMPTS TO TRANSFORM SILENT FILMS FOR THE NEW SOUND MARKET

In 1932, director and editor George Roland created a new form of Yiddish cinema, the Yiddish compilation film. Roland filmed a prologue, narration, and epilogue in Yiddish, pieced them together, included old silent films from various sources, and released the product as a new picture. For his first effort, *Joseph in the Land of Egypt,* Roland used segments from the 1914 Italian picture *Joseph in Egypt,* and added his own opening and closing using Yiddish actors. He repeated this procedure in 1933 with *Yidishe Tokhter* (*Jewish Daughter*), also called *A Daughter of Her People*. Actors told the story of Judith Trachtenberg, using silent footage taken primarily from the 1921 German picture *Judith Trachtenberg*. The film was adapted from the Karl Emil Franzos novel about a Jewish woman who marries a Polish aristocrat and tries to live, unsuccessfully, both a Jewish and Polish life. After beginning with the actors sitting around a table, the action shifted to the silent picture as the Yiddish narration continued. This was repeated a third time with *Avrom Ovinu* (*Abraham Our Patriarch*), alternately called *The Eternal Jew* and *The Wandering Jew*. Here, Roland used clips from various Bible-story silent films to tell the story of the Jewish people. That same year, Roland took the Polish-made 1924 silent classic, *Tkies Kaf* (*The Vow*), added prologue and epilogue, and released it as both *Dem Rebins Koyekh* (*The Rabbi's Strength*) and *A Vilna Legend*. Roland took credit as director of the picture and neglected to credit half the original cast. The director of the original film, Zygmund Turkow, then in Brazil, was certainly surprised when he received the following information sheet from New York publicizing the film: "Between the said sheets, on both sides of the page, is a large picture of (Joseph) Buloff with the inscription: 'The eminent Yiddish star-actor in the great Yiddish talkie *Dem Rebins Koyekh.*' On the right side of the page is written, 'Text—Jacob Mestel, Film Direction—George Roland.' On the left in small letters is written, 'An Outstanding Cast.'"[6]

The picture had literally been stolen and recast in a new form. Turkow was further astounded by the fact that of the six cast members mentioned, four were actors who only provided the prologue; the other two were Ida Kaminska and Turkow himself. No mention was made of the other great actors who participated in the original picture, including Esther Rokhl Kaminska and Moyshe Lipman. "It would have been interesting had they [Roland and his producers] guessed that the director of the picture was by chance still alive and living in Brazil."[7]

---

[6] Zygmund Turkow, *Di Ibergerisene Tkufe, Fragmentn Fun Mayn Lebn* (Buenos Aires: Central Farband, 1961), 97.

[7] Ibid.

Joseph Burstyn's Worldkino production company showed more discretion when it took advantage of the new market by adding Yiddish sound narration to silent Yiddish films from the Soviet Union. Michael Rosenberg narrated at least two of these films, *Durkh Trern* (*Through Tears*), released as *Laughter Through Tears,* and *Yidishe Glikn* (*Jewish Luck*), released as *The Matchmaker.* Each had a new score by Sholom Secunda and was very well received. The original cast and directors were all given proper credit.

HENRY LYNN

In 1934, Henry Lynn, an independent businessman and writer, became interested in Yiddish filmmaking and formed Sov-Am Productions. Over the next year and a half he monopolized Yiddish picture production. Very little is known about Lynn, except that he was an avid writer and theater patron, especially of the Yiddish theater. He was involved in many enterprises, and in the forties he owned a plant that manufactured fiberglass and plastic products.

Lynn wrote and directed his first film, *Yidishe Foter* (*Jewish Father*), also known as *A Youth of Russia,* in 1934. Set in pre- and post-revolution Russia, it told the story of a poor man who is having problems adjusting to the new Soviet government. A clear attack on the Soviet Union, the film challenged Soviet morality and the entire Soviet system. He followed *Yidishe Foter* the next year by starring Yiddish-theater matinee idol Boris Thomashefsky in *Bar Mitsve,* which Thomashefsky wrote. Regina Zuckerberg played his wife, believed to be dead ten years. In the story, Israel (played by Thomashefsky) has already made plans to marry a woman who is plotting with her lover to take his money. The film predictably comes to a climax at his son's Bar Mitzvah, when the "dead" wife appears. Filmed in what seems to be a two-room studio, *Bar Mitsve* is static and has poor sound, many out-of-focus shots, and incongruent scene transitions. One of the key issues raised in the film for the American audience is to what extent someone should remain a Jew while becoming an American. The father points out to his son, just before the bar mitzvah, that one is not exclusive of the other. "Study the World's literature—don't be *just* a Jew. . . . Learn new languages—but *don't forget* your own!" The father's admonition was directed at the Yiddish-speaking audience of the day.

Despite its poor technical quality, *Bar Mitsve* did well financially, largely due to Thomashefsky's reputation, and was one of the first American Yiddish pictures to reach European movie theaters. Lynn, hoping to capitalize on the interest in his pictures, immediately made *Shir Hashirim* (*Song of Songs*). Based on a story by Anshel Schorr, with music by Joseph Rumshinsky, the story revolves around a problematic relationship between a niece and her uncle, which breaks a family apart. Similar to *Bar Mitsve* in its poor technical quality, *Shir Hashirim* was not only an artistic disaster, but a financial one as well. It lacked a big name like Thomashefsky to save it.

After a hiatus of nearly two years, Lynn, together with Abe Leff, formed Menorah Pictures in 1937. Leff had worked with Seiden in a number of capacities on many of the early Judea pictures. Together, they co-directed *Vu Iz Mayn Kind?* (*Where is My Child?*), based on a Louis Freiman story. Lynn wrote the screenplay, telling the story of a widowed mother who turns her child over for adoption and then is committed to an asylum for a number of years—twenty years later, she is reunited with him. Though primitively shot, the picture raised the important issue of inhumane treatment of the mentally ill, the only Yiddish film to take on such a difficult subject. Lynn wisely cast the highly respected Celia Adler in the lead so as to guarantee immediate box office returns. George Roland's editing stands out in this picture as a masterful attempt to cover faulty direction and camerawork.

Lynn reemerged in 1938 with a film based on a story by Isidore Zolatarefsky, *Di Kraft fun Lebn* (*The Power of Life*). Starring Michel Michalesco, the film is about a father's sacrifice for his children that goes unappreciated. Lynn followed this the next year with *Haynteke Mames* (*Mothers of Today*), shot in five days. While other Yiddish productions were lavished with money, Lynn had a tighter budget than ever. With a cast that included Esther Field, who played the mother in *Mayn Yidishe Mame* (1930), Max Rosenblatt as the cantor, and Simon Wolf (also the play's author), the film focuses on the collapse of a Jewish family. A cantor's son runs off with a woman of "questionable morality" and steals the deed to his mother's store. The daughter elopes with a gangster and is charged as an accomplice in a murder.

As if that is not enough, the mother goes blind. Lynn failed to take into account the growing sophistication of his audience. Melodrama had become an acceptable vehicle in Yiddish cinema, but all these calamities in one family were a bit *too* much. The financial failure of *Haynteke Mames* all but ended Lynn's filmmaking career.

Ben K. Blake, who had directed a few short-subject films, felt that by using a well-known star he could generate a commercial success in his first feature film effort. He cast Jennie Goldstein, known in Yiddish circles for her vaudeville and theater work, in *Tsvey Shvester* (Two Sisters), written by Sam Cohen. It is the story of one sister's love and the other's greed. This 1938 attempt to portray suffering and disruption of traditional Jewish mores in a changing society is overly melodramatic, to the point of being comical. It, like Lynn's *Haynteke Mames,* tried to take advantage of the great love of the Yiddish theater audience for melodrama, but it failed to draw an audience. Blake, who planned a series of Yiddish films, was not heard from again.

Henry Lynn made one last attempt at Yiddish film production, releasing *A People That Shall Not Die* in 1939. He used segments of Lothar Mendes' 1934 British-made *Jew Suss,* adding new scenes, which he shot, plus footage from other sound and silent films. Using Roland's compilation techniques from the early thirties, he attempted to pass off the picture as "an extravaganza made with a cast of ten thousand." The picture was billed as "the first million-dollar Yiddish film spectacle ever made," and was released as *A People Eternal.* This method of moviemaking and unusual marketing strategy may have succeeded in 1933, but by 1939 it attracted little interest, and a debt-ridden Henry Lynn was forced to stop making pictures.

PRODUCTION, 1935–1937

Rather than continue to knock out twelve to fifteen pictures a year, Joseph Seiden chose to produce *The Voice of Israel* and a few short-subject films like Max Wilner's *Gelebt un Gelakht* (*Live and Laugh*) with Menashe Skulnick in the mid-1930s. In 1935, Seiden made Jacob Gordin's classic, *Yidishe Kinig Lir* (*Jewish King Lear*), directed by Harry Thomashefsky. Slow paced, with one camera set-ups, the picture,

based on Shakespeare's *King Lear,* is about an aging father in 1892
Vilna who divides his fortune among his three daughters as he takes
leave for Palestine. Because of greed, two of the daughters are cut off
from the inheritance and the father, for want of money, is forced to return from the Holy Land as a beggar and wanderer going blind. To
the modern-day viewer, it is dull and over-staged.

In 1936, wanting to expand production, Seiden moved into an
Upper West Side office/studio and hired George Roland to direct.
Roland was not only a director but a master editor, responsible for a
large amount of editing work on foreign versions of Warner Brothers'
pictures. In addition, he had directed Yiddish segments and edited
them into his compilation pictures of 1932–1933. Roland was a multi-
talented actor, painter, musician, lyricist, scenarist, and filmmaker. Seiden, who still felt unprepared to direct, trusted Roland to handle the
job. Their first production was *Libe un Laydnshaft* (*Love and Passion*),
also released as *Love and Sacrifice*—a tearjerker about a woman, falsely
accused of a crime, who must suffer years of agony. Seiden, trying to
have a picture ready for release on Passover in 1936, was desperate:

> On March 9, I didn't have the faintest idea for a story . . . and
> with Passover three weeks away—our best season. Then, that Satur-
> day, in a bookstore on Allen Street, I found this dog-eared little book-
> let. It was out-of-date, had been printed in Poland, and was called
> *Love and Passion.*
>
> I bought *Love and Passion* for twenty cents, spent Saturday after-
> noon rewriting it—oh yes, I do my own scenario—and on Monday
> started casting. I get my casts very easily. I hang around the beaneries
> on Second Avenue; there's always an actor who wants to get in the
> movies. I don't pay him nothing. Over a cup of coffee, I give him a
> smile, a promise, and he's willing.[8]

The film was indeed ready for Passover and did well enough financially
to allow Seiden to fund another picture.

That same year, Seiden hired Leo Fuchs and Yetta Zwerling to act
in a short comedy, *Ikh Vil Zayn a Pensyoner* (*I Want to Be a Boarder*), and

---

[8] "Moviemaker Joe Seiden Keeps Three-Room Studio Humming," *Brooklyn Daily Eagle,* April 7, 1936.

was so pleased with the results that he designed his next feature, *Ikh Vil Zayn a Mame* (*I Want to Be a Mother*), around the two actors. The new feature was a melodrama about an unwed mother who is forced to give her daughter away. Years later, at the child's wedding, the mother reveals herself; this results in a series of complications that finally end happily. Roland again handled direction with a cast of Seiden regulars, including Rose Greenfield, Esta Salzman, and Cantor Leibele Waldman, with Fuchs and Zwerling providing comic relief. The film was shot at night and on weekends—as were all the Seiden pictures of this period—because Seiden's studio was not certified by the fire department. As combustible nitrate film was being used, filming had to be done when the building was empty. Completing films was difficult under those conditions, but Seiden somehow managed.

SIDNEY GOLDIN'S LAST PICTURE

While Seiden was completing *Ikh Vil Zayn a Mame* during the summer of 1936, his former director-in-residence, Sidney Goldin, was preparing his first Yiddish picture since *Uncle Moses* (1932). Just a few months earlier, Joseph Green's Polish-made *Yidl Mitn Fidl* (*Yiddle with a Fiddle*) had proved that a well-budgeted Yiddish picture could turn a nice profit. Pointing to this success, Goldin was able to raise sufficient funds to allow him, for the first time, to make a picture as he wished. *Dem Khazns Zundl* (*The Cantor's Son*), written by Louis Freiman, was based on the life of singer/cantor Moishe Oysher—who left Eastern Europe and attained success as one of America's finest vocalists. Goldin was working for the first time with an ample budget, and he was able to take his crew and actors for on-location shooting near Easton, Pennsylvania. The character, *played* by Oysher, having achieved success, forsakes his new-world girlfriend and returns home to his village sweetheart. Florence Weiss, Oysher's real-life wife, played the American woman; Judith Abarbanel played the childhood sweetheart.

Sidney Goldin died before *Dem Khazns Zundl* was half completed, and independent director Ilya Moteleff was brought in to finish production. Goldin's passing marked the end of an era of filmmaking. He was one of Yiddish cinema's pioneers. He developed Yiddish cinema in Europe and was the key person responsible for its emergence as a talking medium in America. Goldin brought the art of Yiddish cinema from its beginnings to its golden age—a four-year period in which quality classic Yiddish pictures were made. Like Moses, who saw the Promised Land only from a distance, Goldin did not live to witness this feat. Less than one month after Goldin's death in September 1937, Edgar G. Ulmer and Jacob Ben-Ami's *Grine Felder* (*Green Fields*), the first picture of the American golden age of Yiddish cinema, opened in New York City.

THE GOLDEN AGE OF YIDDISH CINEMA, 1937–1940

In 1934, the American film industry shifted gears as a new set of production codes affected the type of movie being made in Hollywood. As American film historian Robert Sklar points out in *Movie-Made America,* the changes were brought about by a change in national mood caused in part by Roosevelt's "New Deal" as well as by the growing influence of the Catholic Legion of Decency, which moved moviemakers toward greater support of a more traditional Anglo-American culture.[9] One of the immediate results was a rash of "respectable" pictures drawn from the past and adapted from classic literature.[10]

The Yiddish pictures in America largely dealt with the changes taking place within the fabric of the Jewish family, usually portrayed by the rebellion of the new generation against the ways of their parents. In Europe, the Yiddish classics typically served as the basis for Yiddish screenplays, while the American audience seemed to demand contemporary drama and melodrama relating to their ongoing lives. By 1937, with more capital available for Yiddish movie production, and stimulated by the changes in Hollywood film production, a similar "classical" film form ushered in the American golden age of Yiddish cinema.

---

[9] Robert Sklar, *Movie-Made America* (New York: Random House, 1975), 175.
[10] *David Copperfield, Anna Karenina, Mutiny on the Bounty,* and *Tale of Two Cities* were all made in 1935.

More time and money was invested in these films, and a superior group of artists, writers, and technicians participated in production. There was a clear effort to give Yiddish cinema an artistic foundation and better technical quality.

As producers sought to make quality Yiddish films, they drew from the classics of Yiddish theater and literature. The subjects of this new group of films usually dealt nostalgically with Jewish life in Eastern Europe, the place many Yiddish-speaking Jews still considered their home. There, in the *shtetl,* Jewish values and culture seemed more clearly defined. In the West, assimilation and acculturation had changed the mores of Jewish existence; the *shtetl* represented a pure Jewish spirit, lost in Americanization. Over the next four years these classics served as the foundation of Yiddish cinema in America.

The first Yiddish film producer to adapt a literary classic for the screen during this period was Roman Rebush. Rebush was like most of the Yiddish film producers in America, a businessman who saw that there was an excellent market for Yiddish pictures. Yet Rebush was also different. He had a dream to raise the production quality of Yiddish moviemaking. Having seen Joseph Green successfully exhibit his Polish-made *Yidl mitn Fidl* in New York in early 1937, Rebush believed that there was a market for good Yiddish pictures. He wanted to produce a Jewish motion picture good enough to draw both Christian and Jewish audiences to the theater. This required a fine writer, a good director, well-known actors, and a film budget far larger than previous Yiddish film efforts. At a time when Jewish film producers were making pictures on the smallest of budgets, Rebush courageously chose to considerably upgrade the product. He defined *good pictures* as films which were well-budgeted and professionally produced.[11] Choosing material from the Yiddish classics, Rebush first made Peretz Hirschbein's *Grine Felder* in 1937, then *Der Zingendiker Shmid* (*The Singing Blacksmith*) in 1938, based on a David Pinski play, and, to follow that, Jacob Gordin's *Mirele Efros* in 1939.

Producers realized that a big name star made their pictures more attractive. Henry Lynn lured actors Boris Thomashefsky and Celia

---

[11] Martin Panzer, "Jewish Movies Come of Age: An Interview with Roman Rebush," *The American Hebrew* (New York, November 17, 1939), 6.

Adler to the screen. Ben K. Blake filmed theater star Jennie Goldstein in *Tsvey Shvester.* However, Blake's and Lynn's pictures were overly melodramatic and of mediocre technical quality. With the advent of the golden age of Yiddish cinema, film productions were finally produced to a higher technical standard, and actors no longer feared that their participation in Yiddish pictures would leave them open to ridicule. In Poland, fine leading actors like Molly Picon, Zygmund Turkow, and Avrom Marevsky participated in Yiddish films. In America, the list included Moishe Oysher, Maurice Schwartz, and Berta Gersten. A star system had emerged in Yiddish cinema.

Peretz Hirschbein's play, *Grine Felder,* had become a classic of Yiddish drama, and it seemed natural to choose it as the first large-budget classic from Yiddish literature to be adapted for the screen. In 1918, the Folksbienne Yiddish Theater presented the world premiere of the play, an event Yiddish theater critic Jacob Fishman claimed "marked the birth of the Yiddish art theater."[12] Rebush felt that *Grine Felder* would do the same for Yiddish films by raising the artistic level and drawing new audiences who had initially spurned Yiddish films. He was correct. This well-funded classic ushered in the golden age of Yiddish cinema in America.

Grine Felder tells the story of a young student who leaves the *yeshiva* in search of a meaningful existence more closely connected with the soil. It is strange that this story of Leyvi-Yitskhok, a rabbinical student leaving the academy to be with the common people, would be the subject of the first Yiddish megapicture. Did its story speak to the Yiddish-speaking, largely urban audience of the time? Were the producers looking past the American audience at the massive Jewish market in Europe hungry for Yiddish pictures? Or was there simply a desire to gravitate to the classics, much the way American moviemakers did in the late 1930s? Whatever the case, the producer was able to involve the best Yiddish theater talent of the day, with Jacob Ben-Ami as director.

When playwright Peretz Hirschbein was asked for permission to adapt his play for the screen, he consented on the condition that

---

[12] Jacob Fishman, B. Levin, and B. Stabinowitz, *Finf Un Tsvantsik Yor Folksbine* (New York: privately published, 1940), 95.

actor/director Ben-Ami would be involved with the production. Ben-Ami, a fine actor and director of theater, was one of the original members of Hirschbein's theater troupe in Odessa. In New York, Ben-Ami's name, along with that of Maurice Schwartz, had become synonymous with quality Yiddish theater. Ben-Ami had played a large part in Hirschbein's work becoming an integral part of Yiddish art theater. It was, therefore, no great surprise to producer Rebush that Hirschbein not only wanted Ben-Ami to direct the film, but envisioned Ben-Ami in the lead role as well. After all, it was Ben-Ami who, a decade earlier, had made the part of Leyvi-Yitskhok famous. Yet, Leyvi-Yitskhok was a *yeshive-bokher,* a young student, and Ben-Ami, already forty-five, could not hope to fool the camera. Hirschbein compromised and agreed to allow the film to be made if Ben-Ami were on the set establishing the necessary *mise-en-scene*— making sure that the film had the proper interpretation. By hiring film director Edgar G. Ulmer as co-director with Ben-Ami, Rebush sought to ensure a technically well-made film. As it turned out, Ben-Ami directed the actors and gave the film his interpretation, while Ulmer worked with the technicians to produce a technically superb movie.

Grine Felder was well received not only by Yiddish speakers, but by the public at large, and it played for twenty weeks in downtown Manhattan. For many Yiddish-speaking Jews, it was a celebration, a chance to return home to the old world, to the *shtetl,* to their roots. Rebush's dream for a quality Yiddish picture had come true. He had proved that the Hollywood formula of adapting a literary classic could be brought to Jewish films. *Grine Felder* was a milestone. At a special screening of the picture in 1938, Peretz Hirschbein told the audience, "Twenty years ago, the play, *Grine Felder,* was the beginning of a better Yiddish theater in America. Let's hope that the film, *Grine Felder,* is a beginning of better Yiddish cinema."[13] It was!

The film was so successful, in fact, that Rebush's Collective Films Producers set out immediately to make a second picture. Rebush chose to adapt another successful play that drew on the Eastern European Jewish experience, David Pinski's *Yankl der Shmid* (*Yankl the Blacksmith*). Re-

---

[13] David Matis, "*Tsu Der Geshikhte fun Yidishe Films,*" *Ikuf-Almanak* (New York, 1961), 460.

bush sensed that his audience, both in America and Eastern Europe, would be attracted to a nostalgic voyage to a Jewish past. *Yankl* is the story of a blacksmith who sees too many women and drinks too much liquor. However, after meeting Tamare, he promises to change his ways. The story, set in a *shtetl*, deals with important issues like alcoholism and fidelity. Though these were not necessarily the most pressing questions in Jewish life at the time, they were still pertinent issues. The film also offered the audience a dreamlike withdrawal from American life.

Rebush chose Moishe Oysher, who had starred in Sidney Goldin's *Dem Khazns Zindl*, to play the blacksmith. A leading singer and actor on the Yiddish stage, Oysher was known for his rich cantorial voice. Rebush hired Yiddish playwright Ossip Dymow to write the screenplay. Dymow's work has a unique visual quality, and it is not surprising that he was approached to write screenplays. After *Yankl*, Dymow adapted Jacob Gordin's *Mirele Efros* and Mark Arnstein's *Der Vilner Shtot Khazn* (*The Vilna Cantor*) to the screen. Edgar Ulmer, with the experience of directing *Grine Felder* under his belt, directed this picture by himself. His experience working with Ben-Ami had been a difficult one, and this time he sought artistic control. The film was released in November 1938 and was fairly well received by the Yiddish-speaking public. The picture was successful largely due to Oysher's voice; each musical interlude was another highlight of the film. Particularly delightful is a *dudele* that Oysher sings with costar and off-screen wife, Florence Weiss, where a superb rapport is visible. The comical stammering of character actor Benjamin Fishbein completes the film.

After Rebush and Ulmer made *Der Zingendiker Shmid*, they went their separate ways; Rebush began making *Mirele Efros*, and Ulmer directed a Ukrainian picture. Once production was completed on the Ukrainian film, Ulmer began preparing for a third Yiddish picture. Ulmer grew more comfortable with the Yiddish language and culture—and with the Eastern-European setting of the stories. He especially admired a stage adaptation of Mendele Mokher Seforim's *Fishke der Krumer* (*Fishke the Lame*), written by journalist Chaver-Pahver.

It was no accident that in 1939 Ulmer was drawn to *Fishke der Krumer*. It is another story of *dos klayne mentshele*, the little man, a figure which dominates Yiddish literature. The anti-hero, with a crippled body, is caught in a whirlwind of events beyond his control, much like the European Jew of that day, about to be trapped in Nazi Europe. Ulmer and Chaver-Pahver chose to call the film *Di Klyatshe* (*The Dobbin*), alluding to Mendele's 1873 allegorical satire of Jewry as the world's scapegoat; in English, the film was called *The Light Ahead*. In this work, the narrator looks out his window to see a poor, undernourished Jew lashing out at a weakened emaciated horse unable to pull his heavy burden. The horse says to his master, "You fool; you too are a beast of burden serving a master, who abuses you and fills you with fear." So, too, is Fishke, a lame man who is ward of the community, abused. He is kept from marrying Hodl, a blind woman, because of their extreme poverty and handicaps. Only when an epidemic strikes, do the rich, fearing a supernatural force, present the couple with wealth, enabling them to marry and have a better life. Ulmer used twenty-year-old actor David Opatoshu to play the lead of Fishke and Helen Beverly to play Hodl. The film is the most visually interesting American Yiddish film, due to Ulmer's use of expressionistic sets and contrived light to contrast the natural and supernatural.

As soon as work was completed on *Der Zingendiker Shmid*, Rebush began adapting Jacob Gordin's *Mirele Efros* for the screen. Gordin's play was a staple of the Yiddish stage. Ossip Dymow, who had worked with Rebush on *Der Zingendiker Shmid*, agreed to adapt the play for the screen together with Josef Berne, a writer/director who was also hired to direct the picture. Rebush cast Berta Gersten as Mirele, a self-sacrificing matriarch, a sort of "Jewish Queen Lear," who triumphs over a rapacious son and daughter-in-law. Gersten knew the play well, having played the part of the daughter-in-law, Sheyndl, on the stage. She followed a long line of fine actresses who played Mirele, going back to tragediennes Kenni Liptzen, Jennie Goldstein, and Esther Rokhl Kaminska who was Mirele in the first filmed version made in Warsaw in 1912. Mirele was a role with which many mothers, Jewish and non-Jewish, could identify—that of a woman pushed aside when her usefulness no longer served the purposes of her children.

Despite good acting and direction, *Mirele Efros* failed from a technical standpoint. The picture has an overabundance of extended long shots, faulty editing, and too few cutaways. In effect, the film is visually stifled. The entire picture was shot inside a studio with little change of scenery. In Rebush's previous two films, Ulmer had insisted on filming a great deal of the action outdoors, consequently enhancing these pictures. Here, no such choice was made and, as a result, *Mirele Efros* was little more than a well-directed recording of the stage play. A powerful story with a great deal of emotion, it is still quite hard-hitting, never failing to draw tears from its audience. This set the stage for Maurice Schwartz's first movie in seven years.

Although scarred thirteen years earlier when, with no experience, he first directed the 1926 silent picture *Tsebrokhene Hertser,* Maurice Schwartz believed he was finally ready to mount a film production by himself. He knew stage direction and acting, but he found it difficult in the earlier film to transfer his understanding of theater to the screen. He waited for the right moment when he could again try his hand at film direction. In the summer of 1939, conscious of widespread interest in the classics and in quality Yiddish cinema, Schwartz made his long-delayed return to filmmaking. Sholom Aleichem's *Tevye der Milkhiker* (*Tevye the Milkman*) had been one of his favorite stage roles, and he was anxious to adapt the play for film. Schwartz had asked film producer/director Joseph Green to make *Tevye* in Poland three years earlier, but Green was not ready. Green felt that there were too many anti-clerical and anti-church elements in the play. Undeterred, Schwartz set up the Maymon Film Company and secured film rights to this and two other plays by Sholom Aleichem. He hoped that *Tevye der Milkhiker* would be the first in a series of films made by the new company (but this never materialized). Schwartz made the film, recreating a Ukrainian *shtetl* just east of Jericho, Long Island—believing the topography was almost identical to that of the countryside which Sholom Aleichem depicted.

Tevye der Milkhiker was adapted from Sholom Aleichem's "Tevye" stories, written between 1895 and 1916. In the original work, Sholom Aleichem tackled a variety of contemporary issues through the stories of each of Tevye's daughters. Schwartz's adaptation focuses only on one of the daughters, Khave, who is in a constant state of turmoil regarding her relationship with Fedye, her Gentile boyfriend. Khave knows full well the impact her relationship has on her parents, and by dealing solely with her, Schwartz focused in on the problem of intermarriage, the issue he found most troubling. For him, as for his audience, it posed the single greatest threat to the continuation of Jewish life. Intermarriage had become synonymous with a renunciation of Judaism, and it is not surprising that Schwartz chose to emphasize its unacceptability within the Jewish community. It is clear that he saw this issue as more compelling than those raised in the stories of the other daughters. In the film, Tevye tells a priest who intimates that Jewish children are joining the church through intermarriage, "I would rather see them perish than see them betray our faith." No such comment appears in the Sholom Aleichem original. The authors of *Fiddler on the Roof*, who produced a film for a world audience almost four decades later, chose to expand the focus to three daughters instead of putting too much emphasis on intermarriage—which they surely felt would not resonate with a non-Jewish audience.[14]

The actors for the film were chosen from Maurice Schwartz's Yiddish Art Theater, by that time one of the great Yiddish theaters in New York. Schwartz picked his niece, Miriam Riselle, who had played Tamare so well in *Der Zingendiker Shmid*, to be Khave. Leon Liebgold, who had a lead role in Polish Yiddish films *Yidl mitn Fidl* and *Der Dibuk*, played Fedye. Schwartz was the director and also played the lead role of Tevye. Schwartz wanted the picture to be theatrically perfect and have a high degree of technical quality. *Tevye der Milkhiker* received good reviews in the press and did very well commercially. Schwartz had finally demonstrated that he could successfully work with film. Unfortunately, with the war in Europe beginning that year, he never had another opportunity.

In 1940, Edgar G. Ulmer made one more Yiddish film, *Amerikaner Shadkhn* (*American Matchmaker*), a hastily made comedy, shot completely in a studio. It was Ulmer's attempt to cash in on the success of the Yiddish film genre, while producing a film at little cost. Despite fine performances by Leo Fuchs and Judith Abarbanel, the film drew poor reviews and failed to attract an audience. This light comedy had the feel of the earlier, quickly-made Yiddish films and was shunned by

---

[14] By closely looking at differences between the Sholom Aleichem original, the Schwartz adaptation, an Israeli version, and the Broadway and Hollywood productions, you gain insight into how the author of each version focused in on completely different themes felt to be of greatest importance to their respective audiences.

the newly sophisticated viewing public who, in a short period of time, had grown accustomed to seeing well-produced classics. Nevertheless, Ulmer added a new level of artistic and technical quality not previously seen in American Yiddish films. Though not initially comfortable with this new film genre, he quickly adapted and became the most cinematically gifted of the American Yiddish moviemakers. Though he never again made a Yiddish film, he gained notice around the world for making low-budget quality cinema.

Independent producers Ira Greene and Ludwig Landy wanted to lavish the Yiddish screen with opulence, and began work on one last elaborate production in 1939. They used elegant sets, expensive costumes, and a wide array of scenes and settings unprecedented in Yiddish cinema. Ossip Dymow developed a screenplay from a play by Mark Arnstein. It is based on the life of Cantor Yoel Dovid Strashunsky, who had left his position as Vilna Cantor for the secular world of the Warsaw Opera. It was to be Moishe Oysher's third and last Yiddish film.

The story is a rebuke of the secular assimilationist life promoted in Hollywood's films, particularly *The Jazz Singer* (1927). In *The Jazz Singer,* Jack Robin (Jakie Rabinowitz) rejects the vocation pushed on him by his traditional father and chooses not to follow in his footsteps to become a cantor. In the end, it is Jack's father who dies and pays the ultimate price for his unwillingness to let Jack sing jazz. In contrast, in *Overture to Glory,* it is the cantor who dies, punished for abandoning his family and the Jewish community. Hollywood portrayed the older generation as too bound to outdated traditions. But Dymow avowed it was wrong for the cantor to leave his Jewishness—his community. Before the picture was even completed, a war which would forever disfigure world Jewry was unleashed. With the potential viewing market for Yiddish films cut by more than half, *Overture to Glory* was released with little hoopla. It drew favorable critical reviews, but it failed to recoup its costs. With the war on, interest in both making and watching Yiddish movies dropped considerably.

Joseph Seiden was the only one who continued making Yiddish movies into 1941. Between 1939 and 1941, he made *Der Lebediker Yosem* (*The Living Orphan*); *Kol Nidre; Ir Tsveyte Mame* (*Her Second Mother*); *Der Groyse Eytse Geber* (*The Great Advisor*); and *Mazl Tov Yidn* (*Mazel Tov Jews*). As had always been his trademark, Seiden's films were quickly and inexpensively made and failed to match in quality the pictures of Rebush, Landy, and Greene. But the golden age of Yiddish cinema had come to an end with *Overture to Glory*. There would continue to be a few more film efforts, but that same high standard would never again be realized. Nazi storm troopers' boots on Polish territory and a changing America were responsible.

AFTER THE WAR

During the war, Joseph Seiden was involved in the production of collapsible masts for rafts, and it was not until 1949 that he again turned his attention to Yiddish filmmaking. With the European market tragically destroyed, a lack of enthusiasm and even some contempt for Yiddish pictures in Israel,[15] and a new generation of non-Yiddish speakers in America, the commercial producers, once so enamored with the Yiddish cinema, lost interest. Seiden's commitment, however, did not waver, and in June of 1949, he set about preparing for his biggest project ever, the filming of Jacob Gordin's *Got, Mentsh un Tayvl* (*God, Man and Devil*). The play depicts the transformation of a traditional Jew into a man of station whose greed destroys everything around him. In this reworking of *Faust*, the devil overpowers the poor man, causing him to divorce his wife, commit a murder, and bring about his own ruin.

Seiden brought together many of the talents performing in Yiddish theater at that time, each of whom had acted in the play. He meant to continue the Yiddish classics filmmaking, begun twelve years before, and hoped that the professionalism of his cast would suffice to accomplish this. Even though the roles were familiar to the stars, the direction was lacking. The film, produced in Seiden's West Side New York studios, is stagebound and overly theatrical. Its ending is primitive, with scenes shot in one take and from one angle, broken up only by an occasional cutaway.

Seiden did not wait to see the response to *Got, Mentsh un Tayvl*. Relentless, he prepared for another picture, Abraham Blum's *Dray*

---

[15] Yiddish language was repudiated by Hebrew advocates in Palestine as contrary to Zionist philosophy.

Tekhter (*Three Daughters*). *Dray Tekhter* is about three daughters and the various joys and sorrows of childhood. The film was made in little over a week. Before postproduction on *Dray Tekhter* was completed, *Got, Mentsh un Tayvl* opened to an extremely poor reception at theaters, and Seiden, who had always worked on a small, tight budget, was overwhelmed at the failure of his first big-name production. There no longer seemed to be an interest in Yiddish movies. Though the film made its way to theaters, Seiden spent little effort in releasing *Dray Tekhter,* and he turned his attention to other ventures.

Meanwhile, producer Martin Cohen came up with the idea of filming a musical revue. Ten different acts, from comedy to singing routines, highlight *Catskill Honeymoon.* It became an immediate success on the elderly and rehabilitation home circuit. This seemed to be the only audience left for Yiddish pictures. Seiden watched the "success" of *Catskill Honeymoon* carefully from the sidelines. He engaged actor Michael Rosenberg in September of 1950 to introduce a series of film clips from old Judea movies and assembled *Monticello, Here We Come.* Seiden tried to exhibit the picture theatrically, but soon realized that "borsht-belt" musical revues, aimed at the elderly Jewish audience, could not sustain Yiddish cinema.

The year 1950 witnessed the demise of Yiddish cinema. And that same year, Maurice Schwartz's Yiddish Art Theater closed its doors after thirty-two years of continuous operation. There were a number of factors—from the advent of television to high production costs—that brought about these endings, but most important was the passing of the Yiddish-speaking audience. What government immigration restrictions had not destroyed in potential audience, the murder of millions of Yiddish-speaking Jews had. No longer could a producer think of spending twenty, fifty, or a hundred thousand dollars on producing a Yiddish picture with any hope of meeting costs, let alone bringing in a profit. Joseph Seiden tried, but even he—who had witnessed the beginnings of the Yiddish sound film in 1929, and who managed to churn out Yiddish pictures year after year—was unable to succeed.

After World War II, Jews no longer sought the distinct flavor of Yiddish entertainment. They were content with the Hollywood films that told the story of ordinary Americans. It would not be until the late 1970s, with a revival of interest in Yiddish culture, that Yiddish films would again be screened in Jewish or Yiddish film festivals. A new generation craved what had been lost, but except for a few student films, there would be no new attempts at Yiddish film production in America.

THE WORLDLY SOUNDS
OF YIDDISH RADIO

Ari Y. Kelman

"The Jewish Philosopher," one of the more colorful and bombastic characters to populate the Yiddish airwaves during the 1930s and 1940s, once warned his audience, "If you want your children to be liberal, give them a Jewish education. If you give them a general education, they will become radical and will lose every connection with the Jewish past." Sponsored by Carnation Milk Products, The Jewish Philosopher used his weekly program to respond to letters allegedly written by listeners seeking advice on all manner of subjects. With vague disdain in his voice, he would read each letter and then respond with monologues full of bluster, outrage, indignation, and anger. Summoning the fire and brimstone typically reserved for preachers, not philosophers, The Philosopher used the sound and style of religion to fuel his program, entertain his audience, and satisfy his sponsors. Whether or not he agreed with the letter or even bothered answering the question it posed, he used a combination of flamboyance, passion, and Jewish wisdom to let his audience know where he stood on the issue at hand.

His appeal likely derived in part from his hyperbolic and often abrasive persona, but it also owed a debt to the ways in which he summoned the sounds of religion without bothering to garner any of its attendant authority; his opinions rarely referred to traditional texts, relying instead on overstatement, well-timed snorts and sighs, and overdramatic declamations. He commanded his audience through melodrama, popular aphorisms, and self-proclaimed insight, rather than by referring to the wisdom of traditional Jewish texts. He owed as much to the theater as he did to the pulpit, and audiences loved him enough to keep him on the air through the 1960s. His on-air persona offered a secular kind of Jewish authority that clearly cared deeply about being Jewish, but did not rely on traditional religious structures for support. Moreover, The Philosopher (whose real name was C. Israel Lutsky), for all of his impassioned diatribes, neglected to mention whether anyone followed his advice in the first place. He proudly provided advice without authority and Jewish wisdom without religion.

Therein lies the paradox of secular culture on the Yiddish airwaves: Yiddish programming frequently *sounded* religious without actually *being* religious. Cantorial concerts, holiday programming, rabbinic sermons, commercials, and original dramas frequently made allusions to Jewish religious traditions, but they neither promoted nor advocated religion as such. Even when stations did air programs with religious content, the intervention of the broadcast medium often interrupted the familiar meanings of the rituals themselves. Few Jewish broadcasts—especially those in Yiddish—could be categorized as decidedly either religious or secular. Rather, Yiddish radio programs used the sounds of religion to foster a sense of Jewishness in America that was not explicitly religious, but that operated within a broader cultural context that included elements that were both religious and secular.

In this context, *religious* and *secular* are not opposites but rather two symbiotic terms that are dynamically related to one another, and this relationship can be better understood by looking at how these terms translate in Yiddish. The Yiddish word for *secular* is *veltlikh*—worldly. In Yiddish, to be secular did not necessarily mean one excluded religion, but rather that one included religion alongside other, more worldly systems of meaning. Given the popularity of cantorial concerts, holiday celebrations, and radio dramas that drew on forms of traditional Jewish life, Yiddish radio sounded quite secular, quite *veltlikh,* even when it was religious. Yet, at the same time, when Yiddish-speaking broadcasters tried to mimic mainstream radio and sound more *veltlikh,* they often sounded more Jewish. Thus, the tension between worldly and religious produced a dynamic stress that created an aural Yiddish culture routed through and around radio.

THE CONTEXT OF YIDDISH RADIO

Yiddish radio is a phenomenon that exists entirely as a part of American radio, as the radio industries in most other countries were controlled almost entirely by the state and thus did not allow for the same diversity of radio interests as American radio did. To be sure, there were occasional broadcasts of Yiddish programs in Poland, and when theater troupes toured Latin America, they often made promotional appearances on radio, but for the most part, the radio industry of the United States allowed for a greater number of Yiddish speakers to reach the airwaves than anywhere else on earth.

Most radio historians date the beginning of radio broadcasting to November 1920, when Pittsburgh broadcaster Frank Conrad aired the results of that year's presidential election.[1] Over the next five years, radio exploded into American homes and into the popular consciousness. Between 1920 and 1925, the sales of radio sets increased from 60,000 to 3,700,000, while during those same years—and this is before anyone even made a dime on advertising or content—radio set sales rose from $2 million to $250 billion.[2] People wanted to listen, even when there wasn't that much to hear, and immigrants were no exception. By the end of the 1920s, families with at least one immigrant parent became the demographic most likely to own a radio. The 1930 census revealed that nearly 70 percent of those families nationwide owned radios, and in urban areas, it occasionally exceeded 80 percent.[3]

Even before the first Yiddish programs, Jewish immigrants were listening to radio programs in English. Daily radio listings began to appear in the Yiddish press in 1923, and, shortly thereafter, images of radios began appearing in advertisements for other products, in political cartoons, and in novelty records, as in Rubin Goldberg's 1923 Columbia recording "*Shloime auf'n radio*" ("Shloime on the Radio"). Radio had entered the cultural lives of Jewish immigrants first in English.

---

[1] Erik Barnouw, *A Tower of Babel: A History of Broadcasting in the United States to 1933* (New York: Oxford University Press, 1966); Susan Douglas, *The Invention of American Broadcasting 1899–1922* (Baltimore: Johns Hopkins University Press, 1987); Susan Smulyan, *Selling Radio: The Commercialization of American Broadcasting, 1920–1943* (Washington: Smithsonian Press, 1994).

[2] Charles Coolidge Parlin, *The Merchandising of Radio* (Philadelphia: The Curtis Publishing Company, 1925), 4–6.

[3] U.S. Bureau of the Census, *Fifteenth Census of the United States: 1930: Volume 6: Population* (Washington: United States Government Printing Office), 53.

The first Yiddish radio programs appeared in New York early in 1926, the same year that NBC debuted its radio network. While NBC and its partners in the big business of radio used their technological and financial muscles to steer the development of the broader industry, Yiddish-speaking broadcasters established footholds on many low-power local stations that broadcast in cities with large Jewish immigrant populations. Typically, these stations—such as WLTH, WFBH, WBBC, and WPCH in New York; WHFC, WGCU, and WCFL in Chicago; WPEN and WRAX in Philadelphia; and KGER in Los Angeles—were owned and operated by local businessmen who turned their investments into on-air echoes of their cities' immigrant populations. Typically, these stations hosted programs in every imaginable immigrant language and cobbled together lineups from loosely affiliated groups of polyglot performers bound together primarily by the fact that they lived in similar neighborhoods and were basically excluded from larger stations that privileged English. Typically, these smaller stations operated with 250 to 500 watts of power, while the larger "clear channel" English stations commanded as many as 50,000 watts. This power differential meant a much smaller broadcast radius and thus deeper, more highly localized connections to their primary audiences. All Yiddish programs, with only one exception, aired on local radio stations; and at least two other programs found audiences in distant cities through the distribution.

A precise measure of Yiddish-language broadcast hours is difficult because of the tenuous relationship between the programs and the medium, and the marginal status of the stations that housed them. Many programs moved stations or simply disappeared after a too-short attempt at on-air success. Stations also folded, or they moved or changed owners—only *sometimes* with their programming intact. That being said, in 1938, Yiddish programming could be heard (on nineteen different stations) in practically every major American city including Tuscaloosa and Birmingham, Alabama. By 1941, the number of stations carrying Yiddish programs climbed to twenty-one, and by 1956 the number peaked at forty-six.[4] Four years later, the number

---

[4] Joshua Fishman, *Yiddish: Turning to Life* (Philadelphia: John Benjamins Publishing Company, 1991). Fishman's data came largely from two studies con-

dropped to thirty-three but included a station in Honolulu, Hawaii. New York, because it housed the greatest Yiddish-speaking population, always boasted the largest number of stations with Yiddish programming and the greatest number of Yiddish broadcast hours, often accounting for more than one-half of the total Yiddish-language output in the United States.

The primary audience of Yiddish radio, for virtually its entire existence, remained the generation of native-Yiddish-speaking Jewish immigrants. Nearly every attempt to create Yiddish-language children's programming failed, although the immigrant audience in New York kept a significant amount of Yiddish programming on the air through the late 1970s. By 1930, the majority of Jews in America were born in America. And, although the younger generations may have listened to Yiddish programming, they never replaced their elders as its primary audience. Even so, the immigrant generation continued to provide a demand for Yiddish programming on radio well into the second half of the twentieth century. Of non-English-language broadcasting in New York, Yiddish accounted for the highest overall number of programs until 1962, when radio station WHOM decided to start carrying Spanish-language broadcasts of every New York Yankees game.[5] This meant that Yiddish slipped to second place, not because the amount of Yiddish programming decreased, but because the amount of Spanish programming increased.

As the primary audience of Yiddish-language programming began to succumb to the passage of time, the amount of Yiddish broadcasting declined precipitously, leaving only two regularly broadcast Yiddish programs on the airwaves by the end of the twentieth century: WEVD's *Forward Hour* and WNUR's *Dos Yiddishe Kol* (*The Yiddish Voice*). However, as Yiddish programs declined, a new generation of listeners began approaching Yiddish music with renewed interest and enthusiasm, giving birth to a new generation of Jewish music programs on the radio and, increasingly, on the Internet.

The cultural connections and resonances born of this trajectory took root primarily during the 1930s and 1940s, as Yiddish-language

---

ducted by the American Council for Nationalities Service on the presence of non-English-language radio in the United States in 1956 and 1960.
[5] *New York Times*, April 17, 1962, 53.

radio programming emerged—albeit on a different scale—alongside English-language programming during radio's golden age. Yiddish radio provided a powerful venue for an internal conversation among millions of Yiddish-speaking Jewish immigrants about how to create Jewish lives in America. Because radio broadcast in English and Yiddish (and other languages as well), it captured these conversations in particular proximity to burgeoning American mass-media culture, and thus provided some much-needed syncopation to the narratives of American Jewish culture, and a finely-tuned harmony to discussions of secular Jewish culture in America.

WHAT SOUNDS JEWISH IN AMERICA?

The first American radio broadcast that contained Jewish content aired on September 6, 1923. Sponsored by United Synagogue of America and conducted primarily in English, the program celebrated Rosh Hashana by carrying a "message in honor of the Jewish New Year" from Rabbi Azriel Goldstein alongside the musical accompaniment of Reverend Jacob Schwartz "with his big choir."[6] One week later, United Synagogue sponsored a second program in honor of Yom Kippur. According to the *New York Times,* the program included a speech "explaining the significance of impending Jewish festivals or holidays, a rendition of the complete musical ritual of the particular service by a leading cantor, and the recital of an appropriate Jewish legend or folk tale from the Talmud."[7] Noting that the actual airdate of the program fell a few days before Yom Kippur, the *Jewish Daily Forward* scoffed at the program and its host station. "It's a bit too early but after all, it's a *goyishe* [Gentile] station."[8]

Would a *yiddishe* program have aired on Yom Kippur? Even the socialist *Forward* took that day off, but something about the program's timing grated against the newspaper's sense of what Jewish radio pro-

---

[6] *Forward,* September 6, 1923.
[7] *New York Times,* August 30, 1923, 6:2.
[8] *Forward,* September 13, 1923.

grams ought to do and how they ought to sound. Behind the *Forward*'s sarcasm lay a deeper concern for the place of Jewish culture on the radio. Clearly, religious law would have prohibited broadcasting a Yom Kippur service live, but the *Forward* also seemed dissatisfied with the prospect of a program that featured "a rendition of the complete musical ritual of the particular service" on a day that was not Yom Kippur. Somehow, neither option sounded right. Thus, instead of sounding either religious or secular, the program made audible the tensions between the two that underpinned the broadcasting of Jewish culture.

One popular strategy for addressing this tension was to emulate the sounds of mainstream, English-language radio. Shortly after the High Holiday programs of 1923, Saul Birns, a successful phonograph dealer in New York, laid out his plans for "the first and only foreign-language broadcasting station . . . through which the millions of Jews who live in New York and in the hundreds of cities and towns around New York City will be able every day to hear on their radio Yiddish music and songs, Yiddish lectures, popular science, and all sorts of musical programs."[9] Birns did not promise to celebrate holidays with religious programming, choosing instead to offer a lineup that mirrored popular English programming of the day. Birns's plan revolved around a worldly Yiddish lineup that echoed English-radio programming but did so in Yiddish.

Although Birns's station never got off the ground, as soon as Yiddish broadcasting began—some two-and-a-half years later with a concert series on WHN and *The Libby's Hotel Program,* a variety show on WFBH—radio performers started looking to their English-speaking counterparts for inspiration. When popular English-speaking performer Rudy Vallee became a sensation thanks to his performances on *The Fleischmann Yeast Hour* (broadcast nationally on the NBC network), which took place at a small restaurant, Yiddish-speaking Rubin Goldberg replied with "a new funny feature" called *di yidishe okhsanya* (*The Jewish Inn*) on local New York station WMCA.[10] After Arthur Tracey found success as the mysterious "Street Singer," a handful of Yiddish

---

[9] *Forward,* October 6, 1923.
[10] *Forward,* October 10, 1928.

radio performers tried the same ploy and performed on pseudony-
mous programs with names like *der geto zinger, der yidish vagabond,* and
so on. English-language amateur hours, comedic sketches, dramas,
quiz shows, variety hours, and court programs all found Yiddish-
language imitators who wanted to entertain Jewish audiences with
their own versions of these popular genres. These Yiddish programs
were worldly from their very inception, as they came out of the ongoing interaction between English-radio programming and Yiddish-
speaking audiences and performers.

Yet, when these performers went looking for music, they turned
primarily to three sources: Yiddish theater, Yiddish folksong, and Jewish sacred music. Typically, Yiddish radio programs brought all of these
musical styles together, thus keeping the sacred and the secular—the
religious and the worldly—in conversation. Cantors, who specialized
in the vocal performance of sacred music, appeared with some regularity as guest stars on Yiddish radio programs, and even as figures in
advertisements for radio dealers.[11] Cantor Leybele Waldman even
earned the title of "Radio Cantor" for his frequent appearances on New
York radio stations, while a cadre of female performers, such as Frey-
dele Oysher, Perele Feyg, and Jean Gornish, who performed as *"sheyndele di khazente,"* built successful careers performing sacred music on
the radio. The appearance and popularity of these women on the air
further illuminated the tensions between religious and worldly. Owing
to the religious prohibition against women assuming positions of ritual leadership, these women found a parallel pulpit on the air to those
closed to them in synagogues. Even though their music was traditional,
their appearances as performers of that music were anything but.

The group of female performers of sacred music was informally
known as the *khazentes,* which is itself a feminized version of the mascu-
line *khazen* (cantor). Their popularity called for such a neologism because traditional Jewish law prohibits women from assuming a
leadership role in a religious context. Unlike their male counterparts,

---

[11] Vim's, a popular appliance franchise in New York, paid popular Yiddish
performers like Aaron Lebedev, Molly Picon, Ludwig Satz, and Cantor Yossele Rosenblatt to appear in their advertisements. *Forward,* February 4, 1928;
Forward, March 10, 1928.

the khazentes did not build their professional reputations on their abilities to conduct religious services, but on their skills as performers of sacred music in secular settings. Ironically, even though male cantors could serve a congregation, once they achieved a certain level of fame, many found that the weekly duties of a cantor conflicted with their concert schedule (and consequently reduced their earnings), so they often made arrangements to lighten their load of responsibilities to their home congregations. With public performances paying better than pulpit work, both male and female performers of sacred music found the radio to be a broader, less religiously-constricted platform on which to perform. Listening to cantorial music on the radio did not necessarily mean that listeners observed religious law, nor did listening to the *khazentes* mean that the audience members did not care about religious law. Rather, the popularity of cantorial music on the radio highlights the ways in which radio opened up new possibilities for religious and secular performances that were not mutually exclusive.

CLARITY OR CONFUSION?

Although performed primarily in Yiddish, these performances often raised heightened cultural tensions born of immigration and adaptation, and instead of providing a neat solution to the occasionally contentious relationship between the religious and the secular, radio often complicated the matter. During the early days of radio, broadcasters tried just about anything to attract an audience. For Yiddish-speaking broadcasters, this included (following the conventions of the Yiddish theater) broadcasting bar mitzvahs and weddings. Rubin Goldberg, an early star of Yiddish radio, broadcast his own wedding and even got Branfman's Sausage Company to sponsor it.[12] Meanwhile, Mirl Trieber and Benjamin Alperovitch won a contest through *Libby's Radio Program* that resulted in the broadcast of their nuptials (and a set of furniture for the couple). However, the intervention of the radio did not mean that the Alperovitches could simply expand their guest

---

[12] *Forward*, April 2, 1928.

list. The introduction of radio into religious or cultural rituals changed the nature of the relationships engendered by those rituals. In other words, radio was not just a medium of communication, but it impacted the very messages that it mediated, and what sounded religious in the studio did not always sound that way to listeners at home.

In July 1926, the English page of the *Forward* published a cartoon that brought a comic touch to this topic. The cartoon depicted Reb Yankev Leib, an elderly Jew, standing over a radio with the Hebrew words *borei pri hagafen* (the blessing over wine) emerging from the radio's horn. In English, the caption reads, "Reb Yankev Leib is torn between conflicting emotions. Should he say 'amen' or applaud the cantor's fine singing?"[13] Reb Yankev Leib understood the content, but he did not understand the medium. He tuned in to a program that appealed to him as a Jewish listener, but he could not make sense of what he heard. Was it a performance or a ritual? Was this entertainment or worship? Had he been in attendance at the live event, there would have been no question, but as a listener he could not quite make sense of this old ritual in its new context. What is the proper response to a real blessing, spoken as part of a real ritual, heard over the radio by a man accustomed to sacrilizing blessings by responding to them in person?

On one level, the question facing Reb Yankev Lieb was simple: Was this a religious event or a secular one? Fortunately, neither the fictional rabbi nor the cartoonist had to answer the question, but the resonance of the question among the Yiddish-speaking population meant that the impact of radio technology on religious Jewish life was more complicated than either broadcasters or listeners could have imagined. Because radio changed the relationship between performer and audience, it subtly changed the social relationships among Jews with respect to these performances. It was possible and even likely that a performance would *sound* religious but not actually *be* religious.

Zvee Skooler—whose career on Yiddish radio spanned some fifty years from the 1930s to the 1980s—provided one of the most articulate examples of this during his weekly appearance on WEVD's *Forward Hour* in 1937 and 1938. In the fall of 1937, Skooler launched an

---

[13] *Forward,* July 4, 1926.

ambitious year-long run of commentaries on the weekly Torah portion. Broadcast on Sunday mornings, Skooler's 10-minute rhyming monologues offered a new twist on the Jewish textual and intertextual traditions by presenting highly literate and hilarious sermonettes that used American popular culture to explain the weekly Torah portion.

Skooler used terms and institutions more familiar to his audience than those of the Bible's traditional text and turned America into the reference point for Jewish tradition. He described the story of Joseph and his brothers as a Hollywood movie and the instructions regarding the Tabernacle as "interior decorating." He parodied the High Holidays by describing a scenario where the Fuller Brush Man approaches the gates of Heaven, and elsewhere, he explained Israelite governance as

> A government system
> Just like ours here at home.
> With three parts
> Under the name
> The Land of Israel—*Jew S A*.[14]

The ironic twist of his rhyme lay in the phrase, "just like ours here at home," where home is America, not ancient Israel, and where, it seems, Skooler was trying to convince his audience that the Jewish vision of government was no different from the American one. For his audience, America really was home, and in America a weekly sermon on the Torah portion—a fairly traditional Jewish textual genre—could find its best expression through unorthodox comparisons between secular popular culture and sacred text. In fact, Skooler's audience was at least as familiar with the former as the latter, and by putting them in conversation, Skooler used a traditional form to broadcast a worldly explanation of Jewish life in America in which Judaism was not held apart from the colloquial, popular, and familiar aspects of American life.

Playwright Marc Schweid offered a similar take on the relationship between Judaism and American Jewish life by imagining a version

---

[14] *Kibbitzers Incorporated* (radio script), Sunday, September 4, 1938, Box 7, File 75, Zvee Skooler Collection, YIVO Archives, New York.

of Jewish immigration as homecoming, in which religion could make Jews feel more at home in America rather than less so. Schweid, a modestly successful writer for the theater who began writing for radio in 1934, began dramatizing letters from the popular *Forward* feature, *A bintel brief,* for WEVD. In 1936, he launched a weekly series called *yidn in der geshikhte fun amerike* (*Jews in American History*). Beginning with the arrival of the "Jewish Mayflower" in 1654, the program dramatized episodes in American history, highlighting the role of Jews in the growth of New Amsterdam, in the American Revolution, and so on.

In the fourth episode, Schweid broke with his chronology to offer an account of the popular myth that Native Americans are one of the lost tribes of Israel. Schweid opened the episode with a lengthy introduction about the myth and its history before setting the stage in a "little Indian house, a wigwam," where Mingo "the peaceful Indian" and his wife, Puhatami, prepared food for their "Holy Fruit" holiday "that is similar to *sukkot*," the Jewish fall harvest holiday. As Schweid's narration faded, the story opened on Mingo intoning a traditional Indian chant, "Hal-hal-hal, le-le-le, lu-lu-lu, yah-yah-yah." The story followed Aaron Levi, Columbus's Jewish navigator, as he stumbled upon Mingo and Puhatami, only to discover that the Native Americans actually spoke a version of Hebrew, believed in a God called "Yoheyvah," and even shared the collective memory of the Temple in Jerusalem.[15]

By making Native Americans into Jews, Schweid imagined Jewish immigration as a kind of homecoming. Not only were the original Americans actually Jews, but so were the first immigrants. For a new generation of immigrants, this could have sounded tremendously reassuring—that they, too, had come home to America. Despite the obvious differences (Native Americans did not speak Yiddish, did not come from Eastern Europe, pass through Ellis Island or other such portals, or even share the Sephardic Jewishness of Aaron Levi). Religion became the common ground for Levi and Mingo, and, by association, for Schweid's audience. Yet, Schweid's Native Americans did not

---

[15] *Yidn in der geshikhte fun amerike* (radio script), Episode 4, Box 1, Marc Schweid Collection, YIVO Archives.

practice Judaism, and neither did the fictionalized Levi. Instead, Schweid used religion to anchor a kind of ethnic unity between two parties of long-lost Jewish relations. Without the "first fruits holiday" it would have been unlikely that Levi would recognize the Native Americans' "Jewishness," but Levi was not looking for a *minyan*. Schweid used religion, but only to apply it in more worldly terms.

Yiddish radio broadcasters approached holidays the same way, treating both Jewish holidays and American holidays with equal devotion and respect. Particularly for an immigrant population, the adoption of patriotic holidays such as Abraham Lincoln's Birthday, Thanksgiving, and Independence Day took on great significance in their lives. Every year, Yiddish-speaking radio programs devoted themselves to celebrating these moments, often with elaborate performances, orations, and other such tributes. One year, WEVD invited an African-American choir to perform in honor of Lincoln's birthday while Zvee Skooler and Yehuda Bleich contributed annual rhyming tributes to every American holiday from Father's Day to May Day to Graduation Day. Yet, they also made accommodations for Jewish holidays, as when Rokeach moved its high-profile Tuesday night broadcast featuring Molly Picon and Joseph Rumshinsky to Monday because the first night of Passover fell on Tuesday.[16] And the following year, the ownership of radio station WMIL in Long Beach, New York requested special consideration from the Federal Radio Commission to suspend broadcasting on Yom Kippur, out of respect for its audience's religious inclinations. The FRC granted the station's request.

What emerged out of the adoption of American holidays was a particular rhythm to the Yiddish broadcast schedule that placed religious, civic, and social holidays on equal footing. To be sure, only Jewish holidays required canceling or rescheduling a broadcast, but on the radio, a holiday was a holiday no matter where it came from, and every holiday had something to say about contemporary Jewish life. Skooler celebrated Graduation Day in 1936 by reminding his audience to celebrate, despite the fact that the Depression meant no jobs for graduates. Almost a decade later, Molly Picon offered the following

---

[16] *Forward,* March 30, 1931.

interpretation of Purim in a 1944 episode of *Molly Picon's Theater of the Air*. In this episode, Picon played a school teacher:

> Now listen children, Purim is a very important holiday, especially today, because now, just as in days of Haman, there are wicked men who would annihilate our people. Now there is also a Haman who seeks to obliterate us from the earth. But you know that history repeats itself and this new Haman will come to the same end as the old one. . . . Our first enemy's name was Haman, which begins with "H" and then there followed a list of Hangmen whose names all began with the same letter. Himmler, Hess, Hirohito, and Hitler. But they will all finish up as the first Haman did.[17]

Picon and her Yiddish-speaking colleagues rarely missed an opportunity to make holidays speak to contemporary Jewish life. For Picon and other Yiddish-speaking performers, religious holidays became more important because of their connections to the wider world.

Yiddish-speaking radio broadcasters fostered a dynamic relationship between secular and sacred sounds on the radio. For them and their audiences, being Jewish necessarily incorporated the religious tradition, even as it was not restricted to that tradition. While broadcasts of weddings, holiday celebrations, rhyming sermons, and mythic histories all sounded religious on the surface, embedded in those narratives are harmonies and allusions to broader notions of Jewish life in America in which the religious and the secular were not distinct, but dynamically engaged with one another. While some broadcasters intentionally mimicked the styles of English-language radio, others brought Jewish tradition to bear on their presentations and found the radio an ideal venue for blurring the boundaries between performance and religious ritual, between popular culture and religious text, between myth and identity, and between secular and sacred.

THE SOUNDS OF AUTHORITY

Religion became the basis for a broader definition of Jewish identity in America that was not expressly religious, and audiences lived by

---

[17] *Molly Picon's Theater of the Air* (radio script), March 7, 1944, File 901, Molly Picon Collection, American Jewish Historical Society, New York.

these broader definitions. Many Jews lived in dense Jewish neighbor-hoods but did not regularly attend synagogue. Yet, they still enjoyed hearing recordings and broadcasts that sounded traditional and reli-gious. And radio served up programs that sounded religious, in spades—such as broadcasts of cantorial performances—without actu-ally broadcasting many religious programs.

Of all the characters to be heard on the airwaves in Yiddish, per-haps the most adept at this kind of secular ventriloquism was Nukhem Stutchkoff. Stutchkoff was a prolific writer, churning out weekly episodes of original Yiddish drama for nearly thirty years. At the heart of his most successful program, *Bei tate mames tish* ('Round the Family Table), lay the ongoing struggle for immigrants to create Jewish lives for themselves in America. Technically, *Tish* was not a serial. Each episode featured a different storyline, a different cast of characters, and a different account of the struggles of immigrant life. The precise source of these struggles did not matter as much as Stutchkoff's cul-tural logic that always favored Jewish tradition but not necessarily the Jewish religion. Episode after episode featured stories in which Jewish justice adhered to a cultural rather than a strictly religious definition, and where vindication often took the form of a curse, an accusation, or the mutual recognition of guilt. By the end of each episode, dying grandmothers, naive children, old-fashioned grandparents, and aban-doned mothers all got revenge on those who wronged them.[18]

Even when it was meted out mercilessly, Stutchkoff's version of Jew-ish justice was never far from religion, even when the narrative seemed to reject formal religion. In one episode, a Mr. Bernstein, representing "Big Brothers," sought to save a young Jewish hooligan from a life of crime by upbraiding the parents for their old-world child-rearing ways. "Don't teach him to *doven* (pray) unless you want him to be a rabbi!" he warned. Instead, "Make him a *mentsch* (a good human being)."[19] In

---

[18] Sound Portraits' ten-part radio documentary also dedicated one episode to Nukhem Stutchkoff and his achievements. This story and a handful of other recordings from Stutchkoff's programs can be accessed through the Internet at <www.yiddishradioproject.org>. The full collection of available recordings are housed at the New York Public Library for the Performing Arts.
[19] *Bei tate mames tish* (sound recording), Episode 9, New York Public Library for the Performing Arts.

another episode, Zisl, an elderly religious widow who had escaped
from an old-age home after her son tricked her into moving there,
found herself face to face with the son who betrayed her. After his
apologies and her curses, the episode closed with Zisl's guilt-laden
blessing: "May your children be better to you than you were to me."[20]
In Stutchkoff's radio universe, justice always sounded religious, even
though it was rarely delivered in religious terms.

Yet the appeal of religious authority still resonated among listeners, and Rabbi Shmuel Aaron Rubin's radio program, the *American
bord sholom v'tzedek* (American Board of Peace and Justice), provided
one of the most intriguing examples of this. For nearly thirty years, beginning in the late 1930s, Rabbi Rubin invited listeners to present
their small claims and family squabbles on his program to be adjudi-
cated by himself and an ever-changing panel of "esteemed guests." In
fifteen minutes, the complainants settled their differences and Rabbi
Rubin generated enough material to last a lifetime without having to
hire a single writer.[21]

Rabbi Rubin settled every matter that came before him, whether
or not his cases required rabbinic intervention. He heard complaints
from husbands mad at their wives and from wives dissatisfied with their
husbands. He heard from business partners who felt cheated, from
children trying to decide what to do with their elderly parents, and
once from parents upset because their deceased child didn't receive a
burial plot they felt befit his importance. In one episode, he offered
the following advice to a young woman who was financially strapped
but forced to take care of her father: "You can buy a fridge and you can
buy a house, but you can't buy a father."

Rubin's decisions carried little or no legal weight. He certainly
did not posses the civic authority necessary to adjudicate formal dis-
putes, but that mattered little to the people presenting their cases.

---

[20] *Bei tate mames tish* (sound recording), Episode 15, New York Public Library
for the Performing Arts.
[21] *Jewish Board of Peace and Justice,* YIVO Sound Archives. Sound Portraits' ten-
part radio documentary also dedicated one episode to Rabbi Rubin's programs. This story and a handful of other recordings from Rubin's programs
can be accessed through the Internet at <www.yiddishradioproject.org>.

They came to have Rabbi Rubin, with his symbolic authority, weigh in on what is right and, more importantly, *who* is right and *who* is wrong. Rooted in tradition but bearing no power to enforce it, Rubin's rulings, like Stutchkoff's dramas, echoed religious tradition but better served its audience's desire for drama and justice than for anything formally religious.

C. Yisroel Lutsky took this position even further. Dispensing of the religious title *rabbi* for the more enlightened *philosopher,* Lutsky began his radio career during the 1930s and eventually even contributed an advice column to Philadelphia's *idishe velt* (Jewish World) newspaper before launching his own, ultimately unsuccessful, self-titled publication, *The Jewish Philosopher,* which was to be the mouthpiece of a social movement in which he, again, would be the focus. Whereas Rabbi Rubin tried to conduct his court with quiet dignity, Lutsky was all fire and brimstone, layering his advice with snippets of scripture and folk wisdom. But while Rubin's rulings did not carry the weight of civic law, Lutsky's "philosophies" did not even share the aura of religious law, but instead used his position to deliver advice that echoed religion's authoritative voice. He bombastically delivered his responses clad in the fire and brimstone of religion, complete with editorial snorts and ironic laughter. In a particularly graphic example, Lutsky entertained a letter from a woman seeking advice about her wayward son. Lutsky, who read the woman's letter with great pathos, spared none in his reply, concluding that the boy had ruined the lives of at least three women, and there was no telling how many more lives he would ruin. Accusing the mother of debased and misguided "monkey love" for her son, Lutsky warned, "You remind me that among gangsters there are no bad mothers. The fact is, they're one and the same."[22]

Stutchkoff, Rubin, and Lutsky used religion in different ways. Stutchkoff wove a religious sensibility into the fabric of his narratives. Rubin used his religious title to adjudicate matters over which he had no formal authority, and Lutsky used Jewish folk wisdom clad in the fire and brimstone of religion to foist his opinions on his listeners. Each of

---

[22] "Monkey Love," at <http://yiddishradioproject.org/gems/>

the three echoed religion for their audiences, retooled it for their own programs, and softened, updated, or embellished it wherever necessary. These broadcasters alluded to religion, but they were not religious *per se*. By using the sounds of religion, they helped create a worldly Yiddish aural culture that was engaged with but not reliant on Judaism.

SCHEDULING CONFLICTS

Structurally, the relationship between Jewish religion and secular Yiddish culture manifested in the scheduling of Yiddish radio programs. Owing to the close, often intimate relationship between the stations that carried Yiddish programming and the immigrant audiences they served, the Yiddish broadcast week took on a rhythm that echoed the work and leisure habits of their Jewish immigrant audiences. Looking at the development of the Yiddish broadcast week reveals some sensitivity toward Jewish religious life, yet it was a sensitivity that belied a more worldly notion of Jewish life, in which observance of the weekly Sabbath was less a religious affair than a cultural one.

The first battle for Yiddish audiences is a perfect example of this phenomenon. As Yiddish radio programs began appearing with increasing frequency during the first few months of 1926, the newly constructed Libby's Hotel and Baths, located in the heart of the Lower East Side on the corner of Chrystie and Delancy streets, announced its intention to debut its Yiddish radio program over radio station WFBH on Sunday, May 24. Never one to be outdone, the *Jewish Daily Forward* hastily arranged for its first *Forward Radio Concert* to air on WNYC, on the evening of May 22, a Friday night. While the *Libby's Radio Program* thrived and eventually expanded to two shows each week, the *Forward Radio Concert* folded after only a single episode, only to reappear a few months later and disappear again almost as quickly as it came.

It was not for the lack of an audience that the *Forward Radio Concert* series failed, but for a lack of performers. Friday night was the premier night of the week for Yiddish theater performers. Throughout the 1920s and 1930s, local rabbis complained about the number of Jews who attended the theater instead of the synagogue on Friday nights, and the *Forward* believed that it could replicate the success of live theater by offering a concert on radio. However, the newspaper could not successfully book any talent, as they had already made arrangements to perform on stage. Although the *Forward* launched its program on the Sabbath, it was not this that doomed the program, but rather the already widely accepted practice of going out to the theater on Friday night. Friday night was the biggest night for Yiddish theater because many Jews (and their employers) did not work on Saturday, even if they did not follow any of the other laws of Sabbath observance. It was, according to the American workweek, their day off. Thus, Friday night theater attendance had become a kind of "secular ritual" that not even radio could disrupt.

In contrast, when the *Forward* found a home on the radio in 1932, with the launch of the *Forward Hour* on Sunday mornings on New York's WEVD, many of its listeners responded with quasi-religious words of praise for the program. The tenants of 1876 Bay Parkway in Brooklyn reported, "In our forty-five-family apartment house, thirty-eight of the tenants have radios. Sunday, at eleven o'clock, you will not see any tenants on the stoop." One Itche Feigenboym of the Bronx was so moved by the program that he declared that Sunday should become a *yom tov* (holiday).[23]

The *Forward* hoped the airwaves would spread socialism, but its listeners—like Itche Feygenboym—had already written the program into an emergent Jewish sensibility that balanced religious overtones against the framework of the American workweek. If Sunday were to become a Jewish holiday, it would not be a religious one. Instead, it would resemble more closely the civic holidays that Yiddish radio had already begun to commemorate, or else it would follow the secular ritual of Friday night theater. People, such as those who lived at 1876 Bay Parkway, would still congregate, but not in religious congregations. Sunday was already a civic holiday in America, so what better way to celebrate than by gathering with one's Yiddish neighbors, calling it a *yom tov* and tuning in to hear Zvee Skooler and the gang?

Yiddish radio required its own *yom tov*—ironically a transgression of religious law governing other *yom tovim*—because most Yiddish-speaking broadcasters usually took Saturday off. There were always

---

[23] *Forward*, September 22, 1932.

Yiddish programs on Saturday, but the number of offerings was far lighter than on any other day of the week. Thus, while most Yiddish radio broadcasters scheduled their weekly *yom tov* on Saturday, it did not necessarily evidence their observance of religious law. Rather, Yiddish radio's silence *sounded* religious because it coincided with the Sabbath. Meanwhile, the other immigrant communities that shared the airwaves with Yiddish programs wanted *their* Sabbath off, too, leaving the Sunday airwaves wide open for Yiddish-speaking broadcasters to celebrate their *yom tov* on the air. As a result, Sunday became the marquee day for Yiddish radio broadcasters. Practically every major Yiddish program with a big-name sponsor aired on Sunday, such that, during the 1930s and 1940s, audiences in New York City could hear Yiddish programming practically uninterrupted from 9:00 in the morning until 9:00 in the evening. This trend repeated, albeit to a lesser degree, in Yiddish radio's other large markets.

Yiddish radio's Sunday broadcast was particularly enticing for sponsors, because many English-language stations gave Sundays over to shows that illustrated their commitment to the public interest, leaving their usual sponsors in search of a vehicle for their advertising dollars. English-language stations generally used Sundays as the repository for programs that focused on politics, civic issues, and religion, which could not be sponsored, and, ever conscious of their public profile, radio stations did not want to attract the stigma of keeping its audience away from church or of sullying the day with commercials. Both CBS and NBC promoted religious broadcasting according to a policy that would "interpret religion at its highest and best," and CBS explicitly prohibited the sale of time for religious programs.[24] For sponsors and broadcasters, the day became a lost cause, earning it the nickname, "the Sunday ghetto." For Yiddish radio, by contrast, there were no religious concerns inhibiting sponsors from backing the programs, and no church to keep listeners from. On the Yiddish airwaves, Sundays were a great additional day of rest, where restfulness, enter-

---

[24] Spencer Miller, Jr., "Radio and Religion," *Annals of the American Academy of Political and Social Science,* 177 (January 1935), 129–134.

tainment, and commerce went hand in hand. Secular Sundays were a perfect day for the best funded and most ambitious Yiddish programs.

The vibrancy of Sundays was matched only by the density of Fridays, which brimmed with large numbers of programs tuned to accompany the arrival of the Sabbath. On Fridays, programming began as early as 8:00 AM, and ended around—but not always before— sundown. Fridays hummed with programs like *Shabbesdiker melodies* (Melodies in a Sabbath Mood), *Khazen altman's erev shabbes program* (Cantor Altman's Sabbath Eve Program), and sermons from local clergy on the week's Torah portion and other subjects. "Fridays and WEVD somehow belong together," began Ruth Glazer—a self-styled "occasional commentator on Jewish manners, morals, and cooking"— in a 1955 article for *Commentary*.[25] Glazer recounted how WEVD provided the soundtrack to her Fridays as she cleaned the house, polished the candlesticks, and skimmed fat off the chicken soup. For Glazer, Friday and WEVD "belong together" because "when things reach a real crescendo with a real *balebosta* [housewife], we have a correspondingly heightened mood on WEVD." WEVD's Friday lineup was calibrated to the rhythm of the Jewish workweek, when Jewish housewives "of a certain age" found themselves at home, preparing the Sabbath ceremonial dinner while listening to WEVD. Throughout the article, Glazer waxed poetic about her Friday routine and praised the accompaniment of WEVD, but she never mentioned the Sabbath.

Glazer's observations about Fridays on WEVD echoed the cultural but not necessarily the religious significance of Sabbath. So too, on the Yiddish airwaves in general, Fridays gave audiences a chance to hear sacred music and feel the religious overtones of the Sabbath without experiencing the impulse to observe its strictures. Friday recalled the Sabbath without enforcing it, while Sunday provided the parallel pull of a totally secular day of rest. On Yiddish radio, Fridays and Sundays gave the broadcast week a syncopated Jewish rhythm that together emphasized the subtle cultural harmonies of Jewish life in America over its more easily audible religious overtones.

---

[25] Ruth Glazer, "The World of Station WEVD," *Commentary*, February, 1955.

MAKING THE SACRED SECULAR THROUGH ADVERTISING

With Fridays and Sundays punctuating the rhythm of the Yiddish broadcast week, sponsors filled those days with appeals for every product under the sun. As almost any advertiser knows, quality is not enough to move a product. Advertisers have to be prepared to explain why and how their product best suits the lifestyles of their intended customers. Advertisers on Yiddish radio were no different, and their tactics were not terribly sophisticated. Around the turn of the twentieth century, their predecessors in the Yiddish press found success in a strategy that connected products to particular Jewish events. Mass-produced greeting cards for Rosh Hashanah, matzo for Passover, and candles for the Sabbath or Hanukkah were just the beginning.[26] Creative advertisers found countless ways to graft American consumption patterns onto traditional Jewish life and to convince Jews that buying things was appropriate to their religious celebrations. Crisco, Borden's Condensed Milk, Gold Medal Flour, and Uneeda Biscuits were only a few of the advertisers who used religious iconography to peddle their products to Jewish consumers. Yet, as historian Hasia Diner observed, "America's food, like its culture as a whole, represented something [Jewish immigrants] wanted to embrace. But in doing so, they upset the boundaries between the sacred and the ordinary, Jewish and non-Jewish."[27] Struggles between the religious and the secular were already underway on the palates and plates of Jewish immigrants, so that by the late 1920s, when advertisers found an outlet on the Yiddish airwaves, producers of Jewish food products set about satisfying their audience's emerging secular American tastes.

Even Manischewitz, one of the most prominent manufacturers of Jewish food products and one of the biggest supporters of Yiddish

---

[26] Andrew Heinze, *Adapting to Abundance: Jewish Immigrants, Mass Consumption, and the Search for American Identity*, (New York: Columbia University Press, 1991); Jenna Weissman Joselit, *The Wonders of America: Reinventing Jewish Culture, 1880–1950* (New York: Hill and Wang, 1994).

[27] Hasia Diner, *Hungering for America: Italian, Irish, and Jewish Foodways in the Age of Migration* (Cambridge, MA: Harvard University Press, 2001), 219.

radio in America, tried turning the "bread of affliction" into a perfect American snack. In an advertisement for Manischewitz, broadcast in support of *Bei tate mames tish,* Nukhem Stutchkoff explained the beauty of Manischewitz matzo products.

> Who can we credit for making our matzo, originally a Passover food, into a food that so many Jewish homes can enjoy every day of the year? For this there is only one answer: The B. Manischewitz Matzo Company. B. Manischewitz has brought nearly perfect matzo products to Jews. Jews have seen little as uncommon. It brings a spark to the week of Passover, and a great taste to the rest of the year. A little white piece of Manischewitz Matzo is a reliable resident of every Jewish pantry. [They have] the finest, delightful taste. Their bakedness, their freshness and lightness make them an ideal Jewish food any day of the year, or any time of day, for your own family or even in honor of guests.[28]

The crux of this advertising campaign was its ability to frame matzo within the emergent eating habits of American Jews. Another set of radio advertisements made this even more audible. Noting the absence of Jewish snack foods, Manischewitz introduced the Tam Tam, a six-sided cracker made essentially from matzo. To sell the crackers, Manischewitz hired Nukhem Stutchkoff to write and recite Yiddish advertisements that were recorded and distributed nationally. One such advertisement explains, "America is a land of crackers, so it needs a Jewish cracker with Jewish taste." Now, thanks to Manischewitz, within the "land of crackers . . . American Jews have their own cracker. Tam Tam is its name."[29]

Convincing listeners that they could turn the "bread of affliction" into the perfect vehicle for hors d'oeuvres and light sandwiches was difficult, even in America. But the power of suggestion—that even matzo could fit American patterns of eating and entertaining—resonated

---

[28] *Bei tate mames tish* (sound recording), Episode 12, New York Public Library for the Performing Arts.
[29] "Tam Tam Commercials" (sound recording), no date, Catalog number 22.01A, YIVO Sound Archives.

with an audience seeking Jewish flavor but not Jewish law. By turning Passover's central ritual food into an everyday edible, Manischewitz hoped to take matzo out of its religious context and insert it into the "everyday workweek," where anything more than a spark of Passover would have been too much. On the radio, the tension between the religious and the cultural sounded more prominent because of the proximity of English-language broadcasting, which was never more than a turn-of-the-dial away.

Just as Yiddish-speaking radio performers were keenly aware of the inspiration provided by their English-speaking counterparts, sponsors of Yiddish programs tuned their pitches toward the mainstream as well, treating the Jewishness of their products with a light touch, and opting for a cultural appeal instead. Stuhmer's Bread boasted, asking, "How long, I'm asking you to really remember, how long has Stuhmer's Bread been a welcome member of the Jewish home?" Another reinforced its versatility: "Stuhmer's rye bread is made for the Jewish table. . . . Because it's full of Jewish taste . . . because it's kosher and parve, you can eat it with milk and meat."[30] Sterling Salt emphasized its utility in the Jewish kitchen for both cooking and koshering, while Gulden's promised "a mustard that has brought the maximum taste and flavor to food for the last seventy-seven years," and flaunted its East-Side heritage to its Jewish consumers.[31] Breakstone's sour cream recalled life "in the old country [where] it was known as *smeteneh*. Here we call it sour cream. There, we used to like it on a fresh potato. My own potato dunked in sour cream . . . is there any other food?"[32] Heritage and versatility promised to sell more products to more consumers than *kashruth* alone could. By expanding the appeal of their products beyond just their religious aspects, advertisers helped cultivate a broader sense of what Jewish food sounded like, and fed their

[30] "Stuhmer's Bread Commercial" (radio script), no date, File 245, Zvee Skooler Collection, YIVO Archives. Ellipses in original.

[31] "Gulden's Mustard Commercial 4" (sound recording), no date, YIVO Sound Archives.

[32] "Breakstone Commercial" (radio script), no date, File 245, Zvee Skooler Collection, YIVO Archives.

customers' desires to retain Jewish customs that resonated with religion but were not restricted to it.

CONCLUSION

From advice to advertisements, Yiddish radio programs provided an audible Jewishness that harmonized familiar religious elements with more worldly contemporary sensibilities. Radio broadcast the sounds of Jewish life so that programs with religious content sounded secular and programs with secular content sounded religious. Was a Wednesday night cantorial concert considered a religious event? What about a drama that relied on religious themes as plot devices, but did not otherwise advocate for anything explicitly religious?

Because of its character as a mass medium, Yiddish radio had a larger audience than Yiddish theater, and because American radio was dominated by English-language programming, Yiddish radio had an intimate relationship with mainstream American popular culture. If broadcasting was to help Yiddish culture thrive, it had to echo the worldly environs of its audience and foster an aural culture that drew on both Jewish religious traditions and the more worldly tastes of its audience.

During the formative period of Yiddish radio, which lasted from 1926 until the late 1940s, radio performed the religious and the secular in the same key. The airwaves allowed for little distinction between religious and secular programming, as audiences responded to both religious traditions and secular trends. Yiddish-speaking radio performers and sponsors did not try to extricate one from the other, but rather found complex harmonies, counterpoint, and deep wells of resources and opportunities that amplified their voices on the air and animated their performances. On a structural level, too, this relationship could be heard in the pacing of the Yiddish broadcast week, as few Yiddish-speaking broadcasters worked on Saturday, yet took advantage of Sundays and Fridays to highlight their programs.

Yet, these arrangements did not always conceal or mitigate tensions between religious and secular Jewish life in America. Occasionally, Yiddish programs and schedules exacerbated them, echoing to audiences questions about the complex impact of mass media on Jewish religious life. And, as our world is enriched by the exponential expansion and speed of media, those same questions remain unanswered. The Yiddish airwaves during the second quarter of the twentieth century provided a unique laboratory of communication in which Jewish immigrants articulated and experimented with sounds that suited their worldly lives as Jews in America.

THIS IS NOT EUROPE, YOU KNOW: THE COUNTER-MASKILIC IMPULSE OF AMERICAN YIDDISH DRAMA

Joel Berkowitz

From the moment it entered the modern era, Yiddish drama began commenting on the delicate balance between religion and secularization. Modern Yiddish drama was a direct outgrowth of the *Haskalah,* or Jewish Enlightenment, whose adherents (*maskilim*) called upon Jews to modify traditional practices that set Jews apart and impeded full participation in secular society. The first modern Yiddish dramatists, beginning in the late eighteenth century, consciously turned to drama, among other genres, as a vehicle for expressing their reformist agenda. Dramas written by the maskilim frequently attempted to illustrate the necessity of embracing modernity, and the grave dangers of clinging to traditional ways and beliefs that ran counter to social progress.

Yet a funny thing happened to Yiddish drama on the way to America. Students of American Jewish history and culture are familiar with the assault on tradition that immigration to America often represented.[1] Countless memoirs, novels, plays, films, poems, and songs tell the story of the once-devout Jewish immigrant who fails to remain

---

[1] For just a few examples of the extensive historical literature on this subject, see Hasia R. Diner, *The Jews of the United States, 1654 to 2000* (Berkeley: University of California Press, 2004), 71–202; Henry Feingold, *A Time for Searching: Entering the Mainstream, 1920–1945* (Baltimore: Johns Hopkins University Press, 1992); Irving Howe, *World of Our Fathers* (New York: Harcourt Brace Jovanovich, 1976); Moses Rischin, *The Promised City: New York's Jews, 1870–1914* (New York: Harper Torchbooks, 1970); and Gerald Sorin, *A Time for Building: The Third Migration, 1880–1920* (Baltimore: Johns Hopkins University Press, 1992).

pious—no matter how earnestly he or she resolves to do so—in the face of a barrage of economic and social pressures to look, sound, and act like native-born Americans. This phenomenon might seem like a maskil's dream. Where else could Jews adjust their level of religious observance to their environment more freely than in America? If Yiddish drama had carried on in the maskilic mode, it would have become a cheerleader in the Americanization process. As it happened, however, Yiddish drama often tended to take precisely the opposite stance. In the country where modernization was making far greater inroads in the Jewish community than it ever did in Eastern Europe, Yiddish playwrights repeatedly warned their audiences that the United States was at least as likely to be *amerike ganef* (America, the thief) as *di goldene medine* (the Golden Land). This essay will explore pivotal examples of this counter-maskilic perspective in Yiddish dramas that comment, directly or indirectly, on the American Jewish immigrant experience.

MODERN YIDDISH DRAMA'S ENLIGHTENMENT ROOTS

The story of American drama, like the story of its creators and consumers, begins in Europe. In the late eighteenth century, as the Haskalah began, the maskilim wrote in a variety of literary genres in order to advance their cause. The 1790s saw the publication of two comedies by noted maskilim that laid the foundation for modern Yiddish drama: Isaac Euchel's *Reb Henokh, oder, vos tut men damit?* (*Reb Henoch,* or *What's To Be Done With It?,* ca. 1792) and Aaron Halle Wolfssohn's *Laykhtzin und fremelay* (*Silliness and Sanctimony,* ca. 1796).[2] Wolfssohn's play in particular charted a course through the modern Jewish

---

[2] For discussions of dramas written by the maskilim, see *inter alia* Jeremy Dauber, *Antonio's Devils: Writers of the Jewish Enlightenment and the Birth of Modern Hebrew and Yiddish Literature* (Stanford, CA: Stanford University Press, 2004); Max Erik, *Di komedyes fun der berliner oyfklerung* (Kiev: Melukhe-Farlag, 1933); Alyssa Quint, "The Botched Kiss: Abraham Goldfaden and the Literary Origins of the Yiddish Theatre" (Ph.D. Diss., Harvard University, 2003), 155–197; and Meir Viner, *Tsu der geshikhte fun der yidisher literatur in 19tn yorhundert,* 2 vols. (Moscow: 1939; rpt. New York: YKUF Farlag, 1945).

culture wars that many subsequent playwrights took. *Silliness and Sanctimony* is on one level a Jewish *Tartuffe:* a sharp critique of religious hypocrisy embodied in the character of Reb Yoysefkhe, a Polish Jew who comes to Germany to tutor the teenage son of a prosperous family. The tutor puts on a great show of piety for his employer, who is so taken by Reb Yoysefkhe's learning and devotion that he orders his daughter—who has embraced German culture and rejected everything Jewish—to marry Reb Yoysefkhe. She rebels and runs away, but is tricked by a Gentile suitor and sold off to a brothel. At the eleventh hour, she is rescued by her enlightened uncle, who also discovers that Reb Yoysefkhe had not only been a regular customer of the brothel, but had used its services on credit (pawning sacred ritual objects as collateral), and promised the madam that he would soon marry into a wealthy family and easily manage to pay off a month's worth of visits.

Using vivid symbolism, Wolfssohn dramatizes the danger posed by religious hypocrisy, represented by a lustful, greedy schemer who is learned enough to take advantage of a well-off but Jewishly ignorant man like his employer, by dazzling him with a barrage of Talmudic quotations torn out of context. At the same time, however, Wolfssohn—personally invested as he was in the Haskalah—managed to voice the potential pitfalls of that enterprise. His play presents silliness (*laykhtzin*) as being just as great a threat as sanctimony (*fremelay*); the daughter would not have been vulnerable to an untrustworthy suitor had she not become so jaded by a life filled with empty activities.

In subsequent generations, Yiddish playwrights would repeatedly create analogous conflicts between deeply (even fanatically) religious characters and more worldly ones, each seeing the other's outlook as inimical to the Jewish people as a whole. And like Wolfssohn, playwrights would not always take the seemingly obvious side of the secularized characters at the expense of the traditional ones. In Israel Aksenfeld's *Der ershter yidisher rekrut in rusland* (*The First Jewish Recruit in Russia,* ca. 1840), for example—a play still firmly in the pre-professional, Jewish Enlightenment phase of Yiddish drama—the playwright champions greater Jewish participation in institutions like the military, but acknowledges that such participation can have tragic implications. A lighter, more optimistic chord is sounded in the early plays of Avrom Goldfaden, the visionary who launched the modern Yiddish theatre in the 1870s, both by establishing a company and by writing its plays and music. Among his early masterpieces are musical comedies such as *Di bobe mitn eynikl* (*The Grandmother and Her Granddaughter,* 1877), *Shmendrik* (1877), and *Di tsvey Kuni-Leml* (*The Two Kuni-Lemls,* 1880), all of which show enlightened young lovers triumphing over outlandishly backwards characters standing in the way of their happiness.[3]

These early works suggest a couple of different routes a playwright might take through the secular/religious divide: the sort of ambivalence Aksenfeld expresses about the social cost of modernization versus Goldfaden's optimism that nothing but good could come of rational behavior. When the central enlightened character in Aksenfeld's play faces the fact that his advocacy of a government conscription program has led to the lengthy army service of one character, the death of his own daughter, and his wife's descent into madness, he sighs, "I acted only with reason, and forgot that in affairs of the heart, reason fails."[4] By contrast, when the previously fanatical Hasidic father of Goldfaden's *The Two Kuni-Lemls* realizes that he has been outwitted by his enlightened daughter and her university-educated lover, he readily admits the error of his ways, as he explains to his

---

[3] For biographical and critical studies of Goldfaden, see *inter alia,* Zalmen Zylbercweig, ed., *Leksikon fun der nayer yidisher literatur,* 2:77–87; Nachman Mayzel, *Avrom Goldfaden: der foter fun yidishn teater* (Warsaw: Farlag Groshn-bibliotek, 1935); Nokhem Oyslender and Uri Finkel, *A. Goldfadn: materyaln far a biografye* (Minsk: Institut far Vaysruslendisher Kultur, 1926); Quint, "The Botched Kiss"; Nahma Sandrow, *Vagabond Stars: A World History of Yiddish Theater* (New York: Harper & Row, 1977; rpt. 1986 and 1999), 40–69; Jacob Shatzky, ed., *Goldfaden-bukh* (New York: Idisher Teater-Muzey, 1926) and *Hundert yor Goldfadn* (New York: YIVO, 1940); Yitskhok Turkov-Grudberg, *Goldfaden un Gordin* (Tel Aviv: S. Grinhoyz, 1969); Zalmen Zylbercweig, *Leksikon fun yidishn teater* (New York: Farlag Elisheva, 1931), 1:275–367; and Zylbercweig, *Avrom Goldfaden un Zigmunt Mogulesco* (Buenos Aires: Farlag Elisheva, 1936).

[4] Yisroel Aksenfeld, *Der ershter yidisher rekrut in rusland,* in *Y. Aksenfelds verk,* ed. M. Viner (Kharkov: Melukhe-farlag "Literatur un kunst," 1931), 194. All translations from the plays discussed here are my own unless otherwise indicated.

fellow Hasidim: "As long as I thought highly of you, you were honored guests of mine, but now you can take my new son-in-law who I've taken into my home as proof that I've split with you for good. Now I see clearly that they are the wise ones and that the only thing that you know is how to drink brandy. Go in good health!"[5]

The maskilic playwrights were, by definition, critical of certain aspects of traditional Jewish practice. They frequently depicted Hasidic rebbes as inbred, corrupt, and incompetent, and their followers as naive at best, downright idiotic (even monstrously so, in plays by Goldfaden and his teacher, Avrom Ber Gottlober) at worst. They mocked the practice of arranged marriages, with its commodification of family status, which could be traded in for the cash of lower-born but wealthy parents. None of the maskilic plays, however, advocates the wholesale abandonment of tradition. Indeed, those who completely turn their backs on Jewish tradition present targets for satire at least as substantial as those who interpret Jewish law too narrowly or rigidly. The figure of the self-hating Jew thus makes frequent appearances, from Euchel's *Reb Henokh* to Shloyme Ettinger's *Serkele* to Goldfaden's *Kabtznson et Hungerman* (*Pauperson and Hungerman*).

Meanwhile, the changing circumstances of world Jewry began to markedly alter both the style and substance of Jewish literature and drama. The Haskalah was predicated on a central prediction about Jewish-Gentile relations: if the Jews made certain changes in their behavior to make themselves less alien to their Gentile neighbors, then the liberal impulse that was gradually making its way across Europe, leading to the emancipation of the Jews in one country after another, would continue to grow until all Jews willing to enter into this bargain would benefit from it. The pogroms that erupted in southern Russia in the early 1880s, however, made many maskilim reassess this thinking. At this point, after a century of progress in the civil rights of European Jewry, Russian Jews were once again becoming the scapegoat of

---

[5] Avrom Goldfaden, *The Two Kuni-Lemls*, in Joel Berkowitz and Jeremy Dauber, ed. and trans., *Landmark Yiddish Plays: A Critical Anthology* (Albany, NY: State University of New York Press, 2006), 245.

a benighted citizenry. Perhaps, thought many, the maskilim had been deluding themselves about the extent of good will among their Gentile neighbors. Perhaps, the thinking continued, something radically different had to be done to improve the outlook for Eastern-European Jewry. If acculturation was not the answer, three broad avenues of response remained: stay put and make the best of it (with some accepting the status quo, and others challenging it with more radical political responses); establish a Jewish homeland so that Jews would become autonomous economically, politically, and physically; or seek greener pastures elsewhere—in Western Europe or the Americas, for example.

The year 1881, which saw so many other changes in the lives of Eastern-European Jews, also marked changes in the drama they produced and consumed. Playwrights like Goldfaden, who had by this point written several satires aimed at critiquing Jewish fanaticism, now stopped fighting that battle and became more nationalistic. And many of those playwrights, like their audiences, would soon leave Eastern Europe, and before long would be addressing, both obliquely and explicitly, very different conditions. When we join those playwrights who made their way to America, we find them initially exploring American Jewish life through plays set in Europe, and later creating an idiom for examining life in America more directly.

JACOB GORDIN: BRIDGING HASKALAH AND TRADITION

Haskalah drama, which had essentially disappeared in the early 1880s in the wake of the pogroms, made a comeback of sorts a decade later in the work of Jacob Gordin, who found a way to take Yiddish drama in a new direction by wedding classic Western drama with Jewish concerns.[6] Until the early 1890s (when Gordin was already a middle-aged

---

[6] For studies of Gordin's dramaturgy and its reception, see *inter alia* Joel Berkowitz, *Shakespeare on the American Yiddish Stage* (Iowa City: University of Iowa Press, 2002), 31–72; *Leksikon fun der nayer yidisher literatur* (New York: CYCO, 1958), 2:142–153; Kalmen Marmor, *Yankev Gordin* (New York: YKUF, 1953); Shmuel Niger, *Dertseylers un romanistn* (1946), 193–203; Nina Warnke, "Reforming the New York Yiddish Theater: The Cultural Politics of Immi-

man) he had never written for the stage, and had apparently never written in Yiddish. In remarkably short order, Gordin emerged as the most important American Yiddish playwright. By the end of his career, he had written some eighty plays, with at least two dozen of them enjoying substantial critical and commercial success. Gordin had a gift for writing both grand speeches and snappy one-liners, creating characters that the finest actors of his day could flesh out in unforgettable performances, and addressing the most pressing topics of the day in dramatic form that provoked audiences while entertaining them. His willingness to tackle taboo issues often made him simultaneously the darling of the left-leaning critics and the whipping-boy of the Orthodox establishment. But what observers across the political spectrum did not always appreciate was just how conservative, in the aggregate, Gordin's view of Jewish tradition turned out to be.

One way to track changes in Gordin's approach to secular versus religious matters is through two plays that were companion pieces of a sort: his two adaptations of *King Lear*—*Der yidisher kenig Lir* (*The Jewish King Lear,* 1892) and *Mirele Efros* (*Mirele Efros,* 1898, originally billed as *The Jewish Queen Lear*). Nowhere did Gordin stake out his pro-maskilic position more forcefully than in his fifth play, *The Jewish King Lear,* which explicitly pitted maskilim against Hasidim and *misnagdim* (non-Hasidic Orthodox Jews). Gordin's version of Lear is Dovid Moysheles, a successful Vilna businessman who announces in the first scene his decision to divide up his estate among his three daughters and resettle with his wife in the Land of Israel. As in Shakespeare's *Lear,* the eldest daughters flatter their father, while the youngest draws his wrath by refusing to spout such platitudes. Ultimately, Taybele (Yiddish for "little dove") is, in effect, banished from Dovid's kingdom, much to the chagrin of Taybele's teacher and future husband, Yaffe (whose name derives from the Hebrew for "beautiful"):

---

grant Intellectuals and the Yiddish Press, 1887–1910" (Ph.D. thesis, Columbia University, 2001); Zalmen Zylbercweig, ed., *Leksikon fun yidishn teater* (New York: Farlag Elisheva, 1931), 1:391–461; and Zylbercweig, *Di velt fun Yankev Gordin* (Tel Aviv: Farlag Elisheva, 1964). On *The Jewish King Lear* specifically, see also Leonard Prager, "Of Parents and Children: Jacob Gordin's *The Jewish King Lear.*" *American Quarterly* 18 (1966), 506–516.

> Reb Dovidl, please excuse me, but I do not know whether you have heard of the world-famous writer Shakespeare. I know a drama of his entitled *King Lear*. This king, at the same point in his life as you, divided his kingdom. Just as you have expelled your beloved daughter Taybele, so he expelled his beloved daughter Cordelia, who told him the truth. Ach, how dearly that old man paid for what he did. And you are the Jewish King Lear. May God protect you from the fate that befell King Lear.[7]

Yaffe's speech is a quintessentially maskilic one, teaching both the addressee and the audience simultaneously, and using a landmark text from outside the Jewish tradition to do so. Yaffe uses Shakespeare's *Lear* as a parable, much in the way that a rabbi might use a story from the Bible or the Talmud, to warn Dovid Moysheles about the potential dangers of his actions.

It should come as little surprise that Yaffe's warning turns out to be entirely justified; the fact that Dovid misjudged all three of his children scores another point for the Haskalah. Gordin was by no means the first playwright to adapt a drama from another language for Yiddish audiences, but he did figure out a way to make the most of such adaptations, by finding meaningful parallels in the contemporary Jewish world to characters and events in his source material. In this case, one of Gordin's master strokes is the recasting of the conflict among the daughters from *King Lear* in terms of nineteenth-century Jewish communal politics. The eldest daughter, Etele, is married to a *misnagid,* Avrom Kharif (Hebrew for "sharp"). In spite of their self-proclaimed piety, it is their stinginess that forces Dovid to abandon his attempt to settle in Palestine, and later drives him out of their home to wander as a beggar. The middle daughter, Gitele, marries a Hasid who, in stereotypical fashion, finds any excuse he can to drink another shot of whiskey. And lest Gordin's sympathies are not sufficiently clear by this point, the youngest maskilic couple are paragons of virtue. The play makes it clear that piety does not equate with decency.

---

[7] Jacob Gordin, *Der yidisher kenig Lir.* Unpaginated manuscript of 1894 in Jacob Gordin Papers, YIVO Archives.

Gordin also adopts Shakespeare's theme of vision versus blindness, in both the literal and the figurative sense. By the second act, we learn that Dovid "cannot see any more. A curtain has been drawn over his eyes as over the Holy Ark." Where Shakespeare has Gloucester lose his vision in an act of violence, and Lear lose and then regain his moral vision, Gordin combines the physical and figurative components of seeing into one character. Gordin, however, allows his central character to recover both facets of his vision—without suffering the loss of his youngest daughter. During Dovid's wanderings, Taybele and Yaffe have gone off to St. Petersburg (a destination outside the Pale of Settlement, and therefore traditionally off limits to most Jews) to study medicine. When they return to Vilna near the end of the play, they are reunited and reconciled with Dovid, who wanders in from a storm. Just as conveniently, when the young doctors examine the blind old man, they ascertain that his condition can be cured with a simple operation. The Haskalah, in other words, is capable of bringing light into the darkness in more ways than one.

This is an earnest way of conveying a message that Goldfaden and other maskilim did lightheartedly in earlier decades. In maskilic farces like *Shmendrik* and *The Two Kuni-Lemls,* Goldfaden had university-educated youngsters dupe their elders in order to be able to choose their own mates rather than be forced into disastrous marriages, and as in countless comedies in this vein from Plautus to the present, the young lovers prove to be right and their elders misguided. Gordin does not concern himself with arranged marriages here—though he would elsewhere, most notably (and darkly) in *Di shkhite* (*The Slaughter,* 1899). But that aside, his ending turns out to have the feel of a maskilic musical comedy, minus the singing and dancing.

Though Gordin set out to reform the Yiddish stage when he began writing plays, the dénouement of *The Jewish King Lear* is no less obvious than that of the aforementioned Goldfaden farces, and because the latter are leavened with brilliant comic touches, they transcend the specific social points they make, whereas Gordin's play feels far more dated. The comparison is not entirely fair to Gordin, however, who in 1892 was still a novice—a novice who often challenged the expectations of his actors and audiences. As his career developed, he learned valuable lessons about how to balance those expectations with his artistic and social vision—a process that would last nearly two decades, until his death in 1909. One barometer of how his craftsmanship matured is to compare *The Jewish King Lear* to *Mirele Efros* (1898), also based in part on the *Lear* story, but much more loosely so.

The characters' actions in *Mirele Efros* are far more clearly motivated than in *The Jewish King Lear,* where we can usually feel the playwright's heavy hand moving the plot along to suit his purposes. Though *Mirele Efros* also revolves around a conflict between parent and children, none of the figures in the later play is used to represent a particular ideology. Jewish rituals have an important role in the play; preparations for the wedding of Mirele's older son dominate Act I, for example, and the question of whether Mirele will attend her grandson's bar mitzvah after being estranged from his parents for ten years looms heavily over Act IV. Here, however, Gordin keeps the conflict entirely within the family, making no suggestions—certainly not any explicit ones—that any of these characters are meant to represent specific segments of the wider Jewish community.

One can argue that one of the central messages of *Mirele Efros* cuts against the conclusion of *The Jewish King Lear*—that is, against the classic maskilic message of the enlightened children teaching the benighted parents how to behave. In *Mirele Efros,* it is the grasping daughter-in-law, Sheyndele, whose greed disturbs the family harmony—though Mirele's stubbornness and her sons' weakness play no small part in driving a wedge between the generations. The younger generation goes astray here by losing sight of values on which the house of Efros was built: ethical business dealings, giving back a portion of one's riches to the community, putting the greater good before one's personal comfort. It is a message Gordin would return to a couple of years later in another of his best dramas, *God, Man, and Devil,* a Faustian tale depicting the decline of a God-fearing family when Satan brings to life the dormant greed of a pious man, and uses it as the key to open doors to numerous other base desires and indecent acts.

Like his contemporary Henrik Ibsen, whose work he so greatly admired, Gordin was both praised and vilified for the ways in which his plays addressed problematic social issues. His characters cheat on their spouses (*Kreutzer Sonata, The Oath*), beat their wives (*The Slaugh-*

ter), have children out of wedlock (*Sappho*), go mad (*The Slaughter, Homeless*), commit suicide (*Khasye the Orphan*) and murder (*The Slaughter, Kreutzer Sonata*), and reject Jewish teachings in other ways (*Elisha ben Abuye*). Yet in spite of his background as a religious and political reformer, and two decades of provoking traditionalists with his playwriting, Gordin's dramas sided with tradition at least as much as they challenged it. As one historian asks,

> Would Gordin's most loyal *patriótn* [fans] have predicted that
> the Gordin plays that remain most popular are *God, Man, and Devil*
> and *Mirele Efros?* These two plays reinforce, most broadly and simply,
> Jewish values. . . . Gordin wrote good plays. . . . But in retrospect it
> seems that his greatest contribution was precisely that he broadened
> the definition of Jewishness, making it possible for a wider range of
> people, and especially the Russian-Jewish intellectuals, to include
> themselves fruitfully in the definition.[8]

In a way, this was a twofold contribution on Gordin's part, for so much did he influence Yiddish playwriting that we constantly see his innovations in the writings of his peers and successors.

THE VIEW FROM THE LOW ROAD: POPULAR YIDDISH THEATRE AND JEWISH COMMUNAL POLITICS

Gordin wrote squarely in the tradition of those who see art as a tool for improving the world—the Ibsenesque or Shavian approach as opposed to Oscar Wilde's assertion that "the only beautiful things . . . are the things that do not concern us." As such, Gordin's desire to improve the aesthetics of Yiddish drama necessarily meant improving the social content of Yiddish drama, which in his case meant injecting social issues into a drama that he felt had been devoid of such matters before. Gordin was only partly successful in his campaign for reform. He did introduce a new approach to dramaturgy for the Yiddish stage, one that was more cohesive, more socially engaged, and more realistic than

---

[8] Sandrow, *Vagabond Stars,* 162.

most earlier Yiddish drama had been. But he did not "clean the mud off the Yiddish stage," one of the goals he stated in an early essay.[9] The broad comedies, spectacular musicals, and sentimental melodramas that had been popular before Gordin started writing—and which he professed to loathe—continued to be popular among Yiddish audiences. Gordin, in other words, blazed an alternative trail in Yiddish drama rather than paving a road over the pre-existing one.[10]

Popular Yiddish theatre, however, had never been as devoid of social content as Gordin and other intellectual critics suggested; it just addressed social issues in a less self-conscious way, and as popular culture generally does, it tended to reinforce rather than challenge the status quo. The most memorable social commentary being made in drama at the turn of the twentieth century—Ibsen's Nora slamming the door on her domestic life, Shaw's Mrs. Warren describing marriage as a form of prostitution, Chekhov's broken string signaling the end of an era—were made on independent stages, not in the grand popular theatres of the West End, the Champs Elysées, or Broadway. Similarly, when we want to see how Yiddish playwrights were tackling the great social questions of their day, we tend to turn to playwrights with a reputation (if not always justified) for putting aesthetics and contents before commercial considerations.

Yet if we disregard the popular theatre, we miss much of what Yiddish audiences were seeing and hearing about such matters. A full-length study of Yiddish popular theatre needs to be undertaken, but in the meantime, let us take a snapshot of a particular historical mo-

---

[9] "Der suzhet fun mayn tsukunftige [sic] drame," *Arbeter tsaytung,* May 20, 1892.

[10] Gordin, in fact, was not the purist in this regard that his criticism made him out to be. However idealistic and talented he was, Gordin was a practical man of the theatre with a very large family to support, and he knew where his bread was buttered. This meant both writing plays in a way that would not completely alienate actors and audiences with cherished expectations about what they wanted from the theatre, even in his most ambitious plays. It also meant doing as the Romans did, that is, by writing plays—under cover of the pseudonym "Dr. Jacobi from London"—exactly like the ones he claimed to detest. "Dr. Jacobi's" plays constitute a body of popular drama that deserves greater attention in its own right.

ment when American Yiddish musicals were particularly successful at capitalizing on questions of Jewish identity. I have in mind the 1908–09 and 1909–10 seasons, which live in the annals of Yiddish theatre history as a time when a certain type of musical reigned at the box office, much to the dismay of the critics. These were the years of the "yid" play—works with nationalistic titles like Joseph Lateiner's melodrama *Dos yidishe harts* (*The Jewish Heart*), Boris Thomashefsky's and Jacob Ter's musical *Di yidishe neshome* (*The Jewish Soul*), and Thomashefsky's musical *Dos pintele yid* (*The Essential Spark of Jewishness*). The tremendous commercial success of these plays led critics to worry that popular theatre was more likely than ever to eclipse serious drama. As playwright and critic B. Gorin put it, the mass appeal of these plays meant the "rabbi's kaddish for the better drama."[11]

As we shall see, the critics were not entirely correct, and in any case the main threat to serious Yiddish drama was not necessarily *non-*serious Yiddish drama—other factors like the immigration restrictions of the 1920s and the rise of nickelodeons and film would prove far more lethal. In the meantime, though, popular theatre was every bit as popular at the end of the so-called Gordin Era as it had ever been; Gorin claims that *Dos pintele yid,* which ran for half of the 1909–10 season, enjoyed the greatest box-office success of any Yiddish play produced up to that point.[12] Because *Dos pintele yid* effectively recycles many plot twists, song types, and other material from previous Yiddish plays—both from the 1908–09 season and from earlier spectacles by Goldfaden, Joseph Lateiner, and their competitors—and because that play's overwhelming success spawned many imitations, it is as useful a work as any to illustrate how many American Yiddish musicals weighed in on the place of the Jew in the modern world.

Dos pintele yid opens on a momentous occasion: the bar mitzvah of a thirteen-year-old orphan who survived a pogrom in which he lost the rest of his family. After the guests sing a fairly standard song of praise to God, "*Toyre iz di beste skhoyre*" ("Torah is the Best Merchandise"—a familiar Yiddish saying), the orphan describes in detail the horrors

---

[11] B. Gorin, *Di geshikhte fun idishen teater* (New York: Forverts, 1929), 203.
[12] Gorin, 204.

he witnessed during the pogrom. He then leads the singing of the title song, which begins with the notion of universal persecution of the Jews:

In yedn land, in yedn ort	In every land, in every place,
Hert dos yidl nor eyn vort:	The little Jew hears just one word:
A yid bistu, gey dir.	You are a Jew, now go.[13]

The first lines of the song are filled with words of exile and estrangement: *fremder* and *ger* (both words for "stranger"), *vandert* (wanders), until the Jew's ability to endure comes to the fore. He "doesn't grow tired" and "laughs at his enemies when God is with him." This essence of Jewishness is his *pintele yid*—his Jewish core, one might say. The song exhorts Jews to cherish "the essence of Jewishness," and drives the message home with a trio of monosyllabic commands:

Dos pintele yid iz zeyer git,	The essence of Jewishness is very good,
Koved un shtolts makht es dir,	It brings you honor and pride,
yid—	Jew—
Akht es un shets es un hit.	Revere, respect, and guard it.[14]

The chorus of the song similarly moves from suffering to endurance. First come words like *gelitn, gematert, gepaynikt*—all verbs denoting suffering and persecution, culminating in the gruesome image of all the enemies of the Jew having "bathed in his blood." The Jew, however, remains courageous in the face of all this suffering. The song even manages to be playful with this idea; its most daring rhyme comes at the end of the refrain, as the words that are sung cascade down the scale:

---

[13] Boris Thomashefsky, *Dos pintele yid, operete in 4 akten* (Warsaw: Yavne, 1911), 12. B. Gorin claims that Moyshe Zeifert in fact wrote the play, but chose not to have it credited to him (Gorin, 204). Ezra Lahad notes in his bibliography of published Yiddish plays that "the writer is Moyshe Zeifert, who sold his rights to Thomashefsky." See Lahad, *Ha-makhazot be-yidish be-makor u've-targum: bibliografiyah* (Haifa: self-published, n.d.), 207.

[14] Ibid., 12.

Dos kleyntshiker yisrolikl	Little Yisrolik
Lakht fun dir Amalekl,	Laughs at you, Amalek,
Un blaybt tray dem pintele yid.	And remains true to his essence.[15]

Amalek, biblical enemy of the Israelites, is a byword for all those who seek to destroy the Jews, and Jews are commanded to remember him— that is, to be wary of new incarnations of him that may arise at any time. It is therefore startling to hear the song address him with the diminutive *Amalekl;* doing so cuts the mythical enemy down to size, and the final line again asserts the Jew's ability to endure.

The second verse introduces a Zionist strain that reappears at various points in the play and further reinforces an idea seen elsewhere: that of the Haskalah as failure, since it was predicated, at least in part, on the belief that the Jews can enjoy true freedom in any land that is not their own. So the song summons the Jews to Zion, insisting that "there is the *pintele*'s home."[16] The play's hero and heroine, Yankev and Miriam, return to this Zionist idea later in the play, with Yankev exhorting other Jews to reject having to be a stranger everywhere, and Miriam leading a song recalling Israel's ancient glory and looking toward a future where Jews will find a way to recover that glory. We might expect from the repetition of this idea that these characters will find a way to escape their problems in the *shtetl* and find a way to make it to Palestine, but the play ultimately finesses this issue. In a light moment late in the action, we meet two performers from an American circus, who lead a rousing chorus of "*Tri tshirs far di yenki dudel*" which includes the following tribute to Old Glory that would play well in what is now known as red-state America:

Di fon fun frayhayt flatert	The flag of freedom waves
imer tsu,	eternally,
Keyn besers iz nito, es iz nito,	No better one exists, none exists,
Shrayt tsuzamen imer, imer tsu,	Shout together, forever and ever,
Lebn zol di fon fun royt, vays,	Long live the flag of red, white,
un bloy.	and blue.[17]

---

[15] Ibid., 13.
[16] Ibid.
[17] Ibid., 53.

Jacob Ter's musical *Di yidishe neshome,* which Thomashefsky had produced the previous season, ended with characters opening a package from loved ones who had gone to America; the package contained none other than the American flag, "the flag of freedom,"[18] which was then waved with unabashed patriotism as the finale was sung. *Dos pintele yid* ends with a comparable, though even tackier, gesture: as Yankev leads an exultant cry that "there is peace between Jews and Christians,"[19] a Star of David with the words "dos pintele yid" in electrically lit letters descends from the ceiling, as the bar mitzvah march from earlier in the play is reprised. This particular example of light entertainment hedges its bets about the place of the Jews in the world, with songs extolling both Zion and America, but an ending that also holds out the prospect that Jews can co-exist with their Christian neighbors in Eastern Europe. Or would the audience feel that such things could happen only in an American Yiddish musical?

OY, GELTENYU! AMERICA THE THIEF

Such flag-waving and Yankee Doodling aside, American Yiddish drama as a whole will turn out to be far more ambivalent about the prospect of living a meaningful Jewish life in America. Perhaps it is no accident that such unabashed patriotism as that expressed above appears in works set entirely in Eastern Europe; once we start seeing characters disembark at Castle Garden and Ellis Island, we see them facing the realities of adapting to America, rather than the mere dream of the Golden Land. The gap between dream and reality is given dark overtones in Avrom Goldfaden's epic 1891 melodrama of the modern Jewish experience, *Meshiekhs tsaytn?! (The Messianic Era?!),* which follows its central characters from Eastern Europe to America to Palestine. The setting itself gives some taste of the breadth of the play's movement: "1st Act: in the little village of Fanatovka. 2nd and 3rd

---

[18] Jacob Ter, *Di idishe neshome, oder Berl Kokhlefl,* adapted by B. Thomashefsky (Warsaw: Melodye, 1910), 56.
[19] Thomashefsky, 60.

Acts: in the city of Kiev in Russia. 4th Act: in New York (America). 5th Act: on the ocean. 6th Act: in a colony of Baron Rothschild's in Palestine."[20] In the course of this physical journey, we see the characters change spiritually as well—from traditional small-town Jews to maskilim, radicalized out of their assimilationist impulses by an onstage pogrom, bowing to Mammon in New York and sold off to prostitution rings in Buenos Aires, and ultimately finding Zion to be the only place truly hospitable to both their physical and spiritual selves.

During the first half of the play, we follow Hershele, one of the central characters, from his village to Kiev, where he studies medicine and assimilates so readily that he abandons his Jewish name for the moniker Ivan Ivanovich, until a pogrom bursts his assimilationist bubble and he embraces his Jewishness once again, calling out to the *pogromchiks:* "Come here, come here . . . throw stones at me too! I am a Jew! I am a *zhid!*"[21] But Jewish identity and values will come under a different sort of assault in America, where, in his "office salon," the businessman Mr. Levi reigns with all the warmth of a tsar. It is ten years after the pogrom, which sowed confusion that separated the aptly named banker Leon Markovitsh Shteynherts (Stoneheart) from his wife and children. Now he goes by the surname Levi, and by a Dickensian coincidence unbeknownst to any of the characters, the banker's children, Herman and Lise, are now working for him. Perhaps some of his business in America is legitimate, but a good portion of both his personal and professional affairs is decidedly unkosher. He remarried in America for the sake of money, with the added lure of lust; his new wife is a wealthy widow, and he now has designs on his stepdaughter, the sole heir to his late wife's estate. Even more unsavory is the business he conducts in his office behind his employees' backs. When a shady character comes to the office talking about the "goods" he sells so profitably in Buenos Aires, we know that Levi is connected to the so-called white-slave trade. After unwittingly selling his own daughter to the trader, Levi gloats, "Now that's 'business'—it's not for nothing

---

[20] Avrom Goldfaden, *Meshiekhs tsaytn?!: epokhn-bilder der rusishn yidn* (Cracow: Yoysef Fisher, 1900), 4.
[21] Ibid., 52.

that they say you get rich in America!—making money without lifting a finger."[22]

The drive to make a dollar—quick or slow, honest or otherwise—dominates the American portion of Goldfaden's epic. Here we see two locales, first the office and later the street. One Vanderman comes through the office hawking what he claims is a picture of "Mrs. Lot," photographed "just before she turned around to look at Sodom." More ethically troubling is an exchange in which Levi offers Yuntl the Beggar (another immigrant from the Russian village) a bribe to give false testimony in a court case. Yuntl takes as much money as he can manage to get Levi to pay up front, and then gets him to give a few more cents purely for Yukl's daughter's dowry. When Levi leaves, Yukl deposits the payments into two separate pockets:

> Because this is *mitsve-gelt* [money that fulfills a biblical commandment], I'm putting it in one pocket, and since this is *aveyre-gelt* ["sin-money, or ill-gotten gains"], I'm putting it in another—Oy, Kilimbis, Kilimbis! [his bastardization of *Columbus*]. When I get hold of you, I'll tear out your beard and *peyes!* Why did you invent a land where they give money for sinning? What won't people do for *geltenyu*?[23]

Most of Yukl's lament is a fairly standard response to the commercial pressures that forced or enticed so many immigrants to compromise their traditional practice in order to survive in America. Goldfaden's wry twist is to coin a new word and use it as the springboard for a sardonic song about the things people will do to make a dollar. His coinage is all the more effective because it puns on a common Yiddish diminutive for God, *gotenyu,* which in America loses out to *geltenyu.*

In Goldfaden's New York, few people seem to do an honest day's work. Vanderman does walk around with a sandwich board for awhile, with Hebrew letters in front and English all down his back, but this turns out to be dangerous; in an eerie echo of the Act III pogrom, Vanderman is beset by children who throw stones at him—"Here they also throw stones?" he marvels sadly—and call him "Jew! Sheeny!"[24] Per-

---

[22] Ibid., 57.
[23] Ibid., 63–64.
[24] Ibid., 71.

haps Goldfaden was so disenchanted by his own aborted sojourn in America a few years earlier that he did not even balance the picture of the country's anything-for-a-dollar image with that of a refuge from persecution.

Goldfaden attempts to imbue the American episode with the air of a Greek tragedy—the fall of the House of Shteynherts through the patriarch's greed. By the time he learns his daughter's true identity, she is on a ship to Buenos Aires, and no amount of money can get her back. He murders the slave trader, and when his wife and son beg to learn what happened to Lise, he unhelpfully tells them that the dead man knows. A moment later, Levi shoots himself. His wife wanders the streets deliriously until collapsing in front of a trolley, and Herman is left to search for his sister. Though the coincidences are forced, peripheral spectacles in the streets show something of the old Goldfaden magic, and the point is clear: America is all wallet, no heart.[25]

Goldfaden, of course, was far from the only writer who saw America as a place that sapped Jewish immigrants of their spiritual side— a constant theme in American Jewish writing. Usually, of course, the implications are sobering, if not tragic, as in Abraham Cahan's unhappy rags-to-riches novel of 1917, *The Rise of David Levinsky*. Here are some of the narrator's final thoughts on his material ascent and spiritual demise:

> At the height of my business success I feel that if I had my life to live over again I should never think of a business career. . . . My past and present do not comport well. David, the poor lad swinging over a Talmud volume at the Preacher's Synagogue, seems to have more in common with my inner identity than David Levinsky, the well-known cloak manufacturer.[26]

---

[25] Goldfaden softens this harsh view at least somewhat in his last play, *Ben Ami* (1908). While set entirely in Eastern Europe, the play ends with a pageant in which the heroes inspect groups of soldiers from various nations. America finishes second-best, but the verdict is that such fighters would best serve the Jewish people by serving in a fully Jewish state.

[26] Abraham Cahan, *The Rise of David Levinsky* (1917; rpt. New York: Harper Torchbooks, 1969), 530.

As we shall see, American Yiddish drama often strikes a similarly somber note on this subject, but first it is worth seeing how Sholem Aleichem found dark comedy in such material. In his one-act comedy *Oylem-habe* (*The World to Come*, 1915), Sholem Aleichem sharpens the focus on the tension between material and spiritual needs, showing us a hustler who comes up with a scheme to make money by exploiting the religious ignorance of American Jewish *allrightniks*,[27] as well as their anxiety over what their neglect of spiritual matters might cost them when they go to their final judgment.[28]

As the action begins, we meet Mr. and Mrs. Cherkiss, sitting in neighboring rocking chairs, Mr. Cherkiss "with a cigar in his mouth, his feet up, . . . a well-built man in his middle years, elegantly dressed. Next to him, in the second rocking chair, sits Mrs. Cherkiss, a heavy piece of goods with a three-story goiter."[29] Now that he has reached a certain age, Mr. Cherkiss worries that he has not paid sufficient attention to spiritual matters: "I'm thinking back over my life: how we came to this country thirty years ago, and both peddled, and were Jews just like all the other people. But what are we now? (*Gets up, walks around.*) What sort of Jews are we? No *shabbes*, no *yontev*, no *talis*, no *tfiln*—nothing! Day and night playing poker, or pinochle, or other games, and we don't begin to think about the Other World."[30] Cherkiss's lament is one that

---

[27] Mikhail Krutikov elegantly defines an *allrightnik* as "a successful immigrant who fulfilled his American dream at the price of Jewish ethical values" in *Yiddish Fiction and the Crisis of Modernity, 1905–1914* (Stanford, CA: Stanford University Press, 2001), 131.

[28] Only a small portion of the vast critical literature on Sholem Aleichem focuses on his dramaturgy. See Yekhezkel Dobrushin, *Di dramaturgye fun di klasiker* (Moscow: Emes, 1948); Jacob Weitzner, *Sholem Aleichem in the Theater* (Northwood, Middlesex: Symposium Press, 1994); and Zalmen Zylbercweig, ed., *Leksikon fun yidishn teater* (New York: Farlag Elisheva, 1963), 4:3309–3578.

[29] Sholem Aleichem, *Oylem-habe*, in *Ale verk fun Sholem-Aleykhem*, vol. 6: Komedyes (New York: Sholem-Aleykhem Folksfond, 1927), 267.

[30] Ibid., 267. The Yiddish terms mean, respectively, Sabbath, festival, prayer shawl, and phylacteries. Typical of Yiddish dramas set in America, Cherkiss's dialogue is a mixture of Yiddish and English. Here he uses the English words *life, country, people, nothing,* and *world,* as well as the English-Yiddish amalgam *gepedlt* (peddled).

has been made by many a character in American Jewish literature, but here Sholem Aleichem gives it one of his signature comic twists.

For some perspective, let us look at a comparable moment in H. Leivick's drama *Shmates* (1921), in which an elderly immigrant (modeled on the playwright's uncle[31]) castigates himself for having neglected the study of the Torah:

> REB ELYE.   Am I lacking holy books? They're sitting right on my shelf—I brought them from over there. . . . But I can't deny it, my dear friends: I confess to you that I haven't opened any of them in years. . . .
>
> DAYAN.   So who's stopping you?
>
> REB ELYE.   Ha? What? I'm not allowed to. . . . No excuse, no excuse. . . . What do I mean "I'm not allowed?" All day long, as you know, I sort through *shmates*. . . . And at night—I come home, and I can barely keep my eyes open by the time I'm done with the blessing after the meal, may God bless you . . . and my old woman, may she live to a hundred and twenty, has been bedridden for two years already—her feet, may you be spared such misery—so even on the Sabbath I can't sit and study with a clear head.[32]

Reb Elye insists that he has "no excuse," but at least he has serious competing demands on his time. The Cherkisses, by contrast, joined the *allrightnik* class some time ago, and have plenty of free time, which they have chosen to fill by playing cards. Leivick's Reb Elye has a clear, and very traditional, sense of the consequences of his neglect: "I deserve a whipping, a fiery whipping. And sure enough, I'll get one. Oy-oy, will I get a whipping! One mustn't forget, one mustn't. To forget is the

---

[31] Shmuel Niger, *H. Leyvik, 1888–1948* (Toronto: Gershon Pomerants Esey-Bibliotek, 1951), 211. Niger describes the uncle as "an old Jew who worked in a rag shop and in fact was named Reb Elye."

[32] H. Leivick, *Shmates*, in *Di yidishe drame fun 20stn yorhundert*, vol. 2 (New York: Alveltlekhn yidishn kultur-kongres, 1977), 129–130.

greatest sin."[33] Mr. Cherkiss, on the other hand, takes an American approach to the problem: to buy his way out of it. Cherkiss has hired Mr. Kvotshke (from the verb *kvotshken,* to cluck), "a lively little Jew, with a hungry, restless face, [who] looks half tailor, half reverend."[34] Kvotshke has come up with the perfect exchange: some of Cherkiss's money for half of a pious Jew's share in the world to come.

Kvotshke is effusive in his description of the pious Jew: "You've never seen such a Jew in all your life! He goes around dressed like a Turk, and speaks in the holy tongue. . . . Was in Eretz Israel for ten years, has come here to visit his children, and is going back to Eretz Israel again. . . . A kosher Jew, sits day and night[35] and studies. . . . Either he's studying or he's praying. . . . And fasts . . . every Monday and Thursday . . . knows nothing of financial matters."[36] Once again, a commentator on the American Jewish scene has borrowed a page from the maskilic playbook to critique the decline—or in this case, the corruption—of traditional practice. The maskilim habitually depicted arranged marriage as a heartless, wrongheaded commercial transaction— the exchange of one family's riches with another's *yikhes,* or pedigree— that forced young people into loveless marriages. Here, Kvotshke lays it on thick in order to convince Mr. Cherkiss that his two hundred dollars will be money well spent.

Part of the humor of Sholem Aleichem's sketch is that the exchange of money for some share of piety has a place in traditional Judaism. Arranged marriages are but one example; others include wealthy families supporting Torah scholars in other ways, and wealthy members of the community essentially "buying" honors in the synagogue. But lest we have any doubt that this *mekhires oylem-habe* (sale of Paradise) ceremony is fraudulent, the truth becomes clear as soon as the Pious Jew enters, while the Cherkisses are getting dressed for the ritual. Not only is he not pious, but he is hardly more learned in Jewish matters than the Cherkisses are, and his beard and *peyes* are fake (a problem he is told to cover up by facing the wall while the dupes are

---

[33] Ibid., 130.
[34] Sholem Aleichem, 268.
[35] To add to the aura of holiness, Kvotskhe uses the Hebrew expression *yomam va-layla* here.
[36] Sholem Aleichem, 269.

present). Kvotshke further coaches him to speak as little as possible, and when he does, to mumble snippets of whatever Hebrew he can remember—from the prayer book, Psalms, and other basic sources.

Sholem Aleichem's satire hits full stride when the couple re-enters, Mrs. Cherkiss having pondered the inequity of her husband buying his way into Paradise and doing nothing for her: "He'll sit there like a prince, with all the *allrightniks* and *allrightnitses* in Paradise, playing poker or pinochle with the hussies, and I'll be burning in Hell like a candle."[37] This complaint sets off an elaborate negotiation, with the Cherkisses suggesting what they are willing to pay for another quarter of the Jew's share in Paradise, the Jew responding with unconnected sprinklings of prayers, and Kvotshke pretending to translate the latter into the Jew's demands. After a couple of minutes of this, a sum is agreed to. With two paid "witnesses" in place who are also in on the scam, the "ceremony" finally gets under way. The grifters almost get away with it, but as so often happens, are brought low by their own greed, as they get into an increasingly heated disagreement about the equitable way to divide the proceeds. The Cherkisses, who have again exited to change back into everyday clothes, return to witness the following scene, as described in the closing stage direction:

> The JEW's beard is in the SECOND WITNESS's hand. At that moment, the door opens and MR. CHERKISS appears in a change of clothes, and MRS. CHERKISS enters with a tray, on which are a couple of bottles with drinks and some plates with snacks. Seeing one of the witnesses with a beard in his hand and the JEW without a beard, they understand all that has happened. But in their great amazement, they remain frozen in the door as if welded to it, and look at each other. The silent scene continues for a minute, with everyone frozen in a pose. The curtain falls.[38]

Sholem Aleichem recycled this tableau—inspired by the strikingly similar conclusion of Gogol's classic comedy *Revizor* (*The Inspector General*)—in several of his one-act comedies, but it arguably works best here. After such chicanery and such naiveté, what more need be said?

---

[37] Ibid., 274.
[38] Ibid., 280.

OLD MEN SWIMMING AGAINST THE TIDE

When a traditional Jew has no sons, he worries about who will say *kaddish* for him. When he does have sons, but they move away from the tradition, the worry is just as great, but perhaps even more painful. The anxiety over the direction that the next generation will take is ever-present in American Yiddish drama, and in much of American Jewish letters more broadly. Sholem Aleichem also touches on it in the opening moments of *The World to Come,* in the sort of tart exchange that often turns up in his stories:

> MR. CHERKISS.   May we live to one hundred and twenty, who will say *kaddish* after we're gone?
>
> MRS. CHERKISS.   What do you mean? We don't have sons?
>
> MR. CHERKISS.   Those lumps will say *kaddish?*
>
> MRS. CHERKISS.   Maybe Jake won't say *kaddish,* but Maxele? My little darling!
>
> MR. CHERKISS.   Max will say *kaddish?*
>
> MRS. CHERKISS.   Sure he'll say *kaddish!*
>
> MR. CHERKISS.   I'll betcha he won't! Maybe the first eight days. But later—no sir!
>
> MRS. CHERKISS.   Yes ma'am!
>
> MR. CHERKISS.   No sir!
>
> MRS. CHERKISS.   Yes ma'am!
>
> MR. CHERKISS.   (*A bang on the table.*) When I say no sir, it's no sir![39]

Since Sholem Aleichem's purpose here is to lampoon the idea of treating spiritual matters as commercial transactions, he is more interested in comic effect than in subtle details of his characters' psychology. But in naturalistic plays of the 1920s, Yiddish writers would explore the effect of this anxiety on American Jewish families. Two of the finest Yid-

---

[39] Ibid., 267–268.

dish dramas of that period, H. Leivick's *Shmates* (1921) and Leon Kobrin's *Riverside Drive* (1928; first produced in 1931), offer penetrating portraits of the decline of *yidishkayt* among the children and grandchildren of immigrant Jews. And in both of those works, old men who remain strongly connected to their Jewish roots struggle to pass their ideals on to subsequent generations.[40]

Leivick's Mordkhe Maza and Kobrin's Shloyme Yaffe[41] have much in common. Both are patriarchs of immigrant families. Both are learned in Jewish terms and religious in their observance. Both have kind, loving wives: Mordkhe's Rokhl-Leah and Shloyme's Rivke. Both sets of parents suffer some degree of estrangement from their children as well. The Mazas' traditional, married eldest daughter poses little problem. The fact that their second daughter is marrying the son of Mordkhe's boss creates considerable difficulties, particularly because

---

[40] For critical discussions of Leivick's dramaturgy, see Israel Biletzky, *H. Levik, ha-dramaturgyah ha-khezyonit* (Tel Aviv: Ha-Kibuts he-me'ukhad, 1979); Yankev Gotlib, *H. Leyvik, zayn lid un drame* (Kaunas: Pasaulis, 1939); *Leksikon fun der nayer yidisher literatur* (New York: Congress for Jewish Culture, 1963), 5:107–128; Shmuel Niger, *H. Leyvik;* Zalmen Reyzen, *Leksikon fun der yidisher literatur, prese un filologye* (Vilna: B. Kletskin, 1927), 2:196–202; B. Rivkin, *H. Leyvik: zayne lider un dramatishe verk* (Buenos Aires: Farlag Yidbukh, 1955); Levi Shalit, *Meshiekh-troymen in leyviks dramatishe poemes* (Munich: Eynzam, 1947); and Zalmen Zylbercweig, ed., *Leksikon fun yidishn teater* (Warsaw: Farlag Elisheva, 1934), 2:1059–1075. On Kobrin, see Yoel Entin, Introduction to Kobrin's *Dramatishe shriftn* (New York: Leon Kobrin Bukh-komitet, 1952), xi–xxxvii; *Leksikon fun der nayer yidisher literatur* (New York: Congress for Jewish Culture, 1981), 8:2–5; Shmuel Niger, *Dertseylers un romanistn* (New York: CYCO, 1946); Reyzen, *Leksikon* (Vilna: B. Kletskin, 1929), 3:359–370; and Zylbercweig, ed., *Leksikon* (New York: Farlag Elisheva, 1963), 2:2962–3044. Mikhail Krutikov's assessment of Kobrin's novels of immigration in *Yiddish Fiction and the Crisis of Modernity* (132–144) sheds light on the writer's dramas on that theme as well.

[41] The name Yaffe may be a tacit tribute to Kobrin's mentor, Gordin. Kobrin lauded Gordin effusively in his memoirs, which include an appreciation of *The Jewish King Lear.* "And, in the end, who takes pity on [Dovid Moysheles, the Jewish King Lear]? None other than the impious Taybele and the heretic Yaffe." See *Erinerungen fun a idishen dramaturg: a fertel yorhundert idish teater in amerika* (New York: Komitet far Kobrin's Shriften, 1925), 1:131.

there is labor unrest at the sweatshop. And most painful is the gulf between Mordkhe and his youngest child, twenty-year-old Harry, who speaks in clipped sentences, half Yiddish and half English, and gulps down his dinners so he can go out and play baseball with his friends.

The generation gap presents itself differently in *Riverside Drive,* where Herman Jaffe is a devoted son who has prospered in America and whose parents arrive fresh off the boat to stay with him early in the play. Herman understands his parents—at least their language, if not always their feelings—but few of the other characters do. *Riverside Drive* achieves much of its impact through its bilingual dialogue. The elder Yaffes speak only Yiddish, with newly learned English words sprinkled in. Herman speaks Yiddish with them and English with most of the other characters, who do not know Yiddish and speak English throughout the play. Not only are Herman's three children American-born, after all, but their mother (whom we know, tellingly, only as "Madame Jaffe") is the daughter of a German-Jewish Reform rabbi. Thus, the generation gap is complicated here by the familiar tension between Central and Eastern European Jews. Kobrin adds one additional linguistic flourish to the mix with the character Izzy, one of Herman's employees recruited to help attend to the new immigrants, partly because he speaks Yiddish—sort of. Having been in the country for several years, he has come to mix his Yiddish with a substantial helping of English, so that Shloyme and Rivke constantly have to ask him to explain himself, in exchanges like this (italicized words appear in English or "Yinglish" in the original):

IZZY.   I am a *watchman* in his *shop*. He has three *watchleit,* one on every *floor;* I'm one of them, *you know.*

SHLOYME.   Reb Jew, I don't understand what you're saying.

IZZY.   What's wrong? After all, I'm speaking *plain* Yiddish with you.

SHLOYME.   You're from Pleyn? Where is that located?

IZZY.   Ha? My God, you don't understand Yiddish?[42]

---

[42] Leon Kobrin, *Riversayd drayv* (New York: Folks-bibliotek / Shrayber-sektsye baym YKUF, 1942), 43.

This limited exchange between those who ostensibly speak the same language does not bode well for mutual comprehension between those who have even less in common. But as a fellow immigrant of their generation who speaks at least some sort of Yiddish, Izzy initially strikes the newcomers as a potential source of advice about how to speak to their grandchildren—at least until they learn that he speaks English with his children and grandchildren:

> SHLOYME.   What do you mean? Your children don't speak English either? I thought that only the children of aristocrats didn't speak Yiddish.
>
> IZZY.   What sort of child speaks Yiddish in America?
>
> SHLOYME.   And in *kheyder?*
>
> IZZY.   Ay, Reb Shloyme, this is not Europe, you know![43]

In that "Ay, Reb Shloyme" lies the sigh of countless traditional immigrants, coming to terms with the lesson that all their old assumptions about their religious and cultural traditions, and about family cohesiveness, are being threatened in this new environment.

Nevertheless, Shloyme is at first unintimidated by the challenge of making himself understood, which is one of the main characteristics that distinguishes him from Mordkhe Maza in *Shmates*. Mordkhe is constantly trapped by forces beyond his control. When we first meet him, he is brooding over the fact that his middle child, Annie, has gotten engaged to his boss's son without asking her parents' blessing first. After a painfully awkward meeting with the couple, Mordkhe complains bitterly to his wife about the gulf between him and his children, concluding with the following thoughts:

> If anyone were to hear me talking, he would surely think that God-knows-what took place in this house. True, nothing terrible has happened. It's probably like this everywhere. I know. But I see things differently. I sit in the shop in a corner and sort *shmates* and I want to be left alone. . . . The children are drifting away from me, cutting my

---

[43] Kobrin, 45.

life to pieces. The men in the shop don't understand me either. But do I say anything? *Nu*, good, let it be that way.[44]

When Rokhl-Leah starts sobbing a moment later, Maza cannot or will not help her. Instead, he puts his head in his hands and says the grace after meals. Each of the play's four acts ends with a stage direction describing Maza. In every act but the third, which takes place in the shop, the stage directions are noteworthy for his *lack* of action; Acts II and IV, in fact, end with Rokhl-Leah literally pushing her husband around. Only in the shop, in spite of the resignation he expresses above, does Maza ultimately take action, dragging his co-workers out the door to strike against his employers-*cum*-in-laws.

Shloyme takes the initiative more consistently. He first voices his sense of alienation after a meal at which his daughter-in-law, politely but patronizingly, taught him and Rivke the table manners practiced in well-to-do American homes. For Shloyme, the etiquette lesson is revelatory, as he explains to his wife:

> I still have this beard, and I just thought, that. . . . . . . I've suddenly become a little child, and you too. . . . I think that our daughter-in-law placed the white napkins in the little children's little hands and showed them what to do, so the little children won't make a mess, God forbid. . . . Rivke, when our daughter-in-law did that to us, it seemed to me that I had suddenly lost my *tsores-odem,* my human face. And besides that, the pantomime—pointing to my lips to show me what to do, how to hold the fork . . . and the grandchildren . . . not good, Rivke, not good![45]

If Shloyme were Maza, the thought would end there, with a bitter shrug, but Shloyme has a plan:

> I'll immerse myself in their language. But the question is: why won't they learn the language of their grandfather, the Yiddish language? I mean, she's a rabbi's daughter, after all, and they are his

---

[44] Leivick, 121.
[45] Kobrin, 35–36.

grandchildren! Okay, so they don't wash before eating, don't *bentsh,*
don't *davn,* eat with their heads uncovered—but a Yiddish word, at
least. . . . But just wait, let's quickly learn their language, and they'll
soon become Jews.[46]

Shloyme's anguish about his family situation thus intersects with a
dilemma central to the modern Jewish experience. In a world where
the Jewish community no longer adheres to a shared set of assumptions and behavior, what does it mean to be a Jew? Both plays, in different ways, ask the question: How can the values of the traditional
Jewish world find a place in America?

The eminent critic Shmuel Niger makes the startling assertion
that Leivick's focus on this question made *Shmates,* "all things considered, not an American Yiddish play. On the contrary, it is more the
drama of a proud, old-fashioned Jew's *opposition* to the spirit—or more
accurately, the spiritlessness—of Jewish-immigrant America."[47] Yet this
opposition, as we have seen, was deeply ingrained in American Yiddish
drama by the 1920s, at which time Leivick and Kobrin had reason to
worry about the future of Jewish life in America. The youngest members of each family are caught up in amusements reminiscent of the
daughter's balls, operas, and novels in *Silliness and Sanctimony.* The
teenage grandchildren in *Riverside Drive* become so Americanized as
to be ashamed of their greenhorn grandparents; meetings between
these two generations tend to end with the youngsters running out
of the room, either in fits of laughter or annoyance. And Harry in
Shmates is so consumed with playing baseball that he hardly has time
to say two words to his sisters or parents. The indignities that the young
heap upon the old inspire many an eloquent lament by the plays' old
men, none more fiery than this outburst from Shloyme near the end
of *Riverside Drive:*

> I am somebody! Was somebody! I am Yaffe, Shloyme Yaffe! . . . I
> was a wealthy man, but that's nothing. The *pogromchiks* could have

---

[46] Ibid., 37.
[47] Niger, 209.

taken all my material wealth, but not the wealth of my Jewish soul. . . . And not the hope and belief that a new Jewish generation will grow up in my family. No, the *pogromchiks* couldn't take that away from me! I could have said to them, "*Ten li ha-nefesh ve-ha-rekhush kakh lekha*"— take all that I own, but leave me my Jewish soul. I cannot say that to you, though, for you have taken away my Jewish soul.[48]

Yet even as these playwrights endow their protagonists with the eloquence of biblical prophets, we get the distinct sense that even characters who are sympathetic to their plight feel that they may be overreacting. These old men are compelling figures, but both dramatists resist the temptation to make them into saints or seers. Nor do Leivick and Kobrin take cheap swipes at easy targets. Leivick does not present a cartoonish, fat-bellied capitalist in the sweatshop owner Old Levi, but rather a man who is by turns ruthless and charming, in the vein of Sholem Asch's Uncle Moses. Levi's son turns out to be more humane, even helping, along with Mordkhe's children, to support him so he no longer has to sort rags. And the Yaffes are no King and Queen Lear either. After reaching the painful conclusion that their own grandchildren do not love them, Shloyme and Rivke decide to move in with friends, into "a Jewish house . . . we'll be among Jews like us."[49] Though Madame Jaffe does not even bother to hide her satisfaction at this outcome, Herman is dismayed, and tries to stop them. When this fails, he takes Izzy aside and tells him, "Tell them over there to look after my parents; I will pay."[50]

What answers do such plays offer to the problem of the decline of *yidishkayt* among the children and grandchildren of Eastern European Jewish immigrants in America? *Shmates* offers some hope, but like Maza much of the time, is taciturn about it. The play ends with Maza and Harry finally having something resembling a discussion; it is clear they have a long way to go, but at least Maza may be coming to realize that Harry is not his "enemy," as he earlier complained to a friend. *Riverside Drive* is far more explicit. As Shloyme lashes out in the

---

[48] Kobrin, 72.
[49] Ibid., 75.
[50] Ibid., 76.

final moments of the play at Herman's father-in-law, the (to Shloyme) "half-rabbi and half-priest"[51] Rabbi Schlesinger, he finds an interested audience in one of Adele's suitors, a young lawyer more interested in writing poetry and reading Yiddish literature than in his profession. The young man, visibly moved both by Shloyme's tirades and by the dismissive way in which some of the characters treat the new immigrants, ends the play "even more convinced how necessary are my work for the [Yiddish] schools and the Yiddish language!"[52]

In the aggregate, American Yiddish drama offers a variety of solutions to the question of how to foster meaningful Jewish life in America. Keep Yiddish alive, says *Riverside Drive*. Reach out to the next generation even if you are unsure how to do so, suggests *Shmates*. Respect your elders, chides *Mirele Efros*. Such diversity is itself a sign of secularization, for once *halakhah* (Jewish law) no longer reliably governs Jewish behavior, there is no central authority to oversee how—or even whether—Jews practice their faith. In America, many Jews concerned about preserving *yidishkayt,* but not necessarily in the religious sense, turned to Yiddish drama for answers. The wide range of responses they encountered can perhaps be best summed up in the title *Dos pintele yid:* be true to the essence of who you are as a Jew—however you define that essence. Time and again, these dramas suggest that while Jewish tradition is important, one must keep in mind that "this is not Europe"—in other words, that immigrants from Eastern Europe will need to be not only tenacious, but also adaptable, in order to preserve their traditions in their new home.

---

[51] Ibid., 71.
[52] Ibid., 77.

THE INFLUENCE OF AMERICA
ON MODERN YIDDISH POETRY

Marc Miller

Most studies of Yiddish literature cite Yoysef Bovshover (1873–1915), Dovid Edelshtat (1866–1892), Morris Rosenfeld (1862–1923), and Morris Vinchevsky (1856–1932) as the main representatives of sweatshop poetry. However, despite that fact, scholars dismiss the contributions of this first generation of Yiddish writers in America and relegate them to the status of pre-modern poets of sub-literary quality. Consequently, there are few studies that analyze the poetic qualities of sweatshop poetry. In fact, these writers constitute a vital link in the chain of Yiddish literature. They not only represent the first generation of Yiddish literature in America, but are a bridge between Europe and America, between the ideological poetry of the *haskala* (Eastern-European Jewish Enlightenment) and the apolitical, twentieth-century lyrics of *Di yunge,* the traditional starting point of modern American Yiddish poetry for most literary critics of Yiddish.

In 1907, a new literary group appeared in New York centered around their first publication, a short-lived journal titled *Di yugnt* (*Youth*). These poets, essayists, translators, short story writers, and novelists called themselves *Di yunge* (The Young Ones) and, as self-professed literary "orphans," sought to obliterate the poetry that preceded them in this country. For the most part, they ignored the pioneering accomplishments of the sweatshop poets and attacked the poetic principles embodied in their works. The opinions of *Di yunge* permeated Yiddish literary criticism and, in the following decades, with the rise of the pro-modernist aesthetic in America, sweatshop poetry was forced to the sidelines of the Yiddish canon where it has since remained.

The sweatshop poets were Eastern-European immigrants who came to America in the 1880s with the first wave of mass immigration

from the Russian empire. Working with little accessible literary tradition in the Jewish vernacular, these poets created a school of literature
that appealed to their mostly working-class audience. The main outlet
for their works was the infant Yiddish press that burgeoned during the
last two decades of the nineteenth century. These newspapers were
committed to promoting radical ideologies such as socialism, communism, and anarchism, and they solicited the contributions of the politically committed sweatshop poets. These writers—of whom Bovshover,
Edelshtat, Rosenfeld, and Vinchevsky are the best known—responded
to the great urbanization and industrialization of the Eastern-
European Jewish immigrant community and shaped their works
within the new socio-economic and political landscape of America.[1]

The idea of "art for art's sake" began to dominate American Yiddish letters in the first decade of the twentieth century, with young critics and poets calling for a new type of poetry eschewing politics and
embracing the individual moods of their poetical subjects. Many writers of this and future generations did not believe that a canon based
on these principles could accommodate the sweatshop poets, and,
therefore, these critics chose to dismiss the accomplishments of this
first generation. However, more cogent writers understood the enor-
mous impact sweatshop poetry had had upon its readership, and
sought to acknowledge these older writers, although they did so in a
limited manner. These critics claimed sweatshop writers as pioneers of
modern Yiddish poetry whose works possess historical, but not aesthetic, worth. They agreed that true, aesthetic poetry found its gene-
sis in American Yiddish literature with *Di yunge,* and in those few and
slightly older poets such as Avrom Reyzn (1876–1953) and Yoysef Rolnik (1879–1955), whom *Di yunge* considered literary mentors and precursors to their own set of poetics.

In their various publications, *Di yunge* published several mani-
festos outlining their beliefs.[2] Although they claimed to be creating a

---

[1] For a comprehensive survey of the first generation of Yiddish poets in America, see N. B. Minkov's three-volume study *Pionern fun der yidisher poeziye in
amerike* (New York: Grenich Printing Corporation, 1956).
[2] See Reuven Ayzland, "Di yunge," *Shriftn* 1 (1912), 3–20 and "Di naye ven-
dung in der yidisher poeziye," *Fun mentsh tsu mentsh,* ed. Moyshe-Leyb
Halpern (New York: Farlag Nyu York, 1915), 32–36; Dovid Ignatov "Di yugnt,"

totally new and original set of poetics in Yiddish, they actually formulated their poetic position in direct contrast to their perception of the poetics of sweatshop poetry. *Di yunge* identified sweatshop poetry as the following: poetry connected to political affiliations; poetry which voiced the collective; a loud and noisy poetry filled with bombastic and rhetorical tones; and a poetry which employed clichés and generic, prefabricated ideas. For each of these tenets, *Di yunge* offered their own opposite tendencies: art for its own sake; the highlighting of the voice of the individual; stillness and silence; and a stress on *shtimung* (mood). By creating this diametrically opposed set of principles, *Di yunge* sought to dispense with their popular poetic predecessors—their main competition in vying for the attention of their Yiddish readership.

Unlike most of the writers associated with *Di yunge,* who dismissed sweatshop poetry as merely politically motivated verse, several critics highlighted the achievements of the older poets, emphasizing their historical significance, in particular, as representatives of their time and place. These critics focused their attention on the supposed authenticity of the sweatshop poets as the measure of their poetic importance. One writer who expressed this idea succinctly was Avrom Tabachnik, a prolific critic who wrote extensively on Yiddish literature. In his estimation, Morris Rosenfeld was the only poet to distinguish himself from his cohort because his best poems contained "a more complicated, deeper social-historical meaning—that which later emerged in him under the influence of his time and its characteristic ideas, conflicts, and goals."[3] The poet's authenticity, in this case his reflection and embodiment of his time and place, was also Tabachnik's main criterion for Rosenfeld's poetic greatness. In differentiating Rosenfeld from the other sweatshop poets, the critic dismissed Bovshover and Edelshtat as "bohemian" and "not very creative" respectively, and stated that the main reason Rosenfeld was a great poet

---

Di yugnt 2 (Jan. 1908), 1–2 and "Sheyne grobyungeray un mise grobyungeray," *Shriftn* 1 (1912), 3–11; Yoyl Entin, "A yidisher romantizm," *Troymn un virklekhkeyt,* eds. Y. Adler and Y. Slonim (New York, 1909), 14–24.

[3] Avrom Tabachnik, *Dikhter un dikhtung* (New York: Knight Printing Corporation, 1965), 4–5.

and Vinchevsky was not is that "while Vinchevsky *went* to the masses, Rosenfeld *came* from the masses."[4]

For the Soviet Yiddish critics writing during the interwar period, authenticity was also the benchmark of poetic greatness. In their quest to build a canon of proletarian literature, which would serve the tenets of social realism, these writers focused their literary inquiries mainly on contemporary poets who wrote within the narrow parameters of this mold, and sought pre-revolutionary writers whom they could claim as predecessors to their aesthetic values. For a period of time, the American sweatshop poets served as the basis for the proletarian literature promoted by Soviet Yiddish criticism. These critics focused on the socialist and communist sympathies of these writers, claiming that their works prefigured social realism. However, in the 1930s, during the era of the Great Retreat,[5] when the central government tightened its grip on literature and demanded a heightened level of loyalty from its writers, American sweatshop poetry became vilified. After several decades of publishing laudatory essays, books, and anthologies celebrating the achievements of these pioneer poets, Soviet Yiddish critics attacked sweatshop poetry. Rosenfeld was labeled a traitor for his Zionist verse; Vinchevsky was attacked for his involvement in the Bund and his own "nationalistic" works; and, after the anti-Soviet anarchist activities in Spain, Bovshover and Edelshtat—both active anarchists in their lifetimes—were deemed *persona non grata* in the Soviet canon of Yiddish literature.[6]

The most damaging and influential evaluation of sweatshop poetry is in the works of *Di yunge*. In their various anthologies, journals, and other publications, the writers associated with this group dis-

---

[4] Ibid, 12.

[5] This term was coined by the historian Nicholas Timasheff to describe the post-1932 period following the Cultural Revolution in the Soviet Union. See *The Great Retreat—The Growth and Decline of Communism in Russia* (New York: E. P. Dutton, 1946).

[6] For a schematic survey of the critical reception of American sweatshop poetry in Soviet Yiddish criticism, with a particular focus on Dovid Edelshtat, see Alexander Pomerants, "Politishe kritik," *Di sovetishe harugey malkhes* (Buenos Aires: YIVO, 1962), 302–330.

missed the sweatshop poets and claimed that, except for a few precursors, Yiddish literature in America began with their own achievements. Perhaps the most telling document is the collection edited by the poet Zishe Lande titled *Di yidishe dikhtung in Amerike biz yor 1919* (*Yiddish Poetry in America Until the Year 1919*).[7] Of the twenty-eight poets represented in Lande's anthology there is one from the sweatshop generation, Morris Rosenfeld; three from the next generation, Yoysef Rolnik, A. Liyesen (Avrom Valt), and Yehoyesh (Shloyme Blumgortn); one poet from the fourth generation, A. Leyeles (Aron Glants); and twenty-three from the cohort of *Di yunge*.

The few poems Lande includes by Rosenfeld are not from the poet's sweatshop works. Rather, the editor included excerpts from several of the older poet's obscure works, thus reinventing Rosenfeld in his own attempt to redefine the canon of American Yiddish literature. Regarding the remainder of Rosenfeld's cohort, Lande, in the introduction to his anthology, sums up his opinion of sweatshop poetry in two often-cited quotes: "The national and social movements each had their own rhyme departments," and "The history of Yiddish poetry until the beginning of this century is itself the history of an episode in the labor movement."[8]

What was it about sweatshop poetry that disqualified it from the canon of modern Yiddish poetry? Why was it barely acknowledged by modern critics and anthologizers? Following in the wake of *Di yunge*, a modernist aesthetic came to dominate Yiddish literature in America, and the poetry of the subsequent generation—grouped around the periodical *In zikh* (*Within the Self*)—expressed, among other beliefs, the tenets of literary modernism. This valuing of the modernistic aesthetic in Yiddish reflected the influence of American literature and the New Critics who, beginning in the 1930s, held up poets such as T. S. Eliot and Ezra Pound as examples of American poetry at its best.[9] With

---

[7] Zisho Lande, ed., *Di yidishe dikhtung in Amerike biz yor 1919* (New York: Yidish, 1919).

[8] *Di yidishe dikhtung in amerike biz yor 1919*, iv.

[9] For a study of this period see David A. Hollinger, *In the American Province—Studies in the History and Historiography of Ideas* (Baltimore: Johns Hopkins University Press, 1985).

their emphasis on interiority and personal, often fragmented expression, and their belief in the need for new poetic forms and language to express the chaos and uncertainty of the modern world, promodernist critics and writers sought to create a new model of literature.

Despite the ostensible incompatibility of sweatshop poetry and literary modernism, it was the true modernists of American Yiddish literature—the poets associated with *In zikh*—who rejected *Di yunge*'s denigration of sweatshop poetry. In particular, writers such as Yankev Glatshteyn and N. B. Minkov selected Morris Rosenfeld from his cohort, placing him at the head of Yiddish poetry in America. The chief proponent of Rosenfeld's rehabilitation was Nokhem Borekh Minkov, a prominent poet and critic associated with *In zikh*. In Minkov's 1937 *Yidishe klasiker poetn* (*Classic Yiddish Poets*), he named Rosenfeld one of the classic poets of Yiddish.[10] The critic bracketed Rosenfeld with the canonical prose writers of modern Yiddish literature, Sh.Y. Abramovitch, Sholem Aleykhem, and Y. L. Perets. Minkov did not call Rosenfeld a "pioneer," a term used by other critics to relegate the older poet's accomplishments to merely historical, and not literary, significance. In fact, in the introduction to his seminal, multi-volume study of early American Yiddish poetry, *Pionern fun der yidisher poeziye in amerike* (Pioneers of Yiddish Poetry in America), which he published nearly twenty years after his first study, Minkov explicitly states that the poets discussed in his work are precursors to true, developed American Yiddish poetry of which Rosenfeld is a chief representative. In addition, he argued that although Rosenfeld began his career, both in tone as well as in time, as a pioneer, because he "crossed the border of the era,"[11] he deserved the title of "classic."

In 1956, Yankev Glatshteyn—perhaps the most influential figure in American Yiddish poetry—wrote a review of Rosenfeld's recently published correspondence. Although he considered the older poet a worthy subject of discussion, he believed that Rosenfeld was a minor poet who wrote "approximately ten good poems, and four or five great

---

[10] N. B. Minkov, "Moris Rozenfeld," *Yidishe klasiker-poetn* (New York: Bidermanis Farlag, 1937), 67–98.

[11] N. B. Minkov, *Pionern fun yidisher poeziye in amerike*, vol.1, 14.

ones."[12] Here then, it may seem that Glatshteyn accepted *Di yunge*'s verdict. However, Glatshteyn's major statement on Rosenfeld is a long piece he wrote for the centennial of the poet's birthday.[13] There, Glatshteyn praised Rosenfeld and recanted the statements he had made in his earlier review: "My opinion in 1956 was incorrect."[14] Glatshteyn conceded that, after taking a closer look at the poet's works, he saw that there was much value in his poetry and he now called Rosenfeld "the most original poet of his generation,"[15] "the first Yiddish poet to understand America,"[16] and "the father of American Yiddish poetry."[17]

Glatshteyn is considered one of the most talented and sophisticated Yiddish poets and is held in high esteem by contemporary scholars of Yiddish literature who have influenced the current canon of Yiddish poetry. Although Glatshteyn occupies a central role in this canon, his own reevaluation of Rosenfeld seems to have had little, if any effect on Yiddish scholarship. Indeed, *Di yunge*'s view of sweatshop poetry dominates the Yiddish literary canon. This perception of the first generation of American Yiddish writers is reflected in poetic anthologies, particularly those published in America in English translation.

The first of these anthologies, *Modern Yiddish Poetry*,[18] appeared in New York in 1927. This collection was edited by S. J. Imber, a talented poet of the Galician school of Neo-Romanticism and a nephew of the Hebrew poet N. H. Imber who composed *"Hatikva"* ("The Hope"), the national anthem of the state of Israel. Imber's anthology clearly reflected his preference for the modernist aesthetic. Poets associated with *Di yunge*, such as Reuven Ayzland, M. L. Halpern, Zisho

---

[12] Yankev Glatshteyn, "Moris Rozenfelds briv" (1956), *In tokh genumen*, vol. 1 (Buenos Aires: YIVO, 1960), 152. This is a collection of Glatshteyn's essays culled from the Yiddish press and dated individually.

[13] Yankev Glatshteyn, "Moris Rozenfeld," *Mit mayne fartogbikher* (Tel-Aviv: Farlag Y. L. Peretz, 1963), 329–366.

[14] Ibid., 361.

[15] Ibid., 337.

[16] Ibid., 338.

[17] Ibid., 339.

[18] Imber, S. J., ed. *Modern Yiddish Poetry—An Anthology* (New York: East and West Publishing Company, 1927).

Lande, and Mani Leyb—as well as their European contemporaries, such as Dovid Kenigsberg, Melech Ravitch, Ber Horowitz, and Imber himself—are well represented in this anthology, with at least four poems each. Imber gave similar space to those few American poets whom *Di yunge* considered poetic precursors: writers such as Avrom Reyzn, Yoysef Rolnik, and Yehoyesh. Of the sweatshop generation, only Morris Rosenfeld and Morris Vinchevsky were included, with three poems combined. One of the poems Imber selected from Rosenfeld's oeuvre was his eponymous tribute to the American poet Walt Whitman, the same poem Lande chose for his earlier anthology.[19]

Very few Yiddish poetry collections were published in English translation in the United States until the 1960s, when two oft-cited monographs on the history of Yiddish literature appeared,[20] as well as three well-known anthologies: *America in Yiddish Poetry, The Golden Peacock,* and *A Treasury of Yiddish Poetry.*[21] This last volume was co-edited by Eliezer Greenberg and Irving Howe, the latter an influential critic and historian of American Yiddish literature.[22] Although Howe did

---

[19] "Valt Vitman," *Modern Yiddish Poetry,* 268–269; *Di yidishe dikhtung in amerike biz yor 1919,* 147.

[20] Sol Liptzin, *The Flowering of Yiddish Literature* (New York: Thomas Yoseloff), 1963; Charles Madison, *Yiddish Literature—Its Scope and Major Writers* (New York: Frederick Ungar, 1968).

[21] Joseph Leftwich, ed., *The Golden Peacock–A Worldwide Treasury of Yiddish Poetry.* (New York: Thomas Yoseloff, 1961); Ruth Whitman, ed. and tr., *An Anthology of Modern Yiddish Poetry* (Detroit: Wayne State University Press, 1995); Jehiel B. Cooperman and Sarah H. Cooperman, eds. and trs., *America in Yiddish Poetry–An Anthology* (New York: Exposition Press, 1967); Irving Howe and Eliezer Greenberg, eds., *A Treasury of Yiddish Poetry* (New York: Holt, Rinehart and Winston, 1969).

[22] Irving Howe began his career as a scholar of English literature, writing books on American authors such as Edith Wharton and Sherwood Anderson and had co-edited with Eliezer Greenberg the well-known volume *A Treasury of Yiddish Stories* (New York: Viking, 1954). However, it was not until the 1960s that he began to dedicate himself to the research of Eastern-European Jews, and, in particular, of Yiddish literature. During this decade he began work on his best-selling treatment of the Jewish immigration to and settlement of the Lower East Side in *World of Our Fathers: The Journey of the East European Jews to America and the Life They Found and Made* (New York: Harcourt Brace Jovanovich, 1976), as well as *How We Lived: A Documentary History of Immigrant*

discuss sweatshop poetry in his best-selling monograph *World of Our Fathers*, his anthology offered space only to Morris Rosenfeld. Like the anthologists and critics before them, Howe and Greenberg included many poems by the writers of *Di yunge*, such as Lande, Halpern, Mani Leyb, and H. Leyvik—as well as those precursors whom these poets admired: Yehoyesh, Reyzn, and Rolnik. A similar, pro-modernist approach is evident in subsequent anthologies of Yiddish poetry, including the influential *Penguin Book of Modern Yiddish Verse*, co-edited by Howe, Ruth Wisse, and Khone Shmeruk, and *American Yiddish Poetry*, edited by Benjamin and Barbara Harshav.[23]

Despite the exclusion of sweatshop poetry from the canon of modern Yiddish literature, this first school of American Yiddish writers produced significant achievements with little literary tradition upon which they could rely. The only modern precursors for the sweatshop writers were the poets of the Eastern-European *haskala*. There exists a large corpus of nineteenth-century *haskala* poetry in both Hebrew and Yiddish, and one of the most talented of the *haskala* poets is Y. L. Gordon (Yalag) who wrote in both languages and is best known for his 1863 Hebrew poem *"Hakitsah ami"* ("Awake My People"):

Hakitsah ami ad matai tishana
en gaz halayl hashemesh he'ira
hakitsah sim eynkha aneh ve'ana
uzemankha umekomkha ana hakira.

Awake, my people! How long will you sleep?
The night has passed, the sun shines through.

Jews in America, 1880–1930 [with Kenneth Libo], (New York: R. Marek, 1979). Howe and Eliezer Greenberg co-edited several anthologies of Yiddish literature including *Voices from the Yiddish: Essays, Memoirs, Diaries* (Ann Arbor: University of Michigan Press, 1972); *Yiddish Stories, Old and New* (New York: Holiday House, 1974); and *Ashes Out of Hope: Fiction by Soviet-Yiddish Writers* (New York: Schocken Books, 1977).
[23] Irving Howe, Ruth R. Wisse, and Khone Shmeruk, eds. *The Penguin Book of Modern Yiddish Verse* (New York: Viking, 1987); Benjamin and Barbara Harshav, eds. *American Yiddish Poetry* (Berkeley: University of California Press, 1986).

> Awake, cast your eyes hither and yon
> Recognize your time and your place.[24]

Maskilim, proponents of the Eastern-European Jewish Enlightenment, called upon their readers to shed their traditional, orthodox way of life and embrace secular values, European manners, and modern education and culture. One of the central targets of *haskala* literature—both in poetry and prose—was the religious establishment who, *maskilim* claimed, had led the Jewish people astray. In Yiddish, this motif was expressed by, among others, Y. L. Gordon's brother-in-law, the well-known *haskala* poet Mikhl Gordon.[25]

The poetry of the *haskala* writers, such as Y. L. Gordon, M. Gordon, and Elyokim Tsunzer, was the only Yiddish literary model available to the American sweatshop poets. Morris Rosenfeld expressed these *haskala* values in his first published poem, "*Dos yor 1886*" ("The Year 1886"). Written in the style of high bombast and common sentiment, this poem promoted *haskala* beliefs and was also situated within a popular nineteenth-century genre of Hebrew and Yiddish poetry in which poets examined the previous year on the cusp of a new one.[26] "The Year 1886" is typical of the *haskala* mode of nineteenth-century Hebrew and Yiddish poetry. In this long, raw poem, Rosenfeld addressed the Jewish people, demanding they wake from their stupor and free themselves from the shackles of organized religion:

---

[24] *Kitvei Yehuda Leyb Gordon,* vol. 1 (Tel-Aviv: Dvir, 1929) 17. The English translation cited here is in Michael Stanislawski, *For Whom Do I Toil: Jeudah Leib Gordon and the Crisis of Russian Jewry* (New York: Oxford University Press, 1988), 49.

[25] "Shtey uf mayn folk," Mikhl Gordon, *Shirei M. Gordon—Yidishe lider fun Mikhl Gordon* (Warsaw: Y. Alafin, 1889), 29–35. In a footnote, Gordon remarks that his poem was first published in 1869.

[26] See, for example, H. N. Bialik's "Nokh a yorhundert," *Der yid* 16 (1899); Morris Vinchevsky's "Rikblik af dem yor T[a]RM[a]D," *Lider un gedikhte, 1877–1910* (New York: Mayzel, 1910), 257; Elyokim Zunser, "Der nayntsntn yorhundert," *Tsvantsik yidishe folks lider* (New York: Katzenelenbogn, 1898), 74–80; and Dovid Edelshtat, "Tsum yor 1891," *Edelshtats shriftn* (New York: Hebrew Publishing Company, 1923), 155–156.

Zisnke lidelekh zingt men dir ayn,
in vig "fanatizmus"—shlofstu geshmak.
Men zogt dir, az andersh ken gor nit zayn
ze nor, mayn folk, vi men firt dikh in zak.
Dayonim—rabonim—shvindler der velt!
Zey shpiln farshtelt zeyer role atsind,
zey lozn dikh iber shreklekh gekvelt
un redn dir ayn, az du laydst far dayn zind.[27]

Sweet songs are sung to you,
in the cradle of "fanaticism"—you sleep soundly.
You are told that it can be no other way
just see, my people, how you are being trapped.
Judges [traditional judges of religious courts]—rabbis—
swindlers of the world!
They mask themselves as they play their role,
they leave you terribly tortured
and convince you that you are suffering because of your sins.

The enemy, according to Rosenfeld's speaker, is religion, with the functionaries of the Jewish community willfully misleading the Jewish masses for their own benefit.

This attack on organized religion had little relevance in the new world, where traditional Jewish life was not as strong and religious leaders did not hold the same sway over the Jewish community as they did in the old country. As a result, the sweatshop poets, most of whom were political radicals, switched their collective focus to a new enemy, the wealthy. In particular, the sweatshop writers centered their poetic attacks on those who represented the real power in America, the rich owners of the sweatshops and factories responsible for the long, punishing work hours and poverty-level wages of the immigrant shop workers.

In Rosenfeld's *"Der tsveyfakher may"* ("The Two-Sided May"), the speaker connects the blooming of nature with an impending workers' revolution and concludes with a threat to the upper classes:

---

[27] "Dos yor 1886," *Di nyu yorker yidishe folkstsaytung* (Dec. 17, 1886), 5.

Un aykh zog ikh raykhe tiranen,
zeyer noent iz ayer sof!
Der arbets man iz ufgeshtanen
fun zayn tifn langn shlof. . .
Ir megt im oykh di veg fartsamen
ale mitl vendt on,
dokh zog ikh aykh in varheyts nomen,
az zign vet di frayheyts fon![28]

And I say to you rich tyrants,
your end is very near!
The working man has arisen
from his deep, long sleep . . .
You may block his path,
employ every means,
but I tell you in the name of truth,
that the flag of freedom shall prevail!

Sweatshop poetry is bombastic in tone and contains a common lexicon of figurative language. Specifically, these tropes fall into two metaphoric categories, war and crime. The sweatshop poets continuously refer to the upper classes as *royber* (robbers), *merder* (murderers) and *shvindler* (swindlers), while the workers are *heldn* (heroes) who engage in *krig* (battle) on the *shlakhtfeld* (battlefield). The central quest of the poetic protagonists is *varheyt* (truth), a concept repeated unendingly throughout Rosenfeld's early poetry, as well as by other sweatshop poets. The speakers of these poems emphasize *tsaygn* (pointing to the truth), and the dead proclaim this message from *oylem ho'emes* (The World of Truth) where, according to literary tradition, they are afforded a privileged view of the true nature of things.

The portrayal of the dead revealing truth to the living is part of a long tradition which can be traced back to Homer, Virgil, and Lucian. Rosenfeld revived this tradition within a socialist framework. This connected him to a large corpus of nineteenth-century Hebrew and Yid-

---

[28] *Di blumenkete—a zamlung fun farshidene folks lider un poeziyen* (New York: Folksadvokat, 1890), 36.

dish satire prominent in works such as Yitzkhak Erter's *Gilgul nefesh* (*Transmigration of Soul*), Y. Y. Linetski's *Dos poylishe yingl* (*The Polish Boy*), Sholem Aleykhem's *Di ibergekhapte briv af der post* (*Letters Stolen from the Mail*) and M. L. Lilienblum's *Kehal refa'im* (*Congregation of the Dead*).[29] Rosenfeld's appropriation of this tradition is evident in his protagonist's naïveté on meeting the dead.

Rosenfeld was not a typical sweatshop poet, though he is grouped with this literary generation. A more representative poet was Yoysef Bovshover, who began publishing in 1890 and ceased writing in 1899 when hospitalized for mental illness. During this decade, he composed an impressive corpus of poetry which has been reprinted in numerous collections. In one of his best-known works, "*A gezang tsum folk*" ("A Song to the People"), Bovshover's speaker addresses the working masses, imploring them to realize that they are being exploited by the upper classes. Although he paints a pessimistic image of the present, the speaker does not allow the unjust system to overwhelm him, and in the poem's final stanza, he instructs his audience:

> *Heyb uf dayne oygn, o folk, gey aroys fun di finstere kvorim,*
> *heyb uf dayne oygn tsu mizrekh un mayrev, tsu tsofn un dorem,*
> *un nem di geyarshente oytsres un nem fun dayn arbet di peyres,*
> *un shafendik leb un genisndik shaf in di frayere deyres.*[30]

Raise your eyes, oh people, emerge from your dark graves,
raise your eyes towards the east and west, towards the north
and south,
and take your inherited treasures and take the fruits of
your labor,
and live productively and produce enjoyably in the freer
generations.

---

[29] On the Lucian tradition in the Hebrew literature of the *haskala*, see Shmuel Werses, "*Hedei hasatira shel lukianus be-sifrut ha-haskala ha-ivrit,*" *Megamot ve-tsurot be sifrut ha-haskalah* (Jerusalem: Magnes, 1990), 223–248.

[30] Yoysef Bovshover, *Gezamlte shriftn* (New York: Fraye Arbeter Shtime, 1911), 45. The last word in this stanza is pronounced *doyres* in standard Yiddish. I have presented it as *deyres*, as this is the Lithuanian dialectical pronunciation which Bovshover employs for the sake of rhyme (*peyres/deyres*) as he does in many of his poems.

"A Song to the People," like almost all sweatshop poems, concludes on an optimistic note. The speaker asserts that the physical products of manual labor—its "treasures" and "fruits"—rightly belong to the workers since they themselves produced them.

Though few critics have praised the style of sweatshop poetry, this stanza makes a deep impression on the reader, particularly in its usage of rhyme. In addition to the fact that both rhymes (*kvorim/dorem* and *peyres/deyres*) utilize the rare Hebrew element in Yiddish, the first set of words is especially significant. Unlike the latter couple, in which the two concepts are linked in a grammatical sense—they are the plural forms of *peyre* (fruit) and *dor* (generation)—the former couple is neither semantically nor grammatically connected, thereby providing the reader with an unexpected and interesting association of concepts through rhyme.

Another sweatshop poet who adhered closely to the narrow parameters of this genre was Dovid Edelshtat, whose career was shorter than that of Bovshover. Edelshtat, after composing original poetry in Russian, turned to writing Yiddish verse in 1889. He died in 1892 at the age of 26. Like Bovshover, Edelshtat championed the worker and wrote some of the central texts of sweatshop poetry, including "*In kamf*" ("In Struggle"). It begins this way:

> *Mir vern gehast un getribn,*
> *mir vern geplogt un farfolgt,*
> *un ales derfar vayl mir libn*
> *dos oreme shmakhtende folk.*
>
> *Mir vern ershosn, gehangen,*
> *men baroybt undz dos lebn un rekht*
> *derfar vayl mir emes farlangen*
> *un frayheyt far oreme knekht!*[31]

We are hated and chased,
we are harassed and persecuted,
and all because we love
the poor languishing people.

---

[31] "In kamf," *Edelshtats shriftn,* 15.

We are shot, hanged,
our lives and rights are stolen from us
because we desire truth
and freedom for poor slaves.

Although sweatshop poetry is often criticized for its repetitiveness and adherence to traditional poetic forms, this seemingly uninteresting rigidity often engendered interesting results. "In Struggle" is an example of how the form of a poem helps emphasize its meaning. By employing anaphora, a device often used by sweatshop poets, Edelshtat created a tension that highlights the blight of the workers' vanguard ("we") with whom he identifies. Specifically, he builds on "*mir vern*" ("we are" or "we become"), adding to it the acts of the upper class against the leaders of the workers' revolution, progressively heightening the action. In the first stanza they are persecuted, and in the second they are murdered. The poet further emphasizes this tension with his use of metric regularity which pounds out the rhythm of the poem. As almost all poems of this genre do, "In Struggle" paints an increasingly pessimistic portrait of the current situation, yet ends on an optimistic note, in this case an ominous warning to the oppressors:

Ir kent undz ermordn, tiranen!
Naye kemfer vet brengn di tsayt—
un mir kemfn, mir kemfn biz vanen
di gantse velt vet vern bafrayt.[32]

You can murder us, tyrants!
New fighters will bring about the time—
and we'll fight, we'll fight until
the whole world will be free.

Because most of the poetry in this genre sought to agitate its readers, the final stanza of almost all early sweatshop poems had an upbeat climax.

---

[32] Ibid., 16.

"In Struggle" is one of Edelshtat's best-known poems and also one of the poet's own favorites, a fact he attested to in another of his well-known works, "*Mayn tsavo'e*" ("My Last Will and Testament"):

O, gute fraynd! Ven ikh vel shtarbn,
Trogt tsu mayn keyver undzer fon
Di fraye fon mit royte farbn,
Bashpritst mit blut fun arbetsman.

Un dort unter dem baner roytn,
Zing mir mayn lid, mayn frayes lid!
Mayn lid "In kamf," vos klingt vi keytn
Fun dem farshklaftn krist un yid.[33]

Oh, good friends! When I die,
Bring to my grave our flag
The free flag with red colors,
Sprayed with the blood of the working man.

And there, under the red banner,
Sing to me my song, my free song!
My song "In Struggle" which sounds like the chains
Of the enslaved Christian and Jew.

In most sweatshop poetry, red often symbolizes communism. In "My Last Will and Testament," however, Edelshtat imbued this color with a second meaning, claiming that the flag is red because it has been "sprayed with the blood of the working man." Although the poet composed the bulk of his works in Yiddish, this poem stressed that his message transcended national and religious boundaries, promoting not only freedom for its Eastern-European Jewish immigrant readership, but for "Christian and Jew" alike. This universal message is also central in the works of Morris Vinchevsky.

---

[33] *Edelshtats shriftn*, 40.

Vinchevsky, who began his long, multilingual career in the 1870s as a Hebrew poet and journalist, often writing under the pseudonyms *Ben nets* (Son of a Hawk) and *Yig'al ish haruakh* (Yig'al the Man of Spirit), is credited as the "father" (and, by the Soviet Yiddish critics of the interwar period, the "grandfather") of socialist Yiddish literature. By the end of the 1880s, when writers such as Bovshover, Edelshtat, and Rosenfeld began their own careers, Vinchevsky had already turned to writing in Yiddish and was the dominant figure in the nascent genre of sweatshop poetry. Like his cohort, Vinchevsky's poems resonated among his newly proletarized immigrant audience, and several of his poems—as well as those of his contemporary poets— were recited at political demonstrations and set to music and sung by immigrant workers in the shops.[34] In these poems, the speakers respond to the new, industrialized condition of the Jewish working class and attempt to convince their readers of the justice and inevitability of their message. This optimism is evident in Vinchevsky's *"Di tsukunft"* ("The Future"). It ends with these words:

> *Mutik brider, mutik shvester!*
> *Ot der kamf, der letster, grester,*
> *ruft aykh fun di tukhle nester*
> *afn frayen feld;*
> *alzo, mutik in di rayen,*
> *in di rayen, tsu bafrayen,*
> *tsu bafrayen un banayen,*
> *undzer alte velt!*[35]

---

[34] Before immigrating to America, while working in London sweatshops between 1883–1886, Morris Rosenfeld set his first poems—which were never published—to music and circulated them by hand among his fellow shop workers. There is evidence of this in Rosenfeld's first published poems. For example, in "Der shnayder verkshap," the subtitle instructs the reader that this poem is meant *tsum zingen* (to be sung). See *Di gloke—folks lider und revolutsiyonere gedikhte* (New York: Gordon, 1888), 15–16.

[35] Moris Vinchevsky, *Gezamlte verk*, vol. 2 (New York: Frayheyt, 1927), 87. The word *rayen* (lines) is pronounced *reyen* in standard Yiddish, but, for the poem's rhyme, it is pronounced here in the Central or Polish dialect.

> Be brave brothers, be brave sisters!
> The battle, the final one, the greatest one,
> calls you from your moldy nests
> to the free field;
> therefore, be brave in the lines,
> in the lines, to free,
> to free and rebuild,
> our old world!

Typical of sweatshop poetry, the speaker addresses the situation of the workers through the metaphor of war, a technique frequently used by these poets to amplify their emotional impact. This tone is further emphasized through the poet's use of sentimentalism. In "The Future," Vinchevsky employs sentimental language in likening the workers to family members ("brothers" and "sisters"), and underscores his message through incremental repetition. These techniques of European literature had already been incorporated into Yiddish literature, and Vinchevsky used them to produce momentum and tension within his work, endowing it with a richness of internal rhyme.

Although "The Future"—like many of Vinchevsky's poems—is a call to arms, the poet also wrote several works which do not have optimistic endings and, in fact, conclude on pessimistic notes. He experimented with rudimentary forms of melodrama in poems such as "*Dos ufele in vald*" ("The Baby in the Forest"), "*Shtum, toyb, blind*" ("Dumb, Deaf, Blind") and, in one of his best-known creations, "*Dray shvester*" ("Three Sisters"), set in London where the poet himself lived for several years:

> *Di yingste farkoyft dortn blumen,*
> *di mitlste—bendlekh fun shikh,*
> *un shpet in der nakht zet men kumen*
> *di eltste, vos handlt mit zikh.*[36]

---

[36] Ibid., 42.

There the youngest one sells flowers,
the middle one—shoelaces,
and late at night one can see coming
the oldest one, who sells herself.

Instead of a discourse on an abstract experience, the poet focused on a particular and individualized group of people. Here Vinchevsky employed a trope common to the melodramatic mode—that of innocence and virtue destroyed. However, unlike the formula of this genre which offers resolution, this work does not end with virtue restored:

*Dokh shpet ba der nakht, ven zey kumen
tsum nest, vos zey rufn "a heym,"
banetsn zey bendlekh un blumen
mit trern, vos flisn geheym . . .* [37]

But late at night when they come
to the nest which they call "a home,"
they soak laces and flowers
with tears which flow in secret . . .

In contrast to most sweatshop poems, "Three Sisters" concludes on a pessimistic note. There is little opportunity for the girls to remedy their situation. Instead, the poem ends in tears, a common metaphor of melodramatic literature. Vinchevsky applied it here in a typical manner to represent sadness and added to this metaphor both shameful and harmful elements. The sisters do not cry while they work. Presumably, customers would not want to purchase flowers, shoelaces, or sex from sad girls, and therefore their tears must be wept in private. However, when they are finally permitted to express their sorrow within the privacy of their home, their tears assume a destructive nature as they soak and ruin the merchandise which provides their livelihood.

While Vinchevsky is one of the first Yiddish poets to include melodrama and sentimentalism in his poetry, these elements did not find sustained expression in his works. It is Morris Rosenfeld who fully

[37] Ibid.

incorporated them into his own poetry, thereby creating a new and original aesthetic in Yiddish literature. The poet recast the sweatshop poem, saturating it with concrete emotion and human situation, dramatizing the everyday struggles of the immigrant worker. Although Vinchevsky also sentimentalized and melodramatized his works, his use of these elements was limited. Rosenfeld, by contrast, rose above his sweatshop cohort and, after cementing his popularity among his Yiddish, working-class readership, he attained a level of international fame known only to select Yiddish writers such as Sholem Aleykhem, Sholem Asch, and later, Isaac Bashevis Singer. Rosenfeld became the representative of the Eastern-European masses and was known as the poet of the Jewish ghetto.[38]

With the rise of *Di yunge* in the first two decades of the twentieth century, and the subsequent promotion of a pro-modernist aesthetic in American Yiddish literature, Rosenfeld and his fellow sweatshop poets were dismissed by later poets and critics. Subsequent generations of critics, translators and anthologists have perpetuated this attitude, and sweatshop poetry became a footnote in the modern Yiddish canon. The majority of critics, following the lead of *Di yunge*, ignored most of sweatshop poetry, pausing only briefly on the accomplishments of Morris Rosenfeld. Even those scholars who do acknowledge this first generation of Yiddish writers in America offer little praise for their technical and aesthetic achievements.

The American sweatshop poets created their works out of an almost barren literary tradition. Building upon the *haskala* mode of Eu-

---

[38] The image of Rosenfeld as the authentic representative of this community is evident in the titles of his poetry collections, as well as essays and reviews of his work written around the turn of the twentieth century. See his *Songs from the Ghetto,* tr. Leo Wiener (Boston: Copeland and Day, 1898). Translations of Rosenfeld's works into numerous European languages were based on this edition, many bearing the same title. For studies stressing Rosenfeld's authenticity, see I. F. Marcosson, "A Voice from the Ghetto," *The Bookman* 9.1 (March, 1899), 68; William Morton Payne, "Rosenfeld's *Songs from the Ghetto,*" *The Dial* (Jan. 16, 1899), 54. See also the following reviews of Rosenfeld's works: "Real Poet Found in New York's East Side," *The New York Journal* (March 27, 1898); "Two Poets of New York's Ghetto," *The New York Herald* (July 5, 1903); "A Ghetto Poet," *The Public Ledger* [Philadelphia], (April 25, 1898).

ropean Yiddish poetry, they bridged the literary gap between the old and the new worlds. Since they worked within a new context, they fashioned their poems against the American landscape and established an original school of Yiddish poetry. This first generation of Yiddish writers in the United States appropriated the *haskala* hymn and adjusted it to the American socio-economic landscape. Responding to the sudden mass industrialization and proletarization of the Eastern-European Jewish immigrants in America, they politicized modern Yiddish poetry, permeating it with the values of radical ideologies. Although they have since been stigmatized as propagandistic and artistically sterile, poets such as Bovshover, Edelshtat, Rosenfeld, and Vinchevsky pioneered Yiddish literature in America, and produced works that deserve to be read and evaluated without regard to social or political ideologies.

BREAKING THE SILENCE ON AMERICAN YIDDISH POPULAR MUSIC

Hankus Netsky

The story of Yiddish popular music in America is, of course, the story of Second Avenue—the Jewish Broadway, where prominent Yiddish actors and actresses plied their trade, singing songs with Yiddish lyrics that everyone's grandparents knew by heart, before crossing over to "legitimate" theatre for good. But the details of its story still appear only as the scantiest footnotes in volumes of Jewish history. Still a common source for entertainment at senior centers, as well as a point of departure for various headier artistic endeavors, American Yiddish popular music has fought an uphill battle for years. Summarily dismissed by social- and musical-historians alike, with virtually no English-language print sources exploring its post-1924 history, lately it has been sinking quietly into greater and greater obscurity with the passing of each senior Yiddish actor or actress.

Indeed, the entire concept of American Jewish culture has fallen victim to a revisionist agenda that ignores Yiddish music altogether, as if immigrant boats had docked at the foot of Tin Pan Alley. Perhaps that's typical of America: to treat its ethnic traditions as cultural ephemera that exist only to provide fodder for various mainstream fads. Even acquiring a basic collection of American Yiddish popular music can be a serious challenge, with so many of the thousands of 78-RPM recordings made in its golden age still waiting to be transferred from that original format. Moreover, those recordings that have become available in reissues often appear with strangely "enhanced" sound quality, very little in the way of informative liner notes, and no English translations. This is all the more scandalous in that the American phase of Yiddish music was such a pivotal era in Jewish cultural history— a time when hundreds of composers and thousands of performers

189

made their primary living in an industry that not only served a key function in entertaining Jewish Americans, but was the major contemporary musical source for European Jewish consumers as well.

The era that put America at the forefront of Yiddish musical production followed a thousand years of music-making in Europe, where Yiddish popular music had progressed from medieval recitations of epic poems and ballads to the moralistic preaching and silly shenanigans of the *badkhan* (Jewish folk poet), the rowdy entertainment of the *purimshpiler* (Purim player), and the lively skits of the *broderzingers,* with their biblical yarns and drinking songs. By the end of the nineteenth century, the Yiddish theatre had created new musical compositions that turned both biblical and Shakespearian heroes into matinee idols, or lampooned every possible Jewish stereotype. Meanwhile, the trials of everyday life found their expression through folk songs of every type: songs of love, courtship, and treachery; drinking songs; songs to lampoon the religious or condemn the secular; lullabies; and topical songs about the draft, the landlord, or the wonders of the modern world.[1]

How much of this folk culture would actually survive the passage across the ocean? Mark Slobin examines this question in *Tenement Songs,* his pivotal study of early Jewish-American popular song that follows Yiddish music to America, taking into account the culture in the new land, and evaluating the hybridization that took place on these shores. He finds points of convergence between the tastes of immigrants and other Americans, all expressing themselves through songs about family ties, romance, conflict, marriage, the plight of orphans, and contemporary events. He also observes that Jewish immigrants created new song genres unique to their culture—for example: Zionist songs, Jewish comic songs, folk-song and folk-dance arrangements, and songs stressing traditional values, such as religious observance or morality.[2]

For the immigrant of the early twentieth century, American Jewish culture was a culture in transition, and the composers and actors

---

[1] For more on the story of Yiddish folk song, see Ruth Rubin, *Voices of a People* (New York: Thomas Yoseloff, 1963).

[2] Mark Slobin, *Tenement Songs* (Urbana: University of Illinois Press, 1982), 119–163.

who entertained in that community were also constantly in transition, catering to every changing fashion (if they hoped to survive). Consider the fate of premier *badkhn*-folk singer Eliakhum Zunser, whose works had been all the rage in Europe in the last two decades of the nineteenth century, as reported in Hutchins Hapgood's wonderful 1902 ethnographic study of New York's Lower East Side, *The Spirit of the Ghetto*.[3] In it, we find a sanguine, nearly forgotten Zunser, working as a printer, while Morris Rosenfeld, the "poet of the sweatshops," garners huge popularity as he laments the fate of the worker who holds two jobs and never sees his family, whose "teeth are gnashing" as he observes himself becoming more and more a "slave to the machines."[4]

To the immigrant, Zunser's old country verse had become old hat, while Rosenfeld's themes were the ones that resonated for the seasoned immigrant who had come hoping to find streets of gold. True, the occasional immigrant would strike it rich, like the coal merchant in Arnold Perlmutter and Herman Wohl's Yiddish theatre production, *Di Grine Millionaire* (*The Greenhorn Millionaire*). This would occur, not through long hours of grueling work, but by buying a winning lottery ticket, prompting the hero to sing a toast to the discoverer of this miraculous land, *"Lebn Zol Columbus"* ("Long Live Columbus"). But more often a worker would find common ground with the heroine of *"Di Greene Kuzine"* ("My Greenhorn Cousin"), the woman who comes to America with rosy cheeks and feet that can't help but dance; a few years of employment in New York City turn her into an ashen-faced invalid. As historian Arthur Hertzberg points out, such songs provided a kind of catharsis for workers of their day,[5] giving them a way to vent their grievances without actually stirring the pot too much. It was one thing for an American Jewish worker to express displeasure through song and quite another to actually work to foment revolution.

---

[3] Hutchins Hapgood, *The Spirit of the Ghetto* (New York: Funk and Wagnalls, 1902), 90–103
[4] Morris Rosenfeld, *"Mayn Rue Plats,"* in Eleanor Gordon Mlotek, *Mir Trogn a Gezang!* (New York: Workmen's Circle Education Department, 1977), 150.
[5] Arthur Hertzberg, *The Jews in America* (New York: Simon and Schuster, 1989), 165–167.

Not surprisingly, melodrama and tragedy were themes that resonated deeply for a first American-born generation that endured the pain of their parents' transitions, only to have many of their own hopes dashed during the Great Depression. Herman Yablokoff donned the costume of Pagliacci (or, in Yiddish, *der pyots*), the quintessential tragic clown, to sing "*Papirosn,*" a tale of an orphan boy selling cigarettes on the cold, mean, city streets. Such a song carried an experiential resonance for all too many of his fans. Other songs played out the timely drama of interfaith love. And since no immigrant family was too far removed from scandal, when Jennie Goldstein, the "queen of Yiddish melodrama" sang "*Ikh Bin A Mama*" ("I Am a Mother"), pouring out the despair of a mother standing in the shadows at the wedding of her illegitimate daughter, all could easily feel her pain.

A trip to the Yiddish theatre provided immigrants, who spent their days trying to speak a strange language and learn new customs, an opportunity to engage with the familiar: Europe as imagined in their own collective memories. In "*Ikh Benk Aheym*" ("I Long for Home"), the great character actor and comedian, Ludwig Satz, would remember *shabes* (the Sabbath), the High Holidays, and his hoarse grandfather's singing—not as a component of his current way of life, but as a fond reminiscence of life in the old country. In "*A Khazn A Shiker*" ("A Drunken Cantor"), the virtuosic dramatic actor Maurice Schwartz could transform himself into an unpleasant yet familiar old country stereotype that rang completely true, because he knew every nuance of his character so well. And in "*Mayn Shteytele Belz*" ("My Hometown of Belz"), Isa Kremer, the Kiev opera singer turned Yiddish prima donna, could sadly lament the grim state of her birthplace to remind her 1930s fans that they couldn't go home again.

In "Romania, Romania," Aaron Lebedoff reminded his audience that, back home, the wine was sweeter and the women were more compliant. At least three song hits by different artists lamented that the only truly gifted criminals were the ones left behind in Odessa. For the newly Americanized Jew, these foreign places—including Slutzk, Zlatapol, Yass (Jassy), Warsaw, Petrograd (which, as we learn in the song, is now Leningrad), the entire region of Bessarabia, and virtually any town or *gubernia* (province) that produced a Yiddish performer, lyricist, or playwright—were perpetual symbols of idealistic longing.

Yet, even if Jews were longing for their hometowns, very few actually wished for an older Jewish way of life. Carrying on a sentiment going back at least to Michal Gordon's satirical folk songs of the 1860s, American Yiddish popular songs continued to lambaste the religious. Pesakhe Burstein sang of the blind obedience of Hassidim: "Run, Jews, watch them give the *rebe* all of their money, and ask no questions, light the path to a better world." Nellie Casman poked risqué fun by way of timing and double entendre: "Oy, oy, the *rebetsin* spreads . . . her tablecloth over the table."

With the machinery of Second Avenue and the recording industry firmly in place, an American Yiddish song was not simply a song, but a commodity with unlimited potential, although its spoils didn't necessarily fill the pockets of its creators. Even the hapless Zunser's material eventually found new life, usually under someone else's name, as turned out to be the case with "*Der Socher*" ("The Plow"). This, his popular agrarian anthem, came back as "*A Pastuckhl's Khulem*" ("A Shepherd's Dream"), attributed to Perlmutter and Wohl, a popular Second Avenue songwriting team, and was later recorded as a dance tune by the savvy and entrepreneurial orchestra leader, Abe Schwartz. Yiddish theatre wedding songs, such as "*Lebedik, Freylekh*" ("Lively, Merry") or "*A Freylekhs*" *fun Di Dray Kales* ("A Wedding Dance" from *The Three Brides*) could be heard within a few weeks of their theatre debuts at actual weddings.

As the immigrant generation faded, Jewish Americans abandoned the rhythms of Eastern Europe, and Latin dances became the new currency for those who were aware of popular trends. In the 1920s, the tango was the first new style to hit disproportionately in the Yiddish music world, since Jewish composers and audiences had already been some of it greatest proponents both in Argentina and in Europe. Jewish tangos ranged from simple love songs, such as Secunda's "*Mayn Yiddishe Meydele*" ("My Jewish Girl"), to Olshanetsky's ode to jealous love, "*Ikh Hob Dikh Tsufil Lib*" ("I Love You Much Too Much"), to Herman Yablokoff's heart-wrenching ballad, "*Git Mir Op Mayn Hartz Tzurik*" ("Give Me Back My Heart"), with its story of a lover scorned by his sweetheart's pursuit of another partner with more material wealth. Other composers of this era, including Ilya Trilling and Ruben Osofsky, composed songs with rich harmonic content comparable to that of many chestnuts of "The Great American Songbook."

The Jewish jazz age came next, with numerous compositions eventually following a crossover path that made them attractive to non-Jewish performers and fans, who inadvertently served the purpose of "legitimizing" Jewish culture for the Jews themselves. It was Thomas "Fats" Waller's "Russian Fantasy" that most brilliantly merged the "Jewish minor" sound with the frenetic stomps of the 1920s. And it took Cab Calloway (in at least eight recordings with Yiddish subtexts) to turn the cantor into a truly "hep cat."[6] After World War II, Jewish and Yiddish music entered the repertoires of such mainstream entertainers as Connie Francis (*"Tzena, Tzena"*), Johnny Mathis (*"Eli, Eli"*), Ray Charles ("Where Can I Go?"), Eartha Kitt ("Rumania, Rumania"), Perry Como (*"Kol Nidre"*), and Tom Jones and Jackie Wilson (*"Yiddishe Mama"*). Like Judaism itself, Jewish music had become a normal fact of American life.

The vicissitudes of popular tastes and the pathways to the emotional heartstrings of immigrants were never lost on Yiddish theatre composers. The most celebrated of these was Vilna-born Joseph Rumshinsky (1879–1956), who abandoned his early religious training and his position in a synagogue choir to take a job, at age sixteen, as composer and music director in a theatre. If a *meshoyrer* (synagogue choirboy) could adapt in Europe, why not in America? Almost immediately upon his arrival here in 1907, Rumshinsky became the quintessential Jewish-American chameleon, blazing the creative trail that so many others soon followed. He was the one who showed that it was possible to find novel ways to incorporate virtually every musical and theatrical trend that came along into Second Avenue[7] scores, even while holding on to the signifiers, cadences, and feelings of Jewish culture.

An early example of his American style is *"Mamenyu,"* his elegy to the victims of the grueling 1911 fire at New York's Triangle Shirtwaist

---

[6] A similar situation occurred in the klezmer revival era, when clarinetist Don Byron (an African American) became one of the key innovators. Much was written about how his embracing of klezmer helped legitimize the genre.

[7] While Second Avenue in New York City, with its Yiddish theatres and vaudeville houses, was universally thought of as the Yiddish Broadway, it is worth mentioning that a great deal of creativity also went into productions spearheaded by companies headquartered in other enclaves, including Brooklyn, Philadelphia, Montreal, and Cleveland.

Factory. Tapping into an event that touched every heart in the Jewish immigrant community, lyricist Anshel Schorr set his version of the tale well within the boundaries of a popular turn-of-the-century American genre, the orphan song:

> *Oy vey,* my child! The mama tears her hair. For a piece of bread, a terrible death robbed me of my only child. My little girl lies dead; shrouds instead of a wedding gown! Woe is me! A child of sixteen! *Oy, mamma,* woe is me![8]

As Slobin points out in *Tenement Songs,* such a message might well have been enough to elicit tears from immigrant eyes, but to insure immediate emotional response from his listeners, Rumshinsky turned to the emotional tool he knew best—the power of the cantorial *krekhts* (sob). He set Schorr's lyric not in a normal minor key but in "Jewish minor" (a mode cantors call, in Hebrew, *mi sheberakh*—"one who blessed"), a sound with a prominent descending augmented-second interval, the most characteristic wailing sound of Eastern-European Jewish music.[9]

Rumshinsky's ability to pitch traditionally-based music to an American Jewish audience continued to work to his advantage throughout his career. While his early love songs take their inspiration from the European music hall (*"Dos Lid Der Lib"*—"The Song of Love"), when writing later for a more nostalgic generation, he turned back to a Hassidic folk song template to concoct his most successful love song, *"Sheyn Vi Di L'vone"* ("Beautiful As the Moon").

One of Rumshinsky's closest collaborators was an American-style female Yiddish star who was truly a world apart from her more formal European counterparts. Molly Picon was a girlish Chaplinesque pixie, bridging the worlds of Yiddish and vaudeville. Born in 1898 to a Philadelphia Yiddish theatre wardrobe mistress, she made her stage debut in 1921 as the lead character in the musical, *Yankele* (*Jack*). Between

---

[8] Translation is from Slobin, *Tenement Songs,* 134. Used by permission.
[9] For an impassioned discussion of the emotional power of this mode, see "The Altered Dorian Scale In Jewish Folk Music (On the Question of the Semantic Characteristics of Scales)" in Moshe Beregovski (trans. Slobin), *Old Jewish Folk Music* (Philadelphia: University of Pennsylvania Press, 1982), 549–567.

1924 and 1932, Picon collaborated with composer Joseph Rumshinsky on numerous productions, finally abandoning the partnership in the late 1930s in order to begin her long creative relationship with the American-born Yiddish theatre composer, Abe Ellstein. Equally at home in the role of a Gypsy heartthrob, circus acrobat, or *yeshivah* (religious academy) boy, she went on to become one of America's most versatile twentieth-century stage and movie actresses. Her success as a comedienne earned her the nickname "The Jewish Fanny Brice," while her dramatic abilities led others to dub her "The Jewish Helen Hayes."[10]

Rumshinsky's desire to cater to the tastes of the American marketplace shaped Picon's early repertoire. "*Dos Tsigayner Meydl*" ("The Gypsy Girl") cast her as a dangerous gypsy *femme fatale* singing over a ragtime beat, while "*Yom Pom Pom*" gave her a chance to lampoon various aspects of the American Yiddish theatre, including its noisy audience, its sometimes drunken denizens, and its most pompous star, Boris Tomashevsky. "*Macht Dus Chusidl Bim Bom*" played into popular conceptions of clueless Hassidim, "*A Yiddishe Chasene*" ("A Jewish Wedding") turned her into a wedding jester, and "*Mazel Brukhe*" ("Luck and Blessings") was a song of thanks.

Her later artistic collaborations with Julliard-trained Abe Ellstein, the first major American-born Yiddish popular composer—most significantly, through two of the best Yiddish films of the late 1930s, *Yidl Mitn Fidl* (*Yidl With His Fiddle*) and *Mamele* (*Little Mamma*)—gave us such perennial favorites as "*Abi Gezunt*" ("If You're Healthy") and "*Oy Mama, Bin Ikh Farlibt*" ("Oh, Mother, Am I in Love!"), an ode to the simple things in life. Other Picon-Ellstein classics include "*Farges Mikh Nit*" ("Don't Forget Me"), a Yiddish torch song replete with Jewish guilt, and "*Az Meshiakh iz Gekumen in New York*" ("When the Messiah Comes to New York"), an update of the Yiddish folk song, "*A Sudenyu*" ("A Ritual Banquet")—a modernistic farce replete with biblical characters.

America had a way of transforming the stage personalities of European Yiddish performers that came here. A profound case in point

---

[10] The second title once prompted Helen Hayes to write in the foreword to Picon's autobiography, that she only hoped some day she would be deserving of the appellation, "The *goyish* Molly Picon."

was Menashe Skolnick, who, in Warsaw's theatre world had been a romantic leading man. In America, he became the quintessential *shlemazel* (person with little luck), singing songs with hilariously ironic punch lines that had the audience in stitches time and time again.

The religious lifestyle that had already taken a beating in Europe had an even harder time competing with other American options, as we learn from the story of Seymour Rechtzeit (1911–2002), a durable Yiddish matinee idol whose career spanned virtually the entire era of American Yiddish entertainment. The son of a cantor from Lodz, Rechtzeit came to America as a *vunderkhazn* (boy-wonder cantor), first appearing with cantor Mordechai Hershman in a command performance for President Calvin Coolidge, and later apprenticing for years with superstar Yossele Rosenblatt on the Keith vaudeville circuit. Ultimately uninterested in following in his religious father's footsteps, Rechtzeit pursued a career in Yiddish popular music, in his younger years, closely emulating the formal stylings of the great Boris Tomashevsky. In the 1930s and '40s, his foray into the world of Yiddish radio (performing a staggering eighteen shows each week on WEVD) led him into a close partnership with savvy accompanist Sam Medoff.

Using the Americanized moniker "Dick Manning," Medoff had already composed such hits as "It Takes Two to Tango" and "Fascination." He introduced his Yiddish protégé to the work of his other major client, vocalist Perry Como,[11] who provided Rechtzeit with a blueprint for transforming his approach to Yiddish music into that of a relaxed, but still "kevtchy", American crooner. Manning's formula suited him well in his hit recordings of such chestnuts as "*Mayn Shtetele Belz*" ("My Little Town of Belz") and in the hundreds of other songs he continued to record right up to his death in 2002 at age 91.

One factor that kept the later generation of Yiddish theatre composers writing Yiddish songs was the common belief (within the early-1930s music industry) that such composers could never cross over to the national mainstream. After trying desperately to make a move to Hollywood on the basis of his jazzy 1932 composition, "*Bay Mir Bistu Sheyn*" ("To Me, You're Beautiful"), Sholem Secunda, a gifted

---

[11] Hankus Netsky interview with Seymour Rechtzeit, New York, 1999.

musician with a background similar to that of Rumshinsky's, gave up, convinced by the powers that be that his melodies were simply "too Jewish" to cross over.[12] In a story that has since become show business legend, the despondent Secunda sold the rights for "*Bay Mir*" to his publisher, J & J Kammen, for thirty dollars. A few years later, Tin Pan Alley lyricist Sammy Cahn was watching African-American vaudeville acts at the Apollo Theatre in Harlem, and could hardly believe it when Johnny and George, a popular duo, came out and stole the show singing "*Bay Mir Bistu Sheyn*" in Yiddish—they had learned it from legendary Catskills hostess, Jennie Grossinger. Cahn went right over to the Kammen brothers' office, bought the rights to the song for fifty dollars (twenty dollars profit for Kammen!), wrote some English lyrics, and, when the Andrews Sisters recorded it in 1938, had a hit on his hands bigger than any song the country had known until that time.

The success of Yiddish jazz was good news for Moyshe Oysher (1907–1958), the charismatic Bessarabian-born Yiddish movie star and cantor whose flamboyant lifestyle challenged the boundaries of traditional Judaism as much as his gypsy-like cascades and jazzy flourishes stretched the limits of Jewish musical improvisation. Beginning his career as an actor in Rumania at age six, Oysher rose to fame in the American Jewish community for his role in Yiddish films, including *Yankel Der Shmid* (known in English as *The Singing Blacksmith*). His popular musical duet from that film, "*Hassidic in America*" (featuring his first wife, Florence Weiss) showed just how astute Oysher was in mingling Hassidic chant with the popular scat-singing craze of the day.

But the act that gave Yiddish music a new life in the late 1930s was the Barry (Bagelman) Sisters. A duo that entered the popular mainstream after winning *Feter* (uncle) Nachum Stutchkoff's radio talent contest, Claire and Myrna Barry combined a wholesome, yet stylish, American image with their crystalline voices and natural gifts for harmony. Drafted as teenagers to headline WEVD's popular radio show, *Yiddish Melodies in Swing*, they apprenticed themselves to Oysher, picking up

---

[12] Victoria Secunda, "*Bei Mir Bistu Shein*" (Weston, CT: Magic Circle Press, 1982), 144. Ironically, earlier in his career, Secunda had been present at the audition where it was decided that George Gershwin's musical background was too jazzy for the Yiddish theatre.

both his suave European mannerisms and his jazzy delivery.[13] Pairing up with Abe Ellstein, their recordings of such hits as "*Zug Farvus*" ("Tell Me Why"), "*Zug Es Mir Nokh Amol*" ("Say It to Me One More Time"), and "*Der Neyer Sher*" ("The New Scissors Dance") showed the world that Jewish music could breathe with a truly modern American spirit.

The first decades after World War II were a period of rapid expansion and significant change for America's Jewish community. The move to suburbia created a need for new social institutions and for the construction of an unprecedented number of new synagogues. It was also the era when Judaism entered the mainstream, taking its place next to Protestantism and Catholicism as a "normal" American religion.[14] The age of restrictive quotas directed against Jews was mostly over. Hotels and country clubs lifted their discriminatory barriers, and Jewish Americans found their way into new kinds of professional and academic careers, and eventually into positions of political power. Historian Arthur Hertzberg sums up postwar Jews and their aspirations as he saw them:

> They were numerous and increasingly wealthy, and ever more "Jewish". . . . They regarded the Jewish community as their primary home. Yet, they were deeply ambivalent, often without admitting it even to themselves, about their most Jewish emotions. . . . What they did as Jews—and more revealing, what they chose not to do—had to fit their dominant purpose: to arrive.[15]

Needless to say, Yiddish music didn't quite fit with that dominant purpose. Furthermore, the Nazis' destruction of the Eastern-European Jewish world tainted traditional Yiddish music with a painful sadness. Furthermore, the creation of Israel in 1948 gave the Jewish community a fresh, youth-oriented cultural focus, replete with plenty of enticing music and dance. In his preface to *The Songs We Sing*, a landmark

---

[13] Hankus Netsky interview with Claire Barry, New York, 1988.
[14] Jack Werthheimer, *A People Divided: Judaism in Contemporary America* (New York: Basic Books, 1993), 6.
[15] Hertzberg, op. cit., 316.

educational songbook published in 1950 by the Conservative Movement, editor Harry Coopersmith cataloged the new motives:

> The rise of the Nationalist Movement, culminating, at long last, in the establishment of the State of Israel, the upsurge of religious feeling, especially during the war years, an awakened concern on the part of educators and parents for the development of an integrated Jewish personality through a curriculum providing for emotional as well as intellectual growth—these are the forces most responsible for this renewed outpouring of a rich and variegated folk and art song.[16]

His impressive volume (containing over 260 songs) was indeed variegated with regard to English and Hebrew material, including contributions from such composers as Leonard Bernstein, Isidore Freed, Herbert Fromm, and Judith Kaplan Eisenstein, and arrangements by Darius Milhaud and Kurt Weill. But the only section containing any Yiddish songs, under the caption "Hebrew and Yiddish," contained seventeen songs in Hebrew and only two in Yiddish, *"Rozhinkes Mit Mandlen"* ("Raisins and Almonds") and *"Oyfn Pripetshik"* ("By the Fireplace"). American Jewish educators had evidently moved on from their Yiddish roots.

For those who sought to persevere with *mameloshn* (Yiddish), American Yiddish music took on a more comedic twist, thanks to postwar Jewish comedians who felt truly at home in America. When Mickey Katz decided that cowboys would be a lot funnier if they were aging immigrant Yiddish speakers, he sold 150,000 copies of *"Heym Afn Range"* ("Home on the Range") in less than six months. Nothing was sacred in Katz's world—neither opera ("The Barber of Shlemiel" and "Carmen Katz"), nor rock-and-roll ("K'nock Around the Clock"), nor American novelty ("The Flying Purple *Kishke* Eater"). Never content to hire "klezmers who only scratched or phummphed,"[17] Katz's musicians (including trombonist Si Zentner, drummer Sammy Weiss, and trumpeter Manny Klein) were all thoroughly bilingual, and his

---

[16] Harry Coopersmith, *The Songs We Sing* (New York: The United Synagogue Commission on Jewish Education, 1950).

[17] Yale Strom, *The Book of Klezmer* (New York: A Cappella Books, 2002), 181.

arranger, Nat Farber, was one of Hollywood's most sought-after musicians, serving as musical director for the popular television shows of both Dinah Shore and Carol Burnett. The American Jewish audience certainly approved of Katz's experiment. Even his exclusively instrumental recordings sold over fifty thousand copies.

Yiddish performers of this generation continued to emphasize subjects that resonated with their fan base. Billy Hodes' *"Essn"* ("Food") was an ode to the crudeness of overeating in the Catskills, while the Barton Brothers' song, "Joe and Paul," was a coming-of-age story about the modern post-Bar-Mitzvah boy, masked as a commercial for a clothing store. Its edgy sexual humor was typical of songs of this era. It used Yiddish as an "adult" language that no underage listener would understand:

> Mothers, do you have a young boy at home, around 14 or 15 years old, who likes to see burlesque? He's already buying French post cards. He comes home, goes into the bathroom, closes the door, and goes ahwww, ahwww. Mothers, do me a favor and give that boy a few dollars and send him to cockeyed Jennie. And if you don't know where that is, then ask your husband. He knows that place really well.[18]

For the edification of classier Yiddish denizens of that era, America had become home to plenty of well-known traditional folksingers, including Sidor Belarsky, Masha Benya, Chaim Tauber, and Martha Shlamme, but it was only through the 1950s recordings of Theodore Bikel that a truly contemporary Yiddish folk style emerged. Born in Vienna in 1924, Bikel settled with his family in Palestine in 1938, going on to attend college in England and finally emigrating to the United States in 1954. In his travels, he had collected large numbers of folk songs (many from holocaust survivors) and published some of them in 1960 in his collection, *Folksongs and Footnotes*. Picking up the guitar during his sojourn in Israel, his cosmopolitan persona and flair for languages made him a symbol of the international folk-song movement of the mid-twentieth century, and gave Yiddish songs a secure home within that movement.

---

[18] *Joe and Paul: The Best of the Barton Brothers* (New York: Apollo Records, 1952).

Bikel's contribution was the dramatic yet informal interpretive style he (and his musical collaborators[19]) brought to Yiddish chestnuts, as he imbued them with a contemporary folk sensibility. In his hands, the dilemmas "solved" by the sage in "*A Briv Tsum Lyader Rebn*" ("A Letter to the Rabbi of Lyad") seemed like issues anyone could relate to in their lives. "*Akhtzik Er un Zibitzik Zi*" ("He's Eighty and She's Seventy") became a poignant visit with typical Jewish grandparents and "*Di Zun Vet Arunter Geyn*" ("The Sun Will Go Down") was transformed into a timeless hymn to Jewish perseverance. While his approach initially alienated some of the older purists in the Yiddish-speaking world, his recordings on the Elektra folk label arguably paved the way for the klezmer revival that began in the 1970s.[20]

That revival, also spurred on by the African-American roots movement of the 1960s, gave America's Yiddish song tradition a new lease on life as an alternative to the mainstream Hebrew-oriented Jewish expression that had proliferated since the 1950s. In "The Manifesto," found in her article "Why We Do This Anyway,"[21] contemporary klezmer violinist Alicia Svigals sets forth the idea that the current creative generation of Jewish artists considers it a top priority to advocate "for the seriousness of the Yiddish heritage," asserting that their output must be compatible with the values of "high Jewish self-esteem," and should point the way toward a "Jewish way to become more American."[22] As a result of the efforts and outlook of Svigals and others, a new generation is emerging: a generation that mines the riches of America's Jewish heritage with both great irreverence and unapologetic Jewish pride, using Yiddish as an important component of Jewish a cappella and hip-hop, and organizing festivals of both Ivy League/

[19] Most notable of these was Fred Hellerman who also served as music director for the popular American folk group, The Limelighters.

[20] For a full discussion of this aspect of his career, see Barbara Kirshenblatt-Gimblett, "Sounds of Sensibility" in Mark Slobin, ed., *American Klezmer* (Berkeley: University of California Press, 2002), 129–173.

[21] See Alicia Svigals, "Why We Do This Anyway," in Slobin, *American Klezmer*, 211–219.

[22] Ibid., 219.

collegiate klezmer and Knitting Factory/John-Zorn-style radical Jewish culture.

Montreal-based hip-hop artist Josh Dolgin (a.k.a. DJ Socalled), known for his virtuosic forays into the cantorial and klezmer traditions, is a prime example of an early-twenty-first-century artist who mimes Yiddish recordings. His collaborations with such artists as Theo Bikel, Susan Watts, David Krakaner, and Deborah Strauss, have played to enthusiastic young audiences, even while causing some of Yiddish music's older enthusiasts to scratch their heads. Here, he tells how he arrived at his personal approach to hip-hop:

> When you're making hip-hop, you have to find sounds, breaks, little ruptures of sound that you put into your sampler. . . . I realized that hip-hop is about representing yourself, representing your crew, representing where you're from, who you are, and it has to be like that in order to ring true. So I couldn't sample black musicians. . . . I mean I love funk, but I couldn't sample James Brown and all these great black artists because it wasn't me. So I started to find these old Jewish records, this Yiddish music, and I started to chop it up, and it was funky enough, ready to go. So I started to chop up the beats and write Jewish raps, and soon I found my own Jewish identity, but it was through hip-hop and rap music.[23]

American Yiddish music has survived into another century and still evolves with the creative input of a new generation of traditional and innovative American composers and performers who imbue it with their own sensibilities. Zalmen Mlotek, a brilliant classical musician from a family of Yiddish folklorists and archivists, puts a Broadway-influenced theatrical spin on folk, theatre, and ghetto-cabaret material, often working with Adrienne Cooper, a singer who combines the direct stylings of folk with the dramatic flair of opera. Eleanor Reissa, JoAnne Borts, and Phylis Berk, all veterans of Mlotek's productions, present Yiddish songs in modern cabaret-like settings, while the

---

[23] Excerpted from a panel discussion that took place at Hebrew College's "Festival of Secular Jewish Culture," June 2005, in Newton, Massachusetts.

Klezmer Conservatory Band and the Maxwell Street Klezmer Band take an American-style repertory approach. Performers, including Mike Burstein and Judy Bressler, explore their families' rich Yiddish theatre legacies, and groups—including the Klezmatics and the all-women's band Mikve—use Yiddish to challenge gender stereotypes. Michael Alpert's performances with Brave Old World emphasize the European roots of the music, exporting this approach back to Europe—as do the virtuosic performances of Deborah Strauss and Jeff Warschauer. Meanwhile, mainstream Yiddish singers, including Paul Zim and Israel's David "Dudu" Fisher, continue to record Yiddish repertoire, while Yiddish choral societies persist in flying the secular banner of Judaism as a culture of social activism, often pairing with gospel ensembles and other ethnic choral groups.

In many places, local Yiddish performers, little known beyond their communities, are the keepers of the flame. Such individuals continue to perform as long as their graying fans have the energy to listen. I worked with one of these stalwarts, Boston's Ben Gailing, for fifteen years, producing a radio show that had put down roots in that city in 1931. Born in 1898, Gailing, a veteran of the Maurice Schwartz Yiddish Art Theatre and many other New York-based troupes, continued to perform and deliver weekly Yiddish broadcasts right up until his death in April of 1999.

Yiddish music has truly earned its place at the table in the American society that transformed it, but this is not to say that the breadth of its history is well known. There is still much work to be done: exploring the boxes of letters and scores that sit, neglected, in academic archives; translating the Yiddish autobiographies of significant performers and composers; translating the song lyrics; and digitizing the musical performances that are still found only on decaying shellac and metal discs. It is not clear who, or what institutions, will take up this cause in a truly meaningful way. Only one thing is for certain: the more we look at America's Yiddish music heritage, the more it will teach us about who we are and where we come from.

CONTRIBUTORS

JOEL BERKOWITZ is Chair of the Judaic Studies Department at the University at Albany, SUNY. He is the author of *Shakespeare on the American Yiddish Stage*, editor of *Yiddish Theatre: New Approaches*, and co-editor, with Jeremy Dauber, of *Landmark Yiddish Plays: A Critical Anthology*.

ERIC A. GOLDMAN is adjunct associate professor of media studies at Yeshiva University. He is president of the Jewish video publisher, Ergo Media, based in Teaneck, New Jersey, and author of *Visions, Images and Dreams: Yiddish Film Past and Present* (New York: Holmes and Meier Publishers, 2008).

ARI Y. KELMAN is assistant professor of American Studies at UC Davis. His current scholarship investigates the spiritual and social lives of synagogues, cultures of sound, and the role of sound in creating sacred experiences. He has recently published a series of studies of contemporary Jewish culture and identity in America. His book, *Station Identification: A Cultural History of Yiddish Radio* is to be published by UC Press in 2008.

MARC MILLER was born to a Yiddish speaking family in Chicoutimi, Quebec. Educated in Montreal's Zionist day schools, he went on to earn a Ph.D. in German Studies at Columbia University. Currently, Dr. Miller lives in Northwestern Georgia where he is the C.E.O. of Cabbagetown Properties.

HANKUS NETSKY is a multi-instrumentalist, composer, and Jewish music scholar, who serves as Vice President for education at the National

Yiddish Book Center in Amherst, MA, and teaches jazz and contemporary improvisation at the New England Conservatory in Boston. He is also founder and director of the Klezmer Conservatory Band, an internationally renowned Yiddish music ensemble, and serves as research director of the Klezmer Conservatory Foundation, a non-profit organization dedicated to the preservation and perpetuation of Yiddish and klezmer music traditions.

EDWARD S. SHAPIRO is professor of history emeritus at Seton Hall University and the author of *American Jewry Since World War II*; *We Are Many: Reflections on American Jewish History and Identity*; and, *Crown Heights: Blacks, Jews, and the 1991 Brooklyn Riot.*

DANIEL SOYER is associate professor of history at Fordham University, where he teaches US immigration and urban history. He is the author of *Jewish Immigrant Associations and American Identity in New York, 1880–1939* (hardcover, Harvard University Press; paperback, Wayne State University Press), which won the Saul Viener Prize of the American Jewish Historical Society. More recently, he is editor of *A Coat of Many Colors: Immigration, Globalization, and Reform in the New York City Garment Industry* (Fordham University Press), and co-editor with Jocelyn Cohen of *My Future Is in America: East European Jewish Autobiographies* (New York University Press).

LAUREN B. STRAUSS is a professorial lecturer in the departments of History and Judaic Studies at the George Washington University in Washington, D.C., where she specializes in American Jewish history and Jewish cultural history. Her dissertation, which is currently being edited for publication, was entitled: "Painting the Town Red: Jewish Visual Artists, Yiddish Culture, and Progressive Politics in New York, 1917–1939." Dr. Strauss is co-editor of the anthology *Mediating Modernity: Challenges and Trends in the Jewish Encounter with the Modern World. Essays in Honor of Michael A. Meyer.*

RUTH R. WISSE is Martin Peretz Professor of Yiddish Literature at Harvard University, Professor of Comparative Literature, and Harvard College Professor. Among her books are: *The Modern Jewish Canon: A Journey through Language and Culture*; *A Little Love in Big Manhattan: Two Yiddish Poets*; and *I. L. Peretz and the Making of Modern Jewish Culture.*